Procedural Content Generation for C++ Game Development

Get to know techniques and approaches to procedurally generate game content in C++ using Simple and Fast Multimedia Library

Dale Green

PUBLISHING

BIRMINGHAM - MUMBAI

Procedural Content Generation for C++ Game Development

First published: January 2016

Production reference: 1210116

Published by Packt Publishing Ltd.
Livery Place
35 Livery Street
Birmingham B3 2PB, UK.

ISBN 978-1-78588-671-3

www.packtpub.com

Credits

Author
Dale Green

Reviewer
Glen De Cauwsemaecker

Commissioning Editor
Neil Alexander

Acquisition Editor
Indrajit Das

Content Development Editor
Priyanka Mehta

Technical Editor
Vishal Mewada

Copy Editor
Vedangi Narvekar

Project Coordinator
Izzat Contractor

Proofreader
Safis Editing

Indexer
Priya Sane

Graphics
Kirk D'Penha

Production Coordinator
Shantanu N. Zagade

Cover Work
Shantanu N. Zagade

About the Author

Dale Green is a young software developer who started his professional programming career in VB.NET, writing bespoke solutions to automate business tasks. This included the writing and maintenance of an e-commerce site that sold products on big online marketplaces such as Amazon and Rakuten.

Prior to this, he's been creating computer games since his early high school days. Through self-teaching, Dale has worked with a number of game development tools such as GameMaker, Unity, and Unreal before finding home in C++/DirectX/ OpenGL after undertaking a degree in the subject.

Currently studying computer games programming BSc (Hons) at the University of Huddersfield, he is on track to graduate with a first-class degree. Alongside his studies, he is a teaching assistant who helps deliver course content to fellow undergraduates. He undertook a year of self-employment to publish his first commercial title on Steam, Samphi, through his indie studio, Greeny Games Studio.

As a hobby, Dale also operates the indie game news website named Indie Gamers UK and enjoys playing with new technologies and languages.

Acknowledgment

First and foremost, I'd like to thank my family for their support throughout the project. Their encouragement and support kept me focused, determined, and most importantly, kept my cup filled with tea. Thanks, Mum!

Also thanks to Frank the kitty for trying to help. I assume that's what he was trying to do as he liked to walk on the keyboard so much! In the middle of a sentence, if you find "wwwwwwwwwwwwwwwwwwwww", direct your complaints to him.

Thanks to *Dino Kadric* for his help and support with the earlier chapters.
His guidance and feedback helped tremendously.

I'd also like to thank the editors at Packt who've made the whole process as comfortable as possible. They were always there to offer help and support when needed. I'd especially like to thank *Priyanka Mehta* and *Indrajit Das*.

Most importantly, I'd like to dedicate the book to my amazing gran, *Joey Wheeler*. Despite not knowing what a computer is, she calls my phone "the machine", she's read every word as I wrote them, including the code! Her enthusiasm towards the project rivaled my own, and her support really kept the ball rolling when things got tough. Thanks, granny!

About the Reviewer

Glen De Cauwsemaecker is an open source hacker, traveler, and young entrepreneur who has been playing with technology most of his life. He loves to learn, teach, explore, and make things. Open source, free education, and a global world is what he stands for. He has worked for Fishing Cactus (Belgium), Code Combat (Remote), AirPair (Remote), Exient (UK/Remote). He currently works as a freelancer and entrepreneur on independent and open source projects.

> I would like to thank the author of this book for all the hard work that he put into it. It's a great book that's written with passion and it's a gift to the community. I would also like to thank my girlfriend for her support.

www.PacktPub.com

Support files, eBooks, discount offers, and more

For support files and downloads related to your book, please visit www.PacktPub.com.

Did you know that Packt offers eBook versions of every book published, with PDF and ePub files available? You can upgrade to the eBook version at www.PacktPub.com and as a print book customer, you are entitled to a discount on the eBook copy. Get in touch with us at service@packtpub.com for more details.

At www.PacktPub.com, you can also read a collection of free technical articles, sign up for a range of free newsletters and receive exclusive discounts and offers on Packt books and eBooks.

https://www2.packtpub.com/books/subscription/packtlib

Do you need instant solutions to your IT questions? PacktLib is Packt's online digital book library. Here, you can search, access, and read Packt's entire library of books.

Why subscribe?

- Fully searchable across every book published by Packt
- Copy and paste, print, and bookmark content
- On demand and accessible via a web browser

Free access for Packt account holders

If you have an account with Packt at www.PacktPub.com, you can use this to access PacktLib today and view 9 entirely free books. Simply use your login credentials for immediate access.

Table of Contents

Preface   **xi**

Chapter 1: An Introduction to Procedural Generation   **1**

  Procedural generation versus random generation   **2**

    Procedural generation   2

    Random generation   2

  Introducing randomness   **2**

    Pseudorandom number generation   3

    Why computers can't generate truly random numbers   4

    Generating random numbers in C++   4

    Generating random numbers within a range   6

  Seeds   **7**

    Defining seeds   7

    Using seeds   8

    Generating random seeds during the runtime   9

    Controlled randomness is the key to generating random numbers   10

  The use of procedural generation in games   **10**

    Saving space   10

    Map generation   11

  Texture creation   **12**

    Animation   12

    Sound   13

  Benefits of procedural generation   **13**

    Larger games can be created   13

    Procedural generation can be used to lower budgets   14

    An increase in gameplay variety   14

    An increase in replayability   14

The drawbacks of procedural generation	**15**
More taxing on the hardware	15
Worlds can feel repetitive	15
You sacrifice quality control	15
You may generate an unplayable world	16
It is hard to script set game events	16
A brief history of rogue-like games	**16**
How we'll implement procedural generation	**17**
Populating environments	17
Creating unique game objects	17
Creating unique art	**17**
Audio manipulation	**18**
Behavior and mechanics	18
Dungeon generation	18
Component-based design	**18**
The complete game	**19**
Exercises	**19**
Summary	**20**
Chapter 2: Project Setup and Breakdown	**21**
Choosing an IDE	**21**
Microsoft Visual Studio	22
Code::Blocks	22
Other IDEs	23
Build systems	23
Breaking down the game template	**24**
Download templates	24
The class diagram	24
The object hierarchy	25
Level data	25
Collision	27
Input	27
Simple and Fast Multimedia Library (SFML)	**28**
Defining SFML	28
Why we'll be using SFML	28
Learning SFML	29
Alternatives	29
Polymorphism	**30**
Inheritance	30
Virtual functions	31
Pure virtual functions	32

Pointers and object slicing	33
The roguelike template setup	**36**
Downloading SFML	37
Linking SFML	37
Running the project	39
Adding an item	40
Updating and drawing	40
Exercises	**42**
Summary	**42**
Chapter 3: Using RNG with C++ Data Types	**43**
Setting the game seed	**43**
Setting Boolean values randomly	**45**
Generating a number between 0 and 1	45
Choosing if an item spawns	47
Random number distribution	**48**
Giving the player random stats	**50**
Accessing random elements of a collection	**52**
Spawning a random item	**53**
Generating random characters	**55**
Repeating loops	**58**
Spawning a random number of items	**60**
Exercises	**61**
Summary	**62**
Chapter 4: Procedurally Populating Game Environments	**63**
Potential obstacles	**64**
Keeping within the bounds of a level	64
Avoiding overlapping objects	64
Creating meaningful levels	64
Level tiles	**65**
Defining the spawn area	**66**
Calculating the level bounds	66
Checking the underlying game grid	67
Selecting a suitable game tile	**68**
Randomly selecting a tile	69
Checking whether a tile is suitable	69
Converting to absolute position	70
Spawning items at a random location	**70**
Expanding the spawning system	73
Using enumerators to denote an object type	74
Optional parameters	74

The complete spawn functions   75
Updating the spawn code   78
Randomly spawning enemies   79
Spawning random tiles   **82**
Adding a new game tile   82
Choosing a random tile   83
Implementing the SpawnRandomTiles function   84
Exercises   **85**
Summary   **85**

Chapter 5: Creating Unique and Randomized Game Objects   **87**
Creating a random player character   **87**
Choosing a player class   88
An overview of sprites and textures   89
Setting an appropriate sprite   89
Buffing the player stats   94
Random character traits   95
Returning the player traits array   97
Setting trait sprites   98
Procedurally generating an enemy class   **101**
Procedural items   **103**
Random Gem and Heart classes   103
Random gold class   104
The random potion class   **106**
Creating a random potion   106
Determining potion pickups   109
Exercises   **111**
Summary   **111**

Chapter 6: Procedurally Generating Art   **113**
How procedural generation is used with art   **113**
Using sprite effects and modifiers   114
Combining multiple textures   114
Creating textures from scratch   114
Creating complex animations   115
The benefits of procedurally generated art   **115**
Versatility   116
Cheap to produce   116
It requires little storage   116

The drawbacks of procedurally generated art   **116**
Lack of control   117
Repeatability   117
Performance heavy   117
Using SFML sprite modifiers   **117**
How colors work in SFML   118
Creating sprites of a random color   119
    Selecting a preset color at random   119
    Generating a color at random   121
Creating sprites of a random size   123
Saving modified sprites   **124**
Passing a texture into an image   124
Drawing to a RenderTexture class   125
Saving an image to a file   126
Creating enemy sprites procedurally   **127**
Breaking sprites into components   127
The draw setup   128
Randomly selecting sprite components   129
Loading the default armor textures   131
Choosing the armor tier   132
Rendering the armor textures   133
Rendering the final textures   134
Overriding the default draw behavior   135
Debugging and testing   136
Editing the game tiles   **137**
Exercises   **140**
Summary   **140**
Chapter 7: Procedurally Modifying Audio   **141**
An introduction to SFML audio   **142**
sf::Sound versus sf::Music   142
sf::SoundBuffer   142
Selecting a random main track   **143**
Adding sound effects   **144**
Editing sound effects   **147**
Playing a sound function   **148**
The audio listener   148
Creating a fluctuation in a pitch   150

3D sound – spatialization   **152**

The audio listener   152

The minimum distance   153

Attenuation   154

The position of the sound   155

Fixed positions   155

Moving positions   156

Exercises   **158**

Summary   **159**

Chapter 8: Procedural Behavior and Mechanics   **161**

An introduction to pathfinding   **162**

What is a pathfinding algorithm?   162

Dijkstra's algorithm   163

The A* algorithm   164

A breakdown of A*   **165**

Representing a level as nodes   165

The open and closed list   166

The H, G, and F costs   166

The H value   167

The G value   167

The F value   167

The Manhattan distance   167

Parenting nodes   168

The pseudo-algorithm   169

Coding the A* pathfinding algorithm   **170**

The Tile datatype   171

Creating supporting functions   171

The Level class   171

The Enemy class   172

Variable declarations   173

Precalculating the H values   174

Defining the main loop   175

Finding the adjacent nodes   176

Calculating the G and F costs   180

Calculating the G and F cost   181

Checking for superior paths   181

Creating the final path   184

Implementing A* in the game   **185**

Enabling the enemy to follow a path   185

Calling the pathfinding behavior   187

Viewing our path   188

Procedurally generated level goals   **190**
The variable and function declarations   190
Generating a random goal   191
Checking whether a goal is complete   195
Drawing the goal on the screen   197
Exercises   **199**
Summary   **199**
Chapter 9: Procedural Dungeon Generation   **201**
The benefits of procedural level design   **201**
Replayability   202
A reduction in development time   202
Larger game worlds   202
Considerations   **202**
A lack of control   203
Required computing power   203
Suitability   203
An overview of dungeon generation overview   **204**
Generating rooms   204
Generating a maze   205
Connecting rooms and mazes   206
The recursive backtracker   **206**
Procedurally generating a dungeon   **207**
Changing how we view the maze   207
Updating the Game and Level classes   209
Generating a maze   211
Preparing before the generation of a maze   211
Carving passages   213
Adding rooms   217
Choosing the tile textures   **220**
The if/else approach   220
Bitwise tile maps   220
Calculating the tile values   221
Mapping the tile value to textures   222
Calculating tile textures   223
Creating unique floor themes   226
Adding entry and exit points   229
Setting a player's spawn location   231
Undoing the debug changes   234
Exercises   **235**
Summary   **236**

Chapter 10: Component-Based Architecture 237

Understanding component-based architecture 238
Problems with a traditional inheritance-based approach 238
Convoluted inheritance structures 238
Circular dependencies 239
Benefits of component-based architecture 239
Avoiding complex inheritance structures 240
Code is broken into highly reusable chunks 240
Highly maintainable and scalable 240
The disadvantages of component-based architecture 241
Code can become too fragmented 241
Unnecessary overhead 241
Complex to use 241
An overview 241
Designing the component system 242
C++ templates 243
Using templates 243
Template declarations 244
Using templates 245
Template specialization 246
Function overloading 247
Creating a base component 248
Component functions 248
Attaching a component 249
Retuning a component 250
Creating a transform component 252
Encapsulating transform behavior 252
Adding a transform component to the player 253
Using the transform component 254
Updating the game code 254
Creating a SpriteComponent 255
Encapsulating sprite behavior 256
Adding a sprite component to the player class 258
The updated drawing pipeline 259
Updating the game code 259
Creating an audio component 260
Defining the behavior of an audio component 260
Adding an audio component to the player class 262
Using the audio component 262
Exercises 263
Summary 263

Chapter 11: Epilogue   265
Project breakdown   265
Procedurally populating environments   265
Creating unique and random game objects   266
Procedurally generating art   266
Procedurally modifying audio   266
Procedural behavior and mechanics   267
Procedural dungeon generation   267
Component-based architecture   268
The pros and cons of procedural generation   268
Pros   268
Cons   269
Summary   269
Index   271

Preface

Computer games are a vast medium with dozens of genres that have developed over the past three to four decades. Games are bigger and more immersive than ever, and gamers' expectations have never been higher. While linear games, ones that have a set story and fixed progression, are still commonplace, more and more dynamic and open-ended games are being developed.

Advances in computer hardware and video game technologies are giving a much more literal meaning to the phrase "game world". Game maps are constantly increasing in size and flexibility, and it's thanks to technologies such as procedural generation that it's possible. Two gamers who buy the same game may have very different experiences as content is generated on the fly.

In this book, we're going to introduce ourselves to procedural generation, learning the skills needed to generate content on the fly to create dynamic and unpredictable game systems and mechanics.

Provided with this book is a game template for a rogue-like C++ game. When we get the project compiled and set up in *Chapter 2, Project Setup and Breakdown*, you'll see that it's currently just an empty shell. However, as we work our way through the book, you'll be introduced to the concepts behind procedurally generated content through real-world examples. We will then implement these examples in the empty project.

What this book covers

Chapter 1, An Introduction to Procedural Generation, introduces us to the vast topic that it procedural generation. I've always felt a crucial part of really learning something is understanding why it's done the way it is. Its great knowing how something is done, but knowing its origin and why it's the way it is creates a much more complete picture and a deeper understanding. In this chapter, we'll go right back to the birth of procedural generation and its journey into modern computer games.

Chapter 2, Project Setup and Breakdown, explains how to set up the provided rogue-like game project in your chosen IDE with detailed instructions for both Visual Studio and Code::Blocks. It's written in C++/SFML, and we'll be extending it throughout this book. We'll also cover common issues that you may face and run the project for the first time.

Chapter 3, Using RNG with C++ Data Types, explores random number generation (RNG), including the problems surrounding it and how we can use it with C++ data types to achieve random results during runtime. RNG lies at the heart of procedural generation and is how we emulate computers acting randomly and achieve dynamic results with our algorithms.

Chapter 4, Procedurally Populating Environments, helps us develop our level further by spawning items and enemies in random locations around the map. Procedurally generated environments is a staple in procedurally generated games, and spawning game objects at random locations is a big step toward achieving this.

Chapter 5, Creating Unique, Randomized Objects, explores ways in which we can create unique and randomized game objects. Certain items will be procedurally generated during runtime, which means that there will be a vast number of possible combinations. We'll cover the skills and techniques that were used to achieve this in the earlier chapters. We'll pull it all together and build a procedural system!

Chapter 6, Procedurally Generating Art, steps up our procedural efforts by moving away from the simple setting up of member variables randomly to the creation of procedural art and graphics. We'll procedurally create textures for our enemies and alter the level sprites to give each floor of our dungeon a unique feel.

Chapter 7, Procedurally Modifying Audio, looks at the nearest cousin of art, audio, using similar techniques to create variance in our sounds. We'll also use SFML's audio functions to create specialized 3D sound, bringing more depth to our levels.

Chapter 8, Procedural Behavior and Mechanics, uses everything that we've learned so far to create complex procedural behavior and mechanics in the form of pathfinding and unique level goals. We'll give our enemies the intelligence to traverse levels and chase the player. We'll also create unique level goals with unique rewards for the player to carry out.

Chapter 9, Procedural Dungeon Generation, finishes our work on the game project. We're going to implement what is perhaps the most icon feature of roguelike games: procedurally generated levels. All the way through the book, we've been working with the same fixed level. So, it's about time we started generating them procedurally! We'll also create some variance between levels and implement the goal generator that we created in the previous chapter.

Chapter 10, Component-Based Architecture, takes a look at component-based design, since our work on our template project is now complete. Procedural generation is all about flexibility. So, it makes sense that we'd want to work with the most flexible architecture that we can. Component-based architecture can achieve this, and having a good understanding of this design approach will help you progress and build larger systems in the future.

Chapter 11, Epilogue, takes a retrospective look at the project and the topics that we covered as we finish our procedural journey. For each area of procedural generation that we've used, we'll also identify some jumping-off points should you wish to explore the topic in depth.

What you need for this book

Throughout the course of writing this book, I used Visual Studio Community 2015 for Windows Desktop. It's a great IDE with all the tools that we need to create a C++ game for Windows. It's available for free from Microsoft, so I highly recommend that you download it and use it throughout the course of the book.

Don't worry if you've never used it before; we'll cover the project setup in detail so that you'll become accustomed to the parts of the IDE that we'll be using. I'll also provide the setup instructions for Code::Blocks. If you opt not to use an IDE, you'll need access to a C++ compiler so that you can run the project that we'll be working on in the book.

Who this book is for

This book is aimed at those who have knowledge of game development in C++ and are looking to incorporating procedural generation into their games. It will assume a fairly solid understanding of the fundamentals of programming, such as data types, return types, method calls, and so on. An understanding of the concepts behind game development is also assumed as we won't be looking at the underlying engine.

A game template is provided, and we'll use SFML to extend it throughout the course of the book. No prior experience with SFML is assumed. After completing the book, you will have a solid understanding of what procedurally generated content is, how it is used in games, and the collection of practical skills that will be applied to a real game.

Conventions

In this book, you will find a number of text styles that distinguish between different kinds of information. Here are some examples of these styles and an explanation of their meaning.

Code words in text, database table names, folder names, filenames, file extensions, pathnames, dummy URLs, user input, and Twitter handles are shown as follows: " We called `std::srand()` and set a new seed, but each time we run the program, we're setting the same seed again "

A block of code is set as follows:

```
Stirng myStringLiteral = "hello";
string myString = { 'h', 'e', 'l', 'l', 'o', '\0' };
```

When we wish to draw your attention to a particular part of a code block, the relevant lines or items are set in bold:

```
// If the enemy is dead remove it.
if (enemy.IsDead())
{
    enemyIterator = m_enemies.erase(enemyIterator);

    // If we have an active goal decrement killGoal.
    if (m_activeGoal)
    {
        --m_killGoal;
    }
}
```

New terms and **important words** are shown in bold. Words that you see on the screen, for example, in menus or dialog boxes, appear in the text like this: " In Code::Blocks, add the following to the project's **Build Options** and **Search Directories** tab."

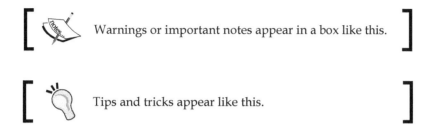

Warnings or important notes appear in a box like this.

Tips and tricks appear like this.

Extra Exercises

At the end of each chapter, there are a number of review questions and further exercises that can be completed. While not crucial to the book, it's advised that you complete them so that you can gauge your understanding of the topics covered and gain more experience.

Reader feedback

Feedback from our readers is always welcome. Let us know what you think about this book—what you liked or disliked. Reader feedback is important for us as it helps us develop titles that you will really get the most out of.

To send us general feedback, simply e-mail feedback@packtpub.com, and mention the book's title in the subject of your message.

If there is a topic that you have expertise in and you are interested in either writing or contributing to a book, see our author guide at www.packtpub.com/authors.

Customer support

Now that you are the proud owner of a Packt book, we have a number of things to help you to get the most from your purchase.

Downloading the example code

You can download the example code files from your account at http://www.packtpub.com for all the Packt Publishing books you have purchased. If you purchased this book elsewhere, you can visit http://www.packtpub.com/support and register to have the files e-mailed directly to you.

Downloading the color images of this book

We also provide you with a PDF file that has color images of the screenshots/ diagrams used in this book. The color images will help you better understand the changes in the output. You can download this file from `http://www.packtpub.com/ sites/default/files/downloads/6713OT_ColoredImages.pdf`.

Errata

Although we have taken every care to ensure the accuracy of our content, mistakes do happen. If you find a mistake in one of our books—maybe a mistake in the text or the code—we would be grateful if you could report this to us. By doing so, you can save other readers from frustration and help us improve subsequent versions of this book. If you find any errata, please report them by visiting `http://www.packtpub. com/submit-errata`, selecting your book, clicking on the **Errata Submission Form** link, and entering the details of your errata. Once your errata are verified, your submission will be accepted and the errata will be uploaded to our website or added to any list of existing errata under the Errata section of that title.

To view the previously submitted errata, go to `https://www.packtpub.com/books/ content/support` and enter the name of the book in the search field. The required information will appear under the **Errata** section.

Piracy

Piracy of copyrighted material on the Internet is an ongoing problem across all media. At Packt, we take the protection of our copyright and licenses very seriously. If you come across any illegal copies of our works in any form on the Internet, please provide us with the location address or website name immediately so that we can pursue a remedy.

Please contact us at `copyright@packtpub.com` with a link to the suspected pirated material.

We appreciate your help in protecting our authors and our ability to bring you valuable content.

Questions

If you have a problem with any aspect of this book, you can contact us at `questions@packtpub.com`, and we will do our best to address the problem.

1

An Introduction to Procedural Generation

When you load an image on a PC, a song on an iPod, or a book on a Kindle, you load it from storage. That image, song, and book already exists as a whole, and whenever you want to access it, you grab the whole previously created thing. In the case of music or a video, you can stream it in chunks, but it still already exists as a whole in storage. Let's compare this to buying a ready-made desk from a furniture store. You get the entire desk as one single thing and that's that; you have a desk.

Now, let's imagine that instead of buying a complete desk, you buy one that's flat-packed. Instead of getting a pre-built desk, you get all the pieces that you need to build one, and instructions on how to do so. When you get home, you can follow those instructions, and you will have a desk. If you feel so inclined, you can even deviate from the instructions and create a unique desk that is different from that of everyone else.

Let's use this analogy in the context of game development by substituting the purchasing of a desk with the loading of a level. In the first case, we loaded the level as a whole, as it was pre-built. However, in the second example, we got all the pieces that we need to build a level and put them together ourselves in whatever order we choose.

This process of something being created via an algorithm or procedure, as opposed to already existing, is called **procedural generation.** The desk was created procedurally as you followed an algorithm to put its pieces together. The same goes for the game level. This can be extended to almost anything. For example, music, images, games, and text can all be procedurally generated.

In this chapter, we will cover the following topics:

- Procedural generation versus random generation
- Generating pseudorandom numbers in C++
- Seeds
- The benefits and drawbacks of procedural generation
- A brief history of rogue-like games
- How to implement procedural generation

Procedural generation versus random generation

I'd like to make a distinction before we go any further. In this book, we're going to talk a lot about procedural generation and random generation. These terms are often used interchangeably, but they are not the same thing. Therefore, let's take a moment to define them.

Procedural generation

Procedural generation is the process of creating content using an algorithm. This in itself has no element of randomness. If the functions, expressions, algorithms, and inputs that are used to generate the content remain the same, then you'll always get the same results. This is due to the fact that computers are deterministic, which is something that we'll cover shortly. Procedural generation is not inherently random.

Random generation

Randomness is induced when we give these algorithms different inputs or alter their expressions. This variance is what creates the variety of the output. When someone says something was procedurally generated, they usually mean procedurally generated utilizing randomness.

Introducing randomness

Computers are **deterministic** machines. This means that if you give them the same input, and perform the same operations, you'll get the same output every time. With respect to the desk example, everyone gets the same pieces, follows the same instructions, and so builds the same desk.

Again, using the context of games, if everyone gets the same assets and algorithms to put them together, we will all get the same game and experience. Sometimes, this is the goal. However, in our case, we want to create game systems that are unpredictable and dynamic. Therefore, we need to introduce an element of randomness to procedural generation.

Pseudorandom number generation

Random number generation is simply the process of picking a number at random. This is pretty straightforward for us, but it is a much tougher task for a computer. In fact, it's impossible for a computer to generate a truly random number without special hardware. You'll understand why this is so in a moment.

The next best thing is pseudorandom number generation. The word *pseudo* literally means *not genuine*. Therefore, pseudorandom number generation can be thought of as a fake random number generation. The numbers appear to be random but are actually the result of complex equations and algorithms that could in fact be calculated in advance.

Bear in mind that not all pseudorandom number generators are built equally. For applications such as trivial simulations and games, fairly linear algorithms can be used and are perfectly suitable. However, pseudorandom number generation is also used in applications such as **cryptography**, and will use much more complex algorithms so that the outcome cannot be determined via patterns created from earlier outputs.

The pseudorandom number generators that we use as developers fall firmly into the first category and are perfectly suitable. Luckily for us, C++ offers a number of ways in which trivial pseudorandom numbers can be generated. Throughout the course of this book, we will use `std::rand()` and `std::srand()`, both of which standard C++ functions that are included in `<cstdlib>` library.

> Learning how to read and extract information from documentation is a skill that I feel is often overlooked. With a multitude of great forums at hand it's easy to go straight to Google for a solution to your problem, but first, always read the documentation. `http://www.cplusplus.com` is a great C++ reference, and SFML is fully documented at `http://www.sfml-dev.org/documentation/`.

Why computers can't generate truly random numbers

We now know that computers can't generate random numbers, and that we generate pseudorandom numbers instead. Let's have a look at why this is so.

The reason behind this is the same as the reason why two computers will reach the same output given the same input and operation; computers are deterministic. Everything that a computer produces is the result of an algorithm or equation. They are nothing more than highly sophisticated calculators. Therefore, you can't ask them to act unpredictably.

True random numbers can be generated, but you need to utilize systems outside the machine. For example, at https://www.random.org/ **you can** generate truly random numbers using atmospheric noise. There are other systems that are akin to this, but unless you are generating random numbers for something important such as security purposes, trivial pseudorandom number generation will suffice.

Generating random numbers in C++

Let's start coding by writing a small program to generate some pseudorandom numbers. To do this, we will use the std::rand() function. It generates a pseudorandom integer in the range between 0 to RAND_MAX. The RAND_MAX variable is a constant defined in <cstdlib>. Its value will vary depending on the library that you are using. On a standard library implementation, it's guaranteed to be at least 32767.

 If you're already familiar with this topic, feel free to skip ahead to the sub-chapter named Seeds.

You can download the code for this program from the Packt website at http://www.packtpub.com/support. It will be present in the Examples folder, and the project name is random_numbers:

```
// Random number generation
// This program will generate a random number each time we press
enter.

#include <iostream>

using namespace std;

int main()
```

```
{
  while (true)
  {
    cout << "Press enter to generate a random number:";
    cin.get();

    // Generate a random integer.
    int randomInteger = rand();

    cout << randomInteger << endl << endl;
  }

  return 0;
}
```

Downloading the example code

You can download the example code files from your account at
http://www.packtpub.com for all the Packt Publishing books
you have purchased. If you purchased this book elsewhere, you can
visit http://www.packtpub.com/support and register to have
the files e-mailed directly to you.

This is a very simple console application that makes a call to `std::rand()` every
time we press the Enter key. This returns us the pseudorandom number, and we
pass it to `std::cout` to display it. That's how easy it is!

```
Command Prompt                                    —  □  ✕

Press enter to generate a random number:
41

Press enter to generate a random number:
18467

Press enter to generate a random number:
6334

Press enter to generate a random number:
26500

Press enter to generate a random number:
19169

Press enter to generate a random number:_
```

Generating random numbers within a range

The previous code generated numbers between 0 and RAND_MAX. That's great, but we'll usually want more control over this in order to generate numbers within a certain range. To do this, we are going to use the **modulo operator**.

 In C++, the modulo operator is the % symbol. This varies between languages, but is generally either % or *Mod*.

The modulo operator returns the remainder of the division between two numbers. So, 9 mod 2 is 1, as 2 goes into 9 four times with 1 left over. We can use this to create a range for the pseudorandom number generation. Let's generate a number between 0 and 249.

To do this, we need to make the following change:

```
// Generate a random integer.
int randomInteger = rand();
int randomInteger = rand() % 250;
```

Run the program a few times now, and you'll see that all the results are limited to the range that we just defined. So now we can generate a number between 0 and n, but what if we don't want our range to start from 0? To do this, we need to make one more change to the line that generates a number:

```
// Generate a random integer.
int randomInteger = rand() % 250;
int randomInteger = rand() % 201 + 50;
```

Remember that the number we used in the mod calculation will generate a number between 0 and n-1, and the number we add afterwards will increase the range by that amount. So here, we generate a number between 0 and 200 and then increase the range by 50 to get a number between 50 and 250.

 If you're not fully comfortable with the math behind what we're doing here, head over to Khan Academy. It's a fantastic resource for learning and has lots of great mathematics-related material.

Run the program and note the first five numbers that are generated. In my case, they are 91, 226, 153, 219, and 124. Now, run it again. You'll notice that something strange happens; we received the exact same numbers.

They were generated in a pseudorandom manner, right? Maybe it was just a fluke. Let's run it again and see what we get. You will get the same result again. To understand what's happening here, we need to take a look at **seeds**.

Seeds

We just created a program to generate pseudorandom numbers, but every time we run it we get the same results. We know that these numbers are the results of complex equations and algorithms, so why are they the same? It's because each time we run the program, we're starting with the same seed.

Defining seeds

A seed provides a starting point for an algorithm. So, in the previous example, yes we're using complex algorithms to generate numbers, but we're kicking off the algorithm at the same point each time. No matter how complex the algorithm is, if you start at the same point, and perform the same operations, you're going to get the same results.

Imagine that we have three people, and each person is about to walk the same path by 5 steps. If they all start from the same square, they will end at the same square:

Now, in the next diagram, we give these three people unique starting positions. Even though they are doing the same actions as before, and are on the same path, their results are different because they started from different locations:

In this analogy, the path is the algorithm, and the starting square is the seed. By changing the seed we can get different results from the same actions.

You will have most likely used seeds before and not even known it. Games that procedurally generate worlds, such as Minecraft and Lego Worlds, give you the option to set a seed manually before generating a world. If your friend generates a world that looks great, they can grab their seed and give it to you. When you input that seed yourself, you kick off the algorithm at the same place that your friends did and you end up with the same worlds.

Using seeds

Now that we know what seeds are, let's fix the previous example so that we don't keep generating the same numbers. To do this, we will use the `std::srand()` function. It's similar to `std::rand()`, but it takes an argument. This argument is used to set the seed for an algorithm. We'll add the call to `std::srand()` before we enter the while loop.

 You only need to set the seed once per run of the application. Once `std::srand()` has been called, all the subsequent calls to `std::rand()` will be based upon the updated initial seed.

The updated code should look like this:

```
// Random number generation
// This program will generate a random number each time we press
enter.

#include <iostream>

using namespace std;

int main()
{
  // Here we will call srand() to set the seed for future rand() calls.
  srand(100);

  while (true)
  {
    cout << "Press enter to generate a random number:";
    cin.get();

    // Generate a random integer.
    int randomInteger = rand() % 201 + 50;
```

```
    cout << randomInteger << endl << endl;
  }

  return 0;
}
```

Now when we run this code we get different results! I got 214, 60, 239, 71, and 233. Don't worry if your numbers don't match mine exactly; they are both CPU- and vendor-specific. So, what will happen if we run the program again? We changed the seed. So we should get different numbers again, right?

Not quite. We called `std::srand()` and set a new seed, but each time we run the program we're setting the same seed again. We're kicking the algorithm off at the same position each time, so we're seeing the same results. What we really want to do is randomly generate a seed during runtime so that the algorithm always starts at a new position.

Generating random seeds during the runtime

There are many ways to achieve this, and your use case will determine which method is suitable. For us, as game developers, something relatively trivial such as the current system time will usually suffice.

This does mean that if you run the program at the exact same time you'll get the same results, but that's almost never going to be a problem for our use. C++ provides us with a nice function to get the current time, `time()`, which is located in `<ctime>`.

Let's update the program one last time and pass `time()` as a parameter in `std::srand()` so that we generate unique numbers with every run:

```
// Here we will call srand() to set the seed for future rand() calls.
srand(100);
srand(time(nullptr));
```

Now, every time we run the program, we get unique numbers! You may have noticed that if you run the program multiple times in succession, the first number is always very similar to the last run. That's because between the runs time doesn't change a lot. This means that the starting points are close to each other and the results reflect this.

Controlled randomness is the key to generating random numbers

The process of generating random numbers is a huge component in creating systems that procedurally generate game content. There are lots of ways in which random data is generated, such as noise maps and other external systems, but in this book, we'll stick to these simple C++ functions.

We want systems that are predictable enough to give us control over them as developers, but they should be dynamic enough to create variations for the player. This balance can be hard to achieve, and sometimes games get it wrong. Later in this chapter, we'll look at some of the things that you have to watch out for when incorporating procedural generation into a game project to avoid this.

The use of procedural generation in games

Now we know what procedural generation is, and that it's the element of randomness we add that lets us create dynamic systems, let's take a look at some examples of how it is used in games. There are countless ways in which it can be utilized; the following are just a few major implementations.

Saving space

Necessity, as the saying goes, is the mother of invention. As developers of today we're spoiled with the hardware that we have at our disposal. Even the most baseline machines that you'll get today will have a hard drive of 500 GB in size and up as standard. This is quite a luxury considering that just a couple of decades ago that would be MB and not GB.

Game distribution was also a very different game back then. Today, we either buy games on a physical disk, with Blu-ray disks offering a whopping 25 GB per layer, or download them off the Internet, where there are no size restrictions at all. Keeping this in mind, now consider the fact that the size of most **Nintendo Entertainment System (NES)** games was a mere 128 to 384 KB! These storage restrictions meant that game developers had to fit lots of content into a small space, and procedural generation was a great way to do this.

Since building large levels and storing them wasn't possible in the past, games were designed to build their levels and resources algorithmically. You'd put all the resources needed on your storage media, and have the software assemble the level at the player's end.

Hopefully now, the earlier desk analogy makes more sense. It's just like how flat-packed furniture is easier to transport, and it can then be built at home. As hardware has developed, this has become less of a problem, but it was a great solution for early developers who had storage concerns.

Map generation

One of the most prominent uses of procedural generation in modern video games is the generation of game maps and terrain. The extent to which this can be used is vast, and ranges from generating simple 2D maps to full 3D worlds and terrain.

When procedurally generating 3D terrain, noise maps, such as the ones generated by **Perlin noise**, are used to represent random distribution by producing an image with areas of both high and low concentration. This data, the variance in concentration and intensity, can then be used in many ways. When generating a terrain, it's commonly used to determine the height at any given position.

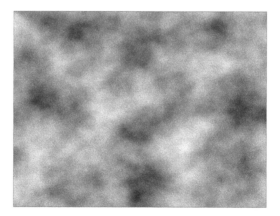

The procedural generation of complex 3D terrain is beyond the scope of this book. However, we will generate 2D dungeons later in this book.

 If you do want to explore 3D terrain generation, read up on terms such as "fractal terrain generation", "height maps", and "noise generation". These will put you on the correct path.

Texture creation

Another prominent example of procedural generation is the creation of textures. Similar to terrain generation, the procedural generation of textures uses noise to create variance. This can then be used to create varying textures. Different patterns and equations are also used to create a more controlled noise that forms recognizable patterns.

Generating textures procedurally like this means that you can potentially have an unlimited number of possible textures without any overhead on storage. From a limited pool of initial resources, endless combinations can be generated, an example of which can be seen in the following image:

Perlin noise is just one example of the many algorithms that are commonly used in procedural generation. The study of these algorithms is beyond the scope of this book, but if you want to further explore the use of procedural generation, it would be a good place to start.

Animation

Traditionally, game animations are created by animators, and then exported as an animation file that is ready for use in the game. This file will store the various movements that each part of a model will go through during animation. It then gets applied to the game character during runtime. The player's current state will determine which animation should be playing. For example, when you press *A* to jump, the player will change to a jumping state, and the jumping animation will be triggered. This system works great, but it is very rigid. Each step, jump, and roll is identical.

However, procedural generation can be used to create real-time, dynamic animation. By taking the current position of the character's skeleton and calculating the multiple forces that are being imparted upon it, a new position can be calculated. The most prominent example of procedural animation is ragdoll physics.

Sound

Although less common than the previous examples, procedural generation is also used to create game sounds. This will commonly be in the form of manipulating existing sounds. For example, sound can be spatialized, meaning it appears to be coming from a specific position when heard by the user.

At a stretch, short, one-shot sound effects may be synthesized, but due to the little benefit that it brings as compared to the amount of work needed to implement it, it's seldom used. It's simply much easier to load premade sounds.

 Sfxr is a small program that generates random sound effects from scratch. Its source is available. So, if sound synthesis interests you, it will serve as a good starting point. You can find the project at `https://github.com/grimfang4/sfxr`.

Benefits of procedural generation

We've looked at some of the key ways in which procedural generation is used in games. So now let's take a look at some of its most important benefits.

Larger games can be created

If your game world is hand-built, it's going to have size restrictions for a number of reasons. Every object needs to be placed manually, every texture/model needs to be handcrafted, and so on. All of this takes time and money. Even the largest handcrafted game's world sizes, such as those seen in The *The Witcher 3: Wild Hunt* and *Grand Theft Auto V*, pale in comparison to what procedurally generated worlds can achieve.

If a game utilizes procedural generation correctly, then theoretically, there is no limit to the world size. For example, *No Man's Sky* is a science-fiction game set in an infinite, procedurally generated galaxy. When you start to get really big maps however, hardware becomes a limiting factor. Areas that have been generated need to be saved to the disk in order to revisit them, and this quickly adds up. For example, to generate the biggest world possible in Minecraft, you will need around 409 petabytes of storage for the level data!

Procedural generation can be used to lower budgets

Making games is expensive. Really expensive. In fact, most AAA games cost tens, if not hundreds, of millions of dollars to make. With budgets that are this high, any option to save money is welcome. Procedural generation can do just that.

Let's say that we are working on a title that needs 100 brick textures. Traditionally, you'd have one of your artists create each brick. While they will have top quality, this will cost both time and money. Alternately, by utilizing procedural generation techniques, you can have an artist create a handful of resources and use them to generate however many resources you need to use.

This is just one example, and the same goes for modeling, design, and so on. There are pros and cons of using procedural generation in this way, but it's a valid option.

An increase in gameplay variety

If your game world is handmade, the experience that players have is going to be fixed. Everyone will collect the same items, the terrain will be the same, and as a result, the overall experience will be the same. The defining feature of procedurally generated games is that experiences differ. There is a sense of unknown to the game, and every time you play, there will be something new waiting that you haven't encountered yet.

An increase in replayability

Let's continue from the last point. If a game is linear, without any procedural generation, the challenge is gone after you've played the game once. You know the plot, you know where the enemies will be, and unless it has an amazing story or mechanics, there's not much reason why you'd want to play the game again.

However, if your game utilizes procedural generation, then the challenge is fresh each time the game is run. The game is always evolving; the environments are always new. If you look at the games that have the greatest replayability, they tend to be the ones that give the player the greatest amount of control. Most of these games will utilize some form of procedural generation to do so.

The drawbacks of procedural generation

As with anything, there are two sides to a story. Procedural generation brings a myriad of possibilities and enhancements to games, but there are considerations to be taken when implementing it.

More taxing on the hardware

As we now know, procedural generation is the creation of content through running algorithms. These algorithms can be intense and require a lot of computing power. If you develop a game that makes heavy use of procedural generation, you need to ensure that a regular consumer PC or console is able to meet its demands.

For example, if you choose to generate trees procedurally in an open world game, there's going to be a big load on the CPU and GPU whenever that area needs to be generated. Lesser PCs might not have the power to do so, and therefore, they may stutter.

Worlds can feel repetitive

Another potential drawback is the fact that worlds can feel repetitive. If you allow your game system to generate incredibly large worlds, but use few and basic algorithms to do so, you'll inevitably have a lot of repetitive areas being generated. Patterns and repeating areas will be very easy to spot, and this will diminish from your game greatly.

You sacrifice quality control

Computers may be faster at crunching numbers than us humans, but there's one thing that we're vastly superior at, and that's creativity. No matter how amazing the procedural algorithm is, you lose the human touch. The little changes and subtleties that a seasoned designer can bring to a project are sacrificed.

It also means that you can't guarantee the same gameplay quality to all players. Some players may generate a really great map that facilitates gameplay, while others may generate a map that actively prohibits it.

You may generate an unplayable world

In extreme cases of the previous point, a level that is completely unplayable may be generated. The risk of this happening depends on how well your procedural content is generated, but it should always be considered.

When generating a 3D terrain map, you may accidently generate a terrain that is too high for the player to climb, or blocks off an area that needs to be accessible. The same goes for a 2D map. Later in this book we'll be generating dungeon rooms randomly. So for example, we need to ensure that each room has a valid entrance and exit.

It is hard to script set game events

Continuing with the previous point, procedural generation is uncertain. If the entire world around you is generated exclusively procedurally and randomly, then it makes it almost impossible to script fixed game events.

Game events are pre-scripted events, and the nature of procedural generation is to create unscripted worlds. Getting the two to work together is a tough challenge. For this reason, games tend to use a mix of procedural generation and premade game development. With this, you get the fixed game events and moments that are needed to drive a narrative, and in between all of this, you create a unique and open world for the player to explore and interact with at their own whim.

A brief history of rogue-like games

Since we're going to implement what we are learning in a rogue-like, let's just take a second to look at their history. It's always great to understand the origins of the things that you are doing!

Rogue is a dungeon crawling game that was first developed by *Michael Toy* and *Glenn Wichman* and initially released in 1980. Every level of the dungeon was randomly generated along with the positions of the object within. Rogue defined the dungeon crawling genre and was the inspiration for many titles that followed. This is why we call games of this type **roguelikes**, because they are literally like Rogue!

Procedural generation has been a key element in roguelikes since their conception. This is why I chose the genre to introduce the topic. Together, we will recreate the iconic features that define the genre, and approach procedural generation with a very practical and hands-on approach.

How we'll implement procedural generation

At the very start of the book I gave a brief overview of each chapter and what we will be covering in it. Now that we've covered what procedural generation is, let's take a look specifically at some of the ways in which we'll be implementing it as we work towards creating our own roguelike game. This list is not exhaustive.

Populating environments

When we load the game for the first time our objects will be in fixed locations. We're going to start our efforts by fixing this, implementing what we've learned in this chapter about random number generation to spawn our objects at random locations.

At the end of this chapter there are a few optional exercises that include generating numbers within a collection of different ranges. I suggest completing them if you're not comfortable with it already, as we'll be relying on it to achieve this.

Creating unique game objects

One of my personal favorite aspects of procedural generation is the creation of unique objects and items. Knowing that there is a wide variety of items in a game is awesome. Knowing that the items don't even exist yet, and that the possibilities are limitless, is even better!

We'll start simply by initializing our object's member variables randomly, and move up to giving our objects unique sprites and properties. We'll also look at creating dynamic classes that can create highly unique objects from a single base class.

Creating unique art

Generating textures and materials from scratch using procedural generation is a very large subject. There are lots of ways by which this can be achieved. Traditionally, we use things such as Perlin noise as their basis function and then build upon it with patterns and colors. We're not going to go into this topic to this extent. Instead, we're going to use the built-in image processing features of **Simple and Fast Multimedia Library** (**SFML**) to create unique textures during the runtime.

Starting with a simple approach, we'll change image properties such as size, color, and scale to create a variation in the existing assets. We'll then use render textures to combine multiple sprite components on the fly to create unique assets for our enemies.

Audio manipulation

As with graphics, SFML offers a number of functions that allow us to modify sounds. Therefore, we'll use these to alter the pitch and volume of our sound effects to create variance. We'll then use advanced functions to create 3D spatialized sound, bringing depth to the scene through our audio.

Behavior and mechanics

It's not just the static items and resources that can be generated procedurally. To add more variance to our gameplay, we'll use some procedural techniques to create dynamic gameplay mechanics. Specifically, we'll create a system that will generate a random goal for the player, and present them with a random reward should that goal be achieved.

We'll also give our enemies some basic **Artificial Intelligence** (**AI**) in the form of **A Star** (**A***)pathfinding, allowing them to chase a player through the level.

Dungeon generation

Towards the end of the book, once we're comfortable using **Random Number Generator** (**RNG**) with procedural systems, and with our game project, we are going to implement the defining feature of roguelikes; randomly generated dungeons.

I've mentioned a few times that procedural generation can be used to create theoretically never-ending game worlds. So, we're going to do just that. We'll implement a system where every room that we visit is generated randomly, and we'll give each floor a distinct feel using the graphics manipulation techniques we'll learn in later chapters.

Component-based design

Procedural generation is all about creating dynamic systems, objects, and data. Therefore, it makes sense that we want the most flexible game framework that we can have so that it incorporates this well. One of the ways to achieve this is through component-based design. Therefore, to end our work, we're going to take a quick look at it, breaking our project down into a more component-based approach.

The complete game

These are the major systems changes that we'll implement. There will be lots in-between, but these examples will cover the major mechanics and skills that we will be using. When we reach the end of the book, you will have a fully working roguelike with an endless dungeon that is randomly generated, randomly generated items that spawn in random locations, procedural textures throughout the dungeon levels, and random enemies, all implemented with a flexible component-based architecture.

You will not only learn the skills needed to implement procedural generation in your own games, but also see how they all work in the context of one-another. Isolated exercises are great, but nothing beats working on a real-world example.

Exercises

To enable you to test your knowledge of this chapter's content, here are a few exercises that you should work on. They are not imperative to the rest of the book, but working on them will help you access your strengths and weaknesses in the material covered.

1. Using the `std::rand()` function with the modulo operator (%), for updating `random_numbers.cpp` to generate numbers that fall within the following ranges:

    ° 0 to 1000

    ° 150 to 600

    ° 198 to 246

2. Come up with a new way of generating a random seed during the runtime. There are lots of ways to do this. So be creative! In my solution, the first numbers were always similar. Find out whether you can generate a random seed that mitigates that.

3. Have a look at your game collection and find out whether you can identify where procedural generation has been used.

4. Which of the following are examples of procedural generation?

    ° Loading a song

    ° Ragdoll physics

    ° Creating unique objects during the runtime

Summary

In this chapter, we learned that procedural generation is the creation of content by using algorithms. This concept can be applied to all digital media and is used in games to create dynamic systems and environments. Procedural generation brings larger games, variety, and dynamism; all at the cost of lesser control, and potentially lesser performance as it is taxing on hardware. Some examples of the most popular uses of procedural generation in modern gaming include terrain generation, texture creation, and procedural animation.

In the next chapter, we will take a look at the project that has been supplied with the book. As we learn to create procedural systems, we will be implementing them in a real game project, with the ultimate goal of creating a roguelike game, a genre that heavily utilizes procedural generation. We will review the game template, the SFML modules that we will be using, and get the project setup. Then, we will compile it on your system.

If you are familiar with C++ game development and have used SFML before, you may already be familiar with the concepts presented in the next chapter. If that's the case, feel free to skim through the chapter to get right into the programming in *Chapter 3, Using RNG with C++ Data Types*.

2
Project Setup and Breakdown

Before we get into the implementation of procedural generation for ourselves, we're going to take a quick tour through the game template that has been provided with the book. Moving forward, the focus will be on the procedural systems that we create, not the underlying template and engine. Given that, it will be beneficial to familiarize ourselves with the templates and engine before we start.

We'll also take a look at **Simple Fast Multimedia Library** (**SFML**), the framework that we'll work with.

In this chapter, we'll cover the following topics:

- Choosing an **Integrated Development Environment (IDE)**
- A breakdown of the provided game template
- An overview of SFML
- Polymorphism
- Project setup and first compile
- Object pipeline

Choosing an IDE

Before we do anything, you're going to need a solid C++ IDE. You may already have one that you prefer to use. If you do have one, that's fine. But if you don't, here's a quick summary of two of my favorites.

Microsoft Visual Studio

Microsoft Visual Studio is an industry-standard IDE from Microsoft. It supports a wide range of languages, and provides a large variety of testing and compatibility tools. It's also tied in with a number of Microsoft services, making it the top choice for development on Windows PCs. The pros and cons to using Microsoft Visual Studio are as follows:

Pros:

- It has a number of free versions available
- A wide range of languages are supported by Microsoft Visual Studio
- It is widely supported by Microsoft
- It has a highly customizable environment with dockable windows
- It has intelligent code completion features
- It is integrated with a number of Microsoft features

Cons:

- Its full version is very expensive
- Its free version is limited
- Works only on Windows PC

Microsoft Visual Studio and a wide range of other Microsoft technologies are available to students for free for the duration of their studies. To find out more about this, visit https://www.dreamspark.com/Student/.

Code::Blocks

The Code::Blocks IDE is a free, open source, and cross-platform IDE for development in C, C++, and Fortran programming languages. It's built around a plugin architecture, meaning it can be highly customized by installing various add-ons to create an IDE that best suits your needs.

Pros:

- It is available for free
- It is available for all Operating Systems
- It is highly customizable through the installation of add-ons

- It supports multiple containers
- It has intelligent code completion features

Cons:

- It has fewer features and tools as compared to what Microsoft Visual Studio offers

Both IDEs have the required features that will allow us to create a game in C++. Therefore, it all boils down to personal preferences. I'll suggest Visual Studio, and it's the one that I'll use throughout the book.

Other IDEs

Visual Studio and Code::Blocks are just two examples of the many IDEs that are available. If you don't prefer either, the following are a number of alternate cross-platform IDEs. All of them are capable of developing C++ code:

- NetBeans (Windows, Mac OS X, and Linux)
- Eclipse (Windows, Mac OS X, and Linux)
- Code Lite (Windows, Mac OS X, and Linux)

Build systems

An alternative to using an IDE is compiling via a build system. These systems decouple the build process from the IDE or code editor that you're using, giving you more control over the process. Build systems allow you to automate various aspects of the build process. It may be something simple, such as incrementing a build number, or advanced, such as automated unit tests.

There are a number of build systems available, including the following:

- Make
- CMake
- MSBuild
- Gradle

We won't cover the setup or use of these systems in the book. So, head to each systems' respective site for documentation and instructions for use.

For more information on build systems and the benefits that they provide, visit `http://www.cs.virginia.edu/~dww4s/articles/build_systems.html#make`.

Breaking down the game template

The best way to learn is by practicing. Examples are great, but there's nothing like getting stuck in and working on a real game. The game template provided will allow us to implement the systems that we're going to learn about in a real game as opposed to them being a collection of isolated exercises.

Familiarizing yourself with this template will not only help make the code examples throughout the book clearer, but also make the exercises at the end of each chapter easier. It will also allow you to use what you're learning to implement your own systems in the project once we're done with it.

Download templates

Before you start, download the game template so that you have the source code available as you run through some of the key points. The template is available for download on the official Packt Publishing website at `http://www.packtpub.com/support`.

We'll set it up shortly, but for now, let's take a quick look at some of its key features.

The class diagram

Included with the project download is an image of the complete class diagram for our solution. If at any point you have any questions about the structure of the template, refer to the diagram.

Class diagrams are a great way of seeing the complete structure of your software. As your game gets bigger and bigger, it will inevitably get more convoluted as inheritance structures grow larger. If you have the tools available to do so, it's a great idea to view a class diagram regularly and keep on top of its structure. It will help you identify where your structure needs work, and where doesn't.

Creating diagrams in Microsoft Visual Studio is restricted to the Professional edition or higher. However, there are various free tools available, such as Doxygen at `http://www.stack.nl/~dimitri/doxygen/index.html` and ArgoUML at `http://argouml.tigris.org/`, which create UML diagrams from source code.

The object hierarchy

All objects in the template follow a set inheritance hierarchy. At the base of all classes is the `Object` class. This provides a `sprite`, a `position`, an `Update()` virtual function, and a `Draw()` virtual function.

All classes extend from this base class, implementing their own behaviors by overriding these virtual functions. In our `main` game class we create containers for the main base classes, grouping all items and enemies into single collections that we can iterate over easily:

```
std::vector<std::unique_ptr<Item>> m_items;
std::vector<std::unique_ptr<Enemy>> m_enemies;
```

A vector of base class pointers allows us to take advantage of polymorphism and store all the classes that inherit from the same parent classes in a single data structure. Don't worry if you're unfamiliar with polymorphism. Towards the end of the chapter we'll take a look at both polymorphism and the object pipeline to add an object to the game.

We're using the `std::unique_ptr` C++11 smart pointer over raw pointers. For more information on smart pointers and their benefits, visit `https://msdn.microsoft.com/en-us/library/hh279674.aspx`.

Level data

The game template that is provided is a `roguelike` template. Given this, the level is described as a grid. The best way to represent a grid in this context is with a 2D array, and to store all the information that we need, we'll use a custom data type named `Tile`, as follows:

```
/**
 * A struct that defines the data values our tiles need.
 */
struct Tile {
```

```
TILE type;          // The type of tile this is.

int columnIndex;    // The column index of the tile.

int rowIndex;       // The row index of the tile.

sf::Sprite sprite;  // The tile sprite.

int H;              // Heuristic / movement cost to goal.

int G;              // Movement cost. (Total of entire path)

int F;              // Estimated cost for full path. (G + H)

Tile* parentNode;   // Node to reach this node.
};
```

This struct allows us to have a single 2D array of the Tile type, which can store all the information that each tile needs. This approach is incredibly common when creating a game of this type. The array is found in the Level class, which is instantiated at the beginning of the game. It encapsulates all the data pertaining to the level.

For now, level data is stored in a simple text file which is parsed during the runtime by performing a simple lookup on an enumerator that defines all the tile types. We will work on an example of this towards the end of the chapter.

The following screenshot shows how the level data is saved:

```
level_data.txt

 1   [06][10][10][10][10][10][10][10][10][10][14][10][16][10][14][10][10][10][12]
 2   [05][19][19][19][19][19][19][19][19][19][05][19][19][19][01][19][19][19][05]
 3   [05][19][06][10][10][10][10][10][10][10][13][19][19][19][19][19][19][19][05]
 4   [05][19][05][19][19][19][19][19][19][19][05][19][04][19][02][10][10][10][13]
 5   [05][19][03][10][10][10][12][19][04][19][05][19][05][19][19][19][19][19][05]
 6   [05][19][19][19][19][19][01][19][05][19][05][19][05][19][19][04][19][19][05]
 7   [05][19][19][04][19][19][19][19][05][19][05][19][05][19][19][05][19][19][05]
 8   [05][19][19][01][19][19][06][10][09][19][01][19][05][19][19][05][19][19][05]
 9   [05][19][19][19][19][19][05][19][19][19][19][19][03][10][10][09][19][19][05]
10   [05][19][06][10][10][10][13][19][19][19][19][19][19][19][19][19][19][19][05]
11   [05][19][05][19][19][19][05][19][19][19][19][19][19][19][19][19][19][19][05]
12   [05][19][05][19][04][19][03][10][12][19][19][02][10][10][10][10][10][10][13]
13   [05][19][05][19][05][19][19][19][01][19][19][19][19][19][19][19][19][19][05]
14   [05][19][05][19][03][12][19][19][19][19][19][19][19][02][10][12][19][19][05]
15   [05][19][05][19][19][05][19][19][19][19][19][19][19][19][19][05][19][19][05]
16   [05][19][01][19][19][03][10][10][12][19][19][19][02][10][10][09][19][19][05]
17   [05][19][19][19][19][19][19][19][05][19][19][19][19][19][19][19][19][19][05]
18   [05][19][19][19][19][19][19][19][05][19][19][19][19][19][19][19][19][19][05]
19   [03][10][10][10][10][10][10][10][11][10][10][10][18][10][10][10][10][09]
```

Collision

Collisions are based on the ID of the tile that you're currently standing on. Every time a player starts to move, the position that they will be in after a successful move is calculated. This position is then used to calculate the grid `tile` that they are placed on. This tile is then used to determine what action should be performed; the action can involve performing a blocking movement, picking up an item, or taking damage.

 This type of collision can lead to the bullet through paper problem, but given the game's speed, this isn't an issue in our case. If you're unaware of what this problem is, look it up online; it may catch you out in later projects!

Input

Input is handled through a custom static `Input` class. It works much like the `Input` class that is provided with SFML, but it combines a number of possible inputs into a single call. For example, when checking whether the left key is pressed, it will check the *A* key, Left arrow key, left *D*-Pad, and analog stick. If this was to be done using the standard `Input` class, you would have to check all four individually. The `Input` class provided streamlines this.

A public `enum` of keycodes is defined in `input.h` and contains the following values that are used to poll input:

```
/**
 * An enum denoting all possible input keys.
 */
enum class KEY
{
  KEY_LEFT,
  KEY_RIGHT,
  KEY_UP,
  KEY_DOWN,
  KEY_ATTACK,
  KEY_ESC
};
```

To check the input, we simply call `Inputs IsKeyPressed(KEY keycode)` statically, passing one of the aforementioned valid keycodes.

Simple and Fast Multimedia Library (SFML)

Whilst you will have experience with C++, you may not have any prior experience with SFML. That's fine, the book doesn't assume any, so now let's take a brief tour through it

Defining SFML

SFML, short for **Simple and Fast Multimedia Library**, is a software development library that provides easy access to multiple system components. It's written in C++ and is split into the following succinct modules:

- System
- Windows
- Graphics
- Audio
- Network

With this architecture you can easily pick and choose how you want to use SFML, ranging from a simple window manager to use OpenGL, to a complete multimedia library that is capable of making full video games and multimedia software.

Why we'll be using SFML

SFML is both free, open-source, and has a vibrant community. With active forums and a selection of great tutorials on the official site, there are plenty of resources available for those who wish to learn. Another compelling reason to use SFML is that it's written in C++ and has bindings for many other languages, meaning you can pretty much code in any language that takes your fancy. There is probably a binding available for the language that you wish to use!

The single most attractive feature of SFML is that it is a multiplatform library. An app written in SFML can compile and run on most common operating systems, including Windows, Linux, and Mac OS X, with the Android and iOS versions coming soon in the market at the time of writing this book.

For your app to be cross-compatible across various platforms, remember that you also have to ensure that your native code or the other libraries used, if any, are also cross-compatible.

Learning SFML

During the course of the book, we'll look at the features and functions of SFML that we'll use to implement our procedural systems, but nothing more. We won't be taking an in-depth look at the library, as that would require a whole book. Luckily, there are a few great books that are published by Packt Publishing dedicated to just that:

- SFML Game Development at `https://www.packtpub.com/game-development/sfml-game-development`
- SFML Essentials at `https://www.packtpub.com/game-development/sfml-essentials`
- SFML Blueprints at `https://www.packtpub.com/game-development/sfml-blueprints`

If you want to learn more about SFML, then these books are a great place to start. There is also a selection of great tutorials on the official SFML site along with active forums. Visit `http://www.sfml-dev.org/learn.php` for more information.

Alternatives

While SFML is a great option for cross-platform game development, it's not the only one. There are a number of great libraries available, each with their own approaches and styles. Therefore, though we'll use SFML for this project, it's advised that you shop around for your next one. You may just run into your new favorite library.

Here are a few suggestions for future reference:

- SDL2 at `https://www.libsdl.org/download-2.0.php`
- Allegro at `http://liballeg.org/`
- MonoGame at `http://www.monogame.net/downloads/`

Polymorphism

Before we get started with the game template, we're going to take a look at polymorphism. It's an important feature of object-orientated programming that we will be taking advantage of in many of the procedural systems that we will create. Therefore, it's important that you have a solid understanding of not only what it is, but also the techniques that are used to achieve it and the potential pitfalls.

 If you already have a strong understanding of polymorphism, feel free to skip this section or head to `https://msdn.microsoft.com/en-us/library/z165t2xk(v=vs.90).aspx` for a more in-depth discussion of the topic.

Polymorphism is the ability to access different objects through an individually implemented common interface. That's a very formal definition. So, let's break that down into the individual techniques and features that are used to achieve it. It's worth noting that while polymorphism is the standard approach in the games industry, it's still a choice among other schools of programming.

Inheritance

Inheritance is perhaps the key component in achieving polymorphism. Inheritance is extending an existing class by inheriting its variables and functions, and then adding your own.

Let's take a look at a typical game example. Let's assume that we have a game with three different weapons: a sword, a wand, and an axe. These classes will share some common variables such as attack strength, durability, and attack speed. It would be a waste to create three individual classes and add this information to each, so instead we will create a parent class that includes all the shared information. Then, the children will inherit these values and use them the way they want.

Inheritance creates an "is a" relationship. This means that since Axe is inherited from Weapon, Axe is a Weapon. This concept of creating a common interface in a parent class and implementing it in unique ways via child classes is the key to achieving polymorphism.

 By interface, I mean the collection of functions and variables that the parent class passes to its children.

The following diagram illustrates this scenario in the form of a simple class diagram:

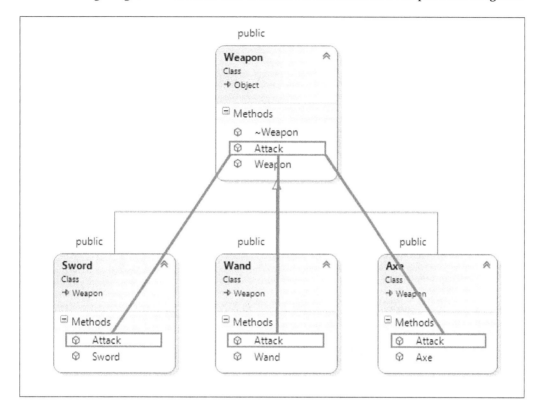

The highlighted `Attack()` functions in the individual weapons are all inherited from the single `Attack()` function defined in the **Weapon** class.

 To maintain proper encapsulation and scope, it's important that our variables and functions are given the correct visibility modifiers. If you're unsure about this or you could do with a quick reminder, head to `https://msdn.microsoft.com/en-us/library/kktasw36.aspx`.

Virtual functions

Continuing with the generic weapon example, we now have a parent class that provides a number of functions and variables that all child classes will inherit. In order to be able to denote our own behavior that is different from that of the parent class, we need to be able to override the parent functions. This is achieved through the use of virtual functions.

Virtual functions are functions that can be overridden by implementing classes. In order for this to be possible, the parent class must mark the function as virtual. This is done by simply prefixing the virtual keyword to a function declaration like this:

```
Virtual void Attack();
```

In a child class, we can then override that function by providing our own definition, provided the signatures of the two functions are identical. This override is done automatically, however, C++11 introduced the `override` keyword to specifically denote where a function will override the function of a parent. The override keyword is optional, but it's considered good practice and it is recommended. It is used as follows:

```
Void Attack() override;
```

C++11 also introduced the `final` keyword. This keyword is used to designate virtual functions that cannot be overridden in a derived class. It can also be applied to classes that cannot be inherited. You can use the final keyword as follows:

```
Void Attack() final;
```

In this case, the `Attack()` function could not be overridden by inheriting classes.

Pure virtual functions

Virtual functions that we just covered allow a function to be *optionally* overridden by an inheriting class. The override is optional, as the parent class will provide a default implementation if one is not found in the child class.

A pure virtual function however does not provide a default implementation. Hence, it must be implemented by inheriting classes. Furthermore, if a class contains a pure virtual function, it becomes abstract. This means that it cannot be instantiated, only inheriting classes, providing they provide an implementation for the pure virtual function, can be. If a class inherits from an abstract class and does not provide an implementation for pure virtual functions, then that class becomes abstract too.

The syntax that is used to declare a pure virtual function is as follows:

```
Virtual void Attack() = 0;
```

In the example of the Weapon parent class, which is inherited by Sword, Axe and Wand, it would make sense to make Weapon an abstract class. We will never instantiate a Weapon object; its sole purpose is to provide a common interface to its children. Since each child class needs to have an Attack() function, it then makes sense to make the Attack() function in Weapon pure virtual, as we know that every child will implement it.

Pointers and object slicing

The last part of the polymorphism puzzle is the use of pointers. Consider the following two lines of code:

```
Weapon myWeapon = Sword();
Std::unique_ptr<Weapon> myWeapon = std::make_unique<Sword>();
```

In the first line, we are not using pointers; in the second one, we are. It is a seemingly small difference, but it produces extremely different results. To properly demonstrate this, we're going to look at a small program that defines a number of weapons.

 If the `Weapon` class contains a pure virtual function, the first line of the preceding code won't be compiled since it will be abstract and cannot be instantiated.

You can download the code for this program from the Packt Publishing website. It will be in the `Examples` folder, and the project name is `polymorphism_example`:

```cpp
#include <iostream>

// We're using namespace std here to avoid having to fully qualify
everything with std::
using namespace std;

int main()
{

  // Here we define a base Weapon struct.
  // It provides a single data type, and a method to return it.
  struct Weapon
  {
    string itemType = "Generic Weapon";

    virtual string GetItemType()
    {
      return itemType;
    }
  };

  // Here we inherit from the generic Weapon struct to make a specific
Sword struct.
```

```
  // We override the GetItemType() function to change the itemType
variable before returning it.
  struct Sword : public Weapon
  {
    string GetItemType() override
    {
      itemType = "Sword";
      return itemType;
    }
  };


  Weapon myWeapon = Sword();

  // output the type of item that weapon is then wait.
  cout << myWeapon.GetItemType().c_str() << endl;
  std::cin.get();

  return 0;
}
```

In this code we created a base struct `Weapon`. We then inherit from it to create a specific implementation named `Sword`. The base `Weapon` struct defines the `GetItemType()` function and `Sword` overrides it to change and then return the item type. This is a pretty straightforward case of inheritance and polymorphism, but there are some important things that we need to know that could otherwise trip us up.

As the code currently stands, the `Weapon` object is instantiated in the following way:

```
Weapon myWeapon = Sword()
```

Let's run the code and see what we get:

Even though we assigned `myWeapon` a `Sword` object, it's a `Weapon` object. What's happening here? The problem is that `myWeapon` is given a fixed type of weapon. When we try to assign it a `Sword` object, it gets passed to the `copy` constructor of `Weapon` and gets sliced, leaving just a `Weapon` object. As a result, when we call the `GetItemType()` function, we call the function in `Weapon`.

For a more in-depth explanation of object slicing, head to
http://www.bogotobogo.com/cplusplus/slicing.php.

To avoid this and make good use of polymorphism, we need to work with pointers. Let's make the following change to the code:

```
// Create our weapon object.
Weapon myWeapon = Sword();
std::unique_ptr<Weapon> myWeapon = std::make_unique<Sword>();
```

Smart pointers such as `unique_ptr` require the `include <memory>`. So don't forget to add this to the top of the file.

Since we've now changed `myWeapon` to a pointer, we also need to change the following:

```
// Output the type of item that weapon is then wait.
cout << myWeapon.GetItemType().c_str() << endl;
cout << myWeapon->GetItemType().c_str() << endl;
```

When working with pointers, we need to use the -> operator to access its variables and functions. Now, let's rerun the code and see what the output is:

This time, we called the overridden function in the Sword struct as intended, and it boils down to the way we defined myWeapon.

Since myWeapon is now a pointer to a Weapon object, we avoid object slicing. Since Sword is derived from Weapon, pointing to a Sword in memory isn't a problem. They share a common interface, so we achieve this overriding behavior. Returning to the initial definition, polymorphism is the ability to access different objects through an individually implemented common interface.

The roguelike template setup

A template is provided with this book for a roguelike game that was created specifically for the book. It's been designed to receive the work that we'll cover, and at the end of the book, you'll have a fully functional roguelike game that implements everything that you will have learned. Now that we've brushed up on our understanding of polymorphism, let's get the template setup. The first step is to download and link SFML.

> The project, as provided, is linked with SMFL 32-bit windows libraries. This should suit most systems. If this is compatible with your system, you can skip the following steps.

Downloading SFML

SFML is available in a number of different precompiled packages. For example, the latest release at the time of writing this book has 12 packages available for Windows alone, so it's important that you download the correct one for your system. The following steps will help you to download and setup SFML:

1. Visit at `http://www.sfml-dev.org/download.php` to find the SFML download page. Unless you specifically need to target a 64-bit machine, choose the 32-bit libraries. A 32-bit program will work fine on a 64-bit machine.

2. Next, you need to choose the right package for your compiler. If you're using Microsoft Visual Studio, you just need to choose the year that matches your version, and if you're using Code::Blocks, or any other IDE for that matter, choose the version of **GNU Compiler Collection (GCC)** that you're using.

3. Once you've identified the correct version for your system, download it and extract the contents of the `.zip` file to where you want SFML to be saved. This location has nothing to do with your project; they don't need to share a directory.

 You can build SFML on your own to create a custom package if you wish or need to do so. For instructions on how to do so, visit `https://github.com/SFML/SFML`.

Linking SFML

There are two ways to link SFML: **static** and **dynamic** libraries. A static library is the one that is compiled into your executable. This means that your executable is bigger, but you don't have to worry about getting the library during the runtime. Dynamic libraries do not get linked into the executable, which results in a smaller executable, but creates dependencies.

 For more information on the difference between `static` and `dynamic` libraries, visit `http://www.learncpp.com/cpp-tutorial/a1-static-and-dynamic-libraries/`.

We're going to link dynamically, which means that to run the game, you will need the .dll files.

To do so, first copy the DLL files that the game will need from the SFML source to the project's executable location. Copy all the files from <sfml-install-path/bin> to <project-location/Debug>.

Next, we have to tell the compiler where the SFML headers are and the linker where the out libraries are. Headers are .hpp files, and libraries are .lib files. This step slightly differs depending on which IDE you're using.

In Microsoft Visual Studio, add the following to the project's properties:

- The path to the SFML headers (<sfml-install-path>/include) to **C/C++ | General | Additional Include Directories**
- The path to the SFML libraries (<sfml-install-path>/lib) to **Linker | General | Additional Library Directories**

In Code::Blocks, add the following to the project's **Build Options** and **Search Directories** tab:

- The path to the SFML headers (<sfml-install-path>/include) to the Compiler search directories
- The path to the SFML libraries (<sfml-install-path>/lib) to the Linker search directories

 These paths are the same in both the Debug and Release configurations. Therefore, they can be set globally for the project.

The final step is to link our project to the SFML libraries that are being used. SFML is made up of five modules, but we won't use all of them. We're using System, Windows, Graphics, and Audio. Therefore, we only need to link to these libraries. Unlike the previous step, the project configuration is important. There are separate libraries for the Debug and Release configurations. Therefore, you need to ensure that you link the correct ones.

In the Debug configuration, we need to add the following libraries:

- sfml-system-d.lib
- sfml-window-d.lib
- sfml-graphics-d.lib
- sfml-audio-d.lib

Now, do the same for the **Release** configuration. However, drop the -d from each. For example, we add `sfml-system-d.lib` in the **Debug** configuration, and we add `sfml-system.lib` in the **Release** configuration.

To add these to Microsoft Visual Studio, they must be added to the project's properties by navigating to **Linker | Input | Additional Dependencies**.

To add these to Code::Blocks, they must be added to the **Link Libraries** list in the project's build options under the **Linker Settings** tab.

 If you have any queries regarding this setup, visit `http://www.sfml-dev.org/learn.php` for a complete breakdown along with images.

Running the project

Now that SFML is linked to our project, we should be ready to perform the first build. The following screenshot shows our currently empty roguelike game:

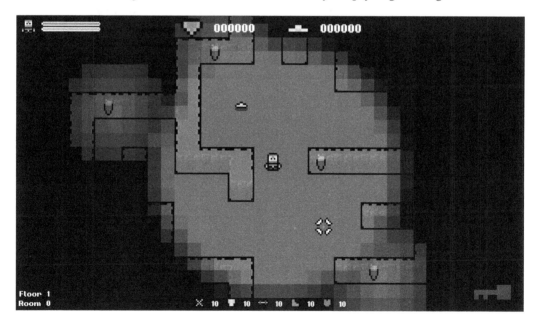

As the project currently stands, we have a runnable application that spawns a player in a fixed room. The first task involves adding an item.

Adding an item

All items that we create need to inherit from the base `Item` class because all game items are stored in a single vector of the `std::unique_ptr<Item>` type. With this data structure we can take advantage of polymorphism, and store all the item subclasses in a single structure; through this, we can update and draw each item.

To add to this vector, simply instantiate a new item via a unique pointer. Then, add it to the vector using the `.push_back()` method. Since we're using unique pointers, we have to use `std::move()` to do so.

 If you're unclear about why we have to use `std::move` here, look up for unique pointers on the Internet.

In the `Game::PopulateLevel` function, let's add a gem item, as follows:

```
// Create a gem object.
std::unique_ptr<Gem> gem = std::make_unique<Gem>();

// Set the gem position.
gem->SetPosition(sf::Vector2f(m_screenCenter.x + 50.f, m_
screenCenter.y));

// Add the gem to our collection of all objects.
m_items.push_back(std::move(gem));
```

All that we have to do is create a new object via a unique pointer, give it a position, and then add it to the list of all the items in the level using the `std::move` function. Easy!

Updating and drawing

Once an item is added to the vector of all the objects, it will be automatically updated:

```
// Update all items.
UpdateItems(playerPosition);
```

This function iterates over all the items, checking whether they have been collected; if this is not the case, it updates them. The `Update()` function of each object has a single parameter named `timeDelta`. This is a float that contains the time that has passed since the last update. It's used in the main outer game loop to keep the game logic fixed at 60 fps.

> To know more about the main game loop, visit `http://gafferongames.com/game-physics/fix-your-timestep/`, which is a great article on the subject.

Items are drawn in a similar way; their container is simply iterated over in the `Game::Draw` function. This loop is as follows:

```
// Have all objects draw themselves.
for (const auto& item : m_items)
{
    item->Draw(m_window, timeDelta);
}
```

The `m_window` variable is a pointer to the render window. Hence, we pass it to each object so that it can use it to draw itself.

Now, if you run the game, you will see the gem in the room along with the gold, as shown in the following screenshot:

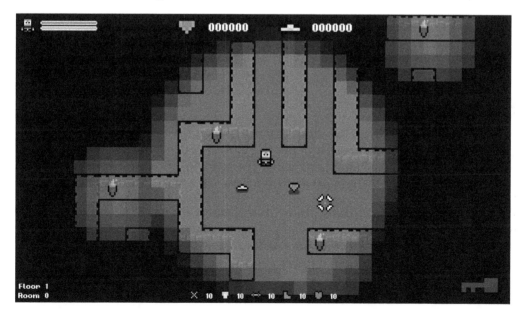

Exercises

To help you test your knowledge of this chapter's content, here are a few exercises that you should work on. They are not imperative to the rest of the book, but working on them will help you assess your strengths and weakness on the material covered.

1. Create a name for your game and change the text of the main window to reflect this change.

2. Consider the following code:

```
class A
{
public:
    int x;
protected:
    int y;
private:
    int z;
};

class B : protected A
{

};
```

    What is the visibility of x, y, and z in `class B`?

3. Add more items to the level.

Summary

In this chapter, we made preparations that are needed in order to start coding the game and create the procedural systems. We looked at the software and libraries that we will use, and the game template that we'll extend. We also took a crash course in polymorphism and the techniques that we will use to achieve it.

We're now ready to start creating our own procedural systems. The groundwork that we just covered isn't terribly exciting, but it is crucial to understanding the work that we're going to cover when moving forward. In the next chapter we're going to use what we learned about random number generation with C++ data types to spawn random items, and give our player random stats.

3
Using RNG with C++ Data Types

In *Chapter 1*, *An Introduction to Procedural Generation*, we learned the fact that pseudorandom number generation is at the heart of random procedural generation. Remember, a procedural system is not random by nature, we need to induce randomness. To start our journey, we're going to look at a range of different C++ data types, and use Random Number Generator (RNG) to give them random values at runtime. This ability to use core C++ data types in a random, yet still controlled, way will be the basis for all our future systems.

In this chapter we'll cover the following topics:

- Setting the game seed
- Enumerators
- Setting Boolean values randomly
- Accessing random elements in an array
- Generating random strings
- Random number distribution

Setting the game seed

Before we do anything we're going to need to set the game seed. Without it we'll get the same results each time our game is run. As we've learned, this simply requires us to make a call to the `std::srand()` function passing a random parameter to be used as the seed. We'll use the current system time as our seed, it's random enough for our purposes.

Where we make the call to the `std::srand()` function is arbitrary so long as it's called before any call to the `std::rand()` function. The file `main.cpp` contains the function `main()`, the entry point of the application. It's here that our game object is created and the main game loop entered, so we'll make our call to the `std::srand()` function here.

Our updated `main()` function should now look like this:

```
// Entry point of the application.
int main()
{
    // Set a random seed.
    std:: srand(static_cast<unsigned int>(time(nullptr)));

    // Create the main game object.
    Game game;

    // Create a Boolean that we can store out result it.
    bool result;

    // Initialize and run the game object.
    result = game.Initialize();

    if (result)
    {
        game.Run();
    }

    // Shutdown and release the game object.
    game.Shutdown();

    // Exit the application.
    return 0;
}
```

Each time we run the game now we will have a random seed set, so our calls to the `std::rand()` yield unique results.

 If you want your game to be consistent between runs you can use a hard-coded value as the seed. Just don't forget to change it back or you'll wonder why things aren't random later down the line!

Setting Boolean values randomly

Perhaps the simplest of all data types is the humble bool. With only two states, true and false, it shouldn't be too hard to set randomly! When represented as integers, the two states have the following properties:

- False = 0 or lower
- True = 1 or higher

Given this, to randomly assign a bool we simply need to generate either the number 0 or 1.

Generating a number between 0 and 1

In *Chapter 1, An Introduction to Procedural Generation*, we covered the generation of random numbers within a specific range. Well we're now going to put that to use. Using the std::rand() function we will generate a number between 0 and 1:

```
std::rand() % 2;
```

> Remember, std::rand() generates a number between 0 and RAND_MAX function. We then calculate the remainder of that result divided by 2. This leaves just the range 0 and 1.

A bool does not have to be set with the true or false keyword. You can assign an integer to a bool and its state will be determined by the integer's value using the rule stated previously. Any number less than 1 is false, and any number above 0 is true. That means we can feed our result straight into a bool:

```
bool myBool = std::rand() % 2;
```

Putting this together, we can create a simple console application that outputs either true or false randomly each time the user presses *Enter*.

You can download the code for this program from the Packt Publishing website. It will be in the Examples folder, and the project name is random_boolean:

```
#include <iostream>

using namespace std;

int main()
{
  // Loop forever.
  while (true)
```

```
    {
        // Generate a number between 0 and 1.
        bool myBool = rand() % 2;
        if (myBool)
        {
            cout << "true";
        }
        else
        {
            cout << "false";
        }
        return 0;
    }
```

This code results in the following output:

Each time we hit *Enter* we get a random Boolean value. Even this simple case of random generation can enable us to start building our procedural roguelike game. Let's apply it straight away to the creation of items when the room is created.

Remember, nowhere in this small example application do we set the seed randomly. As a result, this program will generate the same sequence of values each time it is run.

Choosing if an item spawns

Currently, when we start the game a gem and gold item are always spawned. Let's use this random bool assignment to decide whether or not the two objects are created. To accomplish this we'll encapsulate their spawn code inside an `if` statement, the parameter to which will be the result of our random Boolean assignment.

The `Game::PopulateLevel` method is where out items are spawned. We'll replace the current code with the following:

```cpp
// Populate the level with items.
void Game::PopulateLevel()
{
    // A Boolean variable used to determine if an object should be
spawned.bool canSpawn;

    // Spawn gold.
    canSpawn = std::rand() % 2;
    if (canSpawn)
    {
        std::unique_ptr<Gold> gold = std::make_unique<Gold>();
        gold->SetPosition(sf::Vector2f(m_screenCenter.x - 50.f, m_
screenCenter.y));
        m_items.push_back(std::move(gold));
    }

    // Spawn a gem.
    canSpawn = std::rand() % 2;
    if (canSpawn)
    {
        std::unique_ptr<Gem> gem = std::make_unique<Gem>();
        gem->SetPosition(sf::Vector2f(m_screenCenter.x + 50.f, m_
screenCenter.y));
        m_items.push_back(std::move(gem));
    }
}
```

Now, each time we run the game, it's random whether or not the gem and gold are spawned.

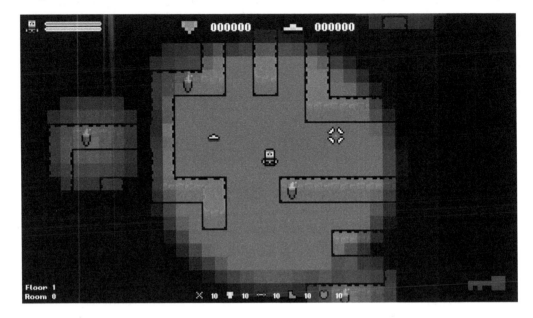

A simple change, but the first step in creating a procedurally generated game. There is no single algorithm or function that makes a game procedural. It's a collection of small techniques such as this that make systems non-predictable and determined at runtime.

Random number distribution

Let's build upon what we know about random number generation to distribute numbers randomly. We'll achieve this by first generating n numbers between 0 and 100. If we add these together we get a random total where each of our individual numbers represents a percentage of that. We can then take that percentage of our goal number to get a random portion. The following code demonstrates this and will make it clearer.

You can download the code for this program from the Packt website. It will be in the
Examples folder, and the project name is random_distribution:

```cpp
#include <iostream>

using namespace std;

// Entry method of the application.
int main()
{
  // Create and initialize our variables.
  int upperLimit = 0;

  // Output instructions.
  cout << "Enter a number, and we'll split it into three random
smaller numbers:" << endl;
  cin >> upperLimit;
  cout << endl;

  float number1Bias = rand() % 101;
  float number2Bias = rand() % 101;
  float number3Bias = rand() % 101;

  float total = number1Bias + number2Bias + number3Bias;

  // Output the numbers.
  cout << upperLimit * (number1Bias / total) << endl;
  cout << upperLimit * (number2Bias / total) << endl;
  cout << upperLimit * (number3Bias / total) << endl;

  // Pause so we can see output.
  cin.get();
  cin.get();

  // Exit function.
  return 0;
}
```

This method ensures that each segment of the number is completely random. There is a slight rounding error to be taken into account, but that's not a problem for our application.

Let's waste no time and apply this new skill to the game!

Giving the player random stats

A classic way in which this random distribution of numbers can be used is to give a player random stats. Traditionally, a character in a game is given n stat points, and it's up to the player to distribute them. Since we're making a procedural game, we'll instead distribute them randomly to create procedurally generated character stats.

To do this we need to hook up the previous code with the assignment of our player's stat variables. Our player stats are currently fixed, and assigned in the following way:

```
m_attack = 10;
m_defense = 10;
m_strength = 10;
m_dexterity = 10;
m_stamina = 10;
```

Let's replace that with the following to randomly distribute the stats. We'll also add a variable to the player so we can change how many stat points the player has to distribute.

To start, add the following variable to the player, and don't forget to add it to our initializer list:

```
int m_statPoints;
```

Now let's use this to give our player random stats:

```
// Randomly distribute other stat.
m_statPoints = 50;

float attackBias = std::rand() % 101;
float defenseBias = std::rand() % 101;
float strengthBias = std::rand() % 101;
float dexterityBias = std::rand() % 101;
float staminaBias = std::rand() % 101;

float total = attackBias + defenseBias + strengthBias + dexterityBias
+ staminaBias;

m_attack += m_statPoints * (attackBias / total);
m_defense += m_statPoints * (defenseBias / total);
m_strength += m_statPoints * (strengthBias / total);
m_dexterity += m_statPoints * (dexterityBias / total);
m_stamina += m_statPoints * (staminaBias / total);
```

Each time we now load the game our player has their stat points allocated randomly. This approach of randomly distributing of a set amount could be used in many other ways, such as sharing loot between players and allocating damage between multiple entities.

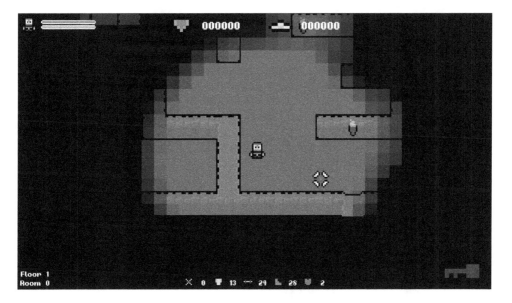

Accessing random elements of a collection

When we have collections of similar objects, they are often stored in structures such as arrays and vectors. Usually when working with these structures we access specific elements, and it's their uniformness and order that make them useful.

To access a specific element we simply supply its index in the collection. Therefore, to access a random element of the array we just supply a random index, which is a simple case of generating a random number.

Let's have a look at an example of this. In the following example we create a vector of strings which we populate with animal names. Each time we press enter we access a random element of the vector by generating a number between 0 and the vectors size.

You can download the code for this program from the Packt website. It will be in the Examples folder, and the project name is random_element:

```cpp
#include <iostream>
#include <vector>

using namespace std;

// Entry method of the application.
int main()
{
  // Create and populate an array of animals.
  vector<string> animals = { "Dog", "Cat", "Bird", "Fox", "Lizard" };

  // Output the instructions.
  cout << "Press enter for the name of a random animal!" << endl;

  // Loop forever.
  while (true)
  {
    // Wait for user input.
    cin.get();

    // Generate a random index.
    int randomIndex;
    randomIndex = rand() % animals.size();
```

```
        // Output the name of the randomly selected animal.
        cout << animals[randomIndex].c_str();
    }

    // Exit function.
    return 0;
}
```

The output of is as follows:

Accessing random elements of a collection is a great tool for creating procedural systems. Anywhere in your game where there is a single object, you can create an array or vector of alternates, and choose one at random at runtime. With this alone you could create a highly randomized game where each run is unique.

Spawning a random item

Currently, when we load our game, set items are spawned. We need to add an element of randomness to do this, and something as simple as a `switch` statement is all that's needed. Where we can, we always want to add options to create random and procedurally generated content.

To randomly spawn our items, we need to generate a random number between `0` and the number of items we have, and then use that in a `switch` statement. As stated previously, there isn't one approach to procedural generation, so there will be other methods to doing this.

Let's add in the number generation and `switch` statements to choose which item to spawn. The updated `Game::PopulateLevel` function should look as follows:

```cpp
// Populate the level with items.
void Game::PopulateLevel()
{
    // A Boolean variable used to determine if an object should be
spawned.
    bool canSpawn;

    // Spawn an item.
    canSpawn = std::rand() % 2;
    if (canSpawn)
    {
        int itemIndex = std::rand() % 2;
        std::unique_ptr<Item> item;
        switch (itemIndex)
        {
            case 0:
                item = std::make_unique<Gold>();
            break;

            case 1:
                item = std::make_unique<Gem>();
            break;
        }
        item->SetPosition(sf::Vector2f(m_screenCenter.x, m_
screenCenter.y));
        m_items.push_back(std::move(item));
    }
}
```

Now we can see that when we run the game, if an object can be spawned it will be either the gold item or the gem. We have a bunch of items in the game, and in the next chapter we'll be extending this system to include them all, populating our entire level from a single function:

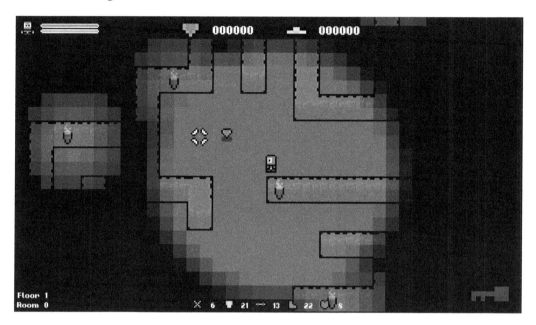

Generating random characters

Since we've covered generating random strings from a set wordlist, let's look at generating random characters. The char data type is a single, one byte character.

A string is actually just a null-terminated sequence of characters, so the following lines of code produce the exact same result:

```
Stirng myStringLiteral = "hello";
string myString = { 'h', 'e', 'l', 'l', 'o', '\0' };
```

Likewise, the following code is semantically correct:

```
char myCharArray[6] = { 'h', 'e', 'l', 'l', 'o', '\0' };
string stringVersion = myCharArray;
```

Since a `char` is one byte, it has the possible integer representations of 0 to 255. Each of these decimal values represents a different character. A lookup table can found in the ASCII table. For example, the character *a* has the decimal value 97. We can use these integers when assigning a `char`, as follows:

```
char myChar = 97;
```

In C++ the maximum decimal value of a `char` is 255. If you go over this it will overflow and loop back through the table. For example, setting a char value equal to 353 will result in the character *a*. An ASCII table can be found at http://www.asciitable.com/.

To generate a random char we therefore need to generate a number between 0 and 255, something we're very familiar with now.

You can download the code for this program from the Packt website. It will be in the `Examples` folder, and the project name is `random_character`:

```cpp
#include <iostream>

using namespace std;

// Entry method of the application.
int main()
{
  // Loop forever.
  while (true)
  {
    // Output instructions.
    cout << "Press enter to generate a random character from the ASCII
standard:" << endl;

    // Pause for user input.
    cin.get();

    // The ASCII characters range from 0 - 127 in decimal.
    int randInt = rand() % 128;

    // To turn that into a char, we can just assign the int.
    char randChar = randInt;
```

```
    // Output the random char.
    cout << "Random Char: " << randChar << "\n" << endl;
}

  // Exit function.
  return 0;
}
```

With this code we're generating a random character from the entire ASCII table. To generate characters within a more specific range, we simply need to cap the number range we generate with.

For example, looking at the ASCII table shows us that the lowercase alphabet starts at 97 and runs until 122. Let's adjust the random number generator to generate values within this range only:

```
// The ASCII characters range from 0 - 127 in decimal.
int randInt = rand() % 128;
int randInt = std::rand() % 128;
int randInt = std::rand() % 26 + 97;
```

Now we can see that the outputs are letters from the lowercase alphabet only, as shown in the following screenshot:

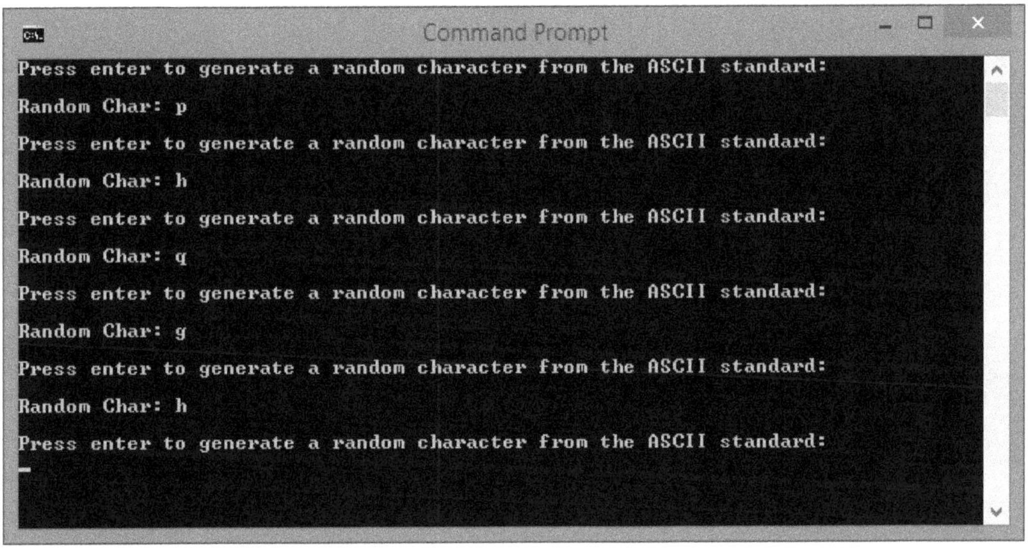

Repeating loops

Another use of generating random numbers is to loop over certain code an undetermined number of times. For example, when we spawn our items we make individual calls to the spawn code. This is fine if we just want to spawn one item every time, but what about when we want to spawn a random number of items.

We need to make a random amount of calls to our code, which we'll later wrap in its own function, and this can be achieved using `for` loops. In a `for` loop we specify how many times we want the loop to iterate, so instead of using a fixed value as we normally would, we can generate a random number to use instead. Each time the code is run, a new random number will be generated, and the loop will be a different size each time.

You can download the code for this program from `http://www.packtpub.com/support`. It will be in folder `Chapter 3`, and is called `random_loops.cpp`:

```cpp
// Include our dependencies.
#include <iostream>
#include <ctime>

// We include std so we don't have to fully qualify everything.
using namespace std;

void HelloWorld();

// Entry method of the application.
int main()
{
  // First we give the application a random seed.
  srand(time(nullptr));

  // Loop forever.
  while (true)
  {
    // Output the welcome message.
    cout << "Press enter to iterate a random number of times:" <<
endl;

    // Pause for user input.
    cin.get();
```

```cpp
    // Generate a random number between 1 and 10.
    int iterations = rand() % 10 + 1;

    // Now loop that number of times.
    for (int i = 0; i < iterations; i++)
    {
      cout << "Iteration " << i << ": ";
      HelloWorld();
    }

    // Output ending message.
    cout << endl << "We made " << iterations << " call(s) to
  HelloWorld() that time!" << endl << endl;
  }

  // Exit function.
  return 0;
}

// Outputs the text Hello World!.
void HelloWorld()
{
  cout << "Hello World!" << endl;
}
```

The output is shown in the following screenshot:

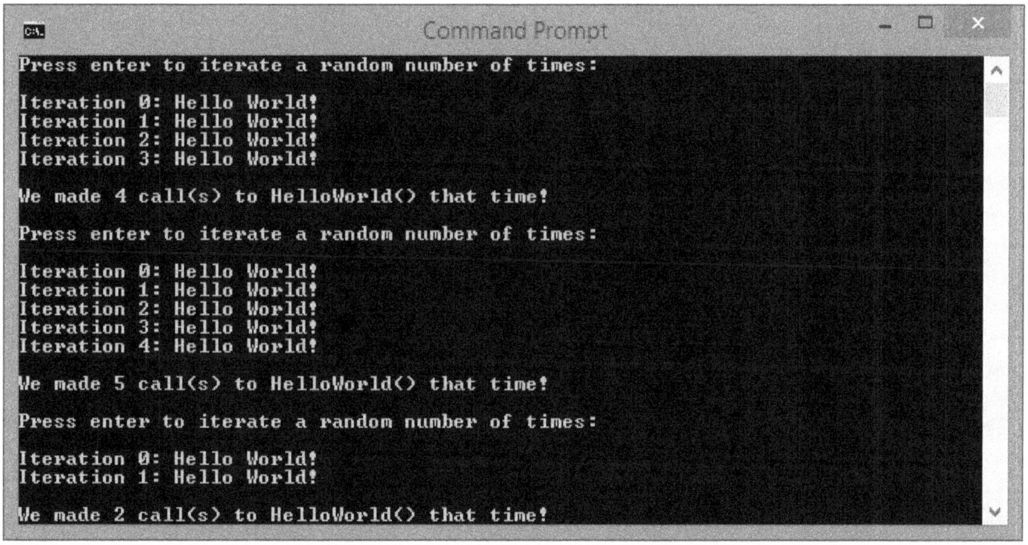

Spawning a random number of items

With our items being spawned in our `Game::PopulateLevel` function, and the ability to call a function a random number of times, let's update the code so we spawn a random number of items when we start the game.

To achieve this, all we need to do is create the same loop as in the previous exercise, and encapsulate our spawn code within it. Let's update `Game::PopulateLevel` with the following:

```cpp
// Populate the level with items.
void Game::PopulateLevel()
{
  // A Boolean variable used to determine if an object should be
spawned.
  bool canSpawn;

  // Generate a random number between 1 and 10.
  int iterations = std::rand() % 10 + 1;

  // Now loop that number of times.
  for (int i = 0; i < iterations; i++)
  {
    // Spawn an item.
    canSpawn = std::rand() % 2;

    if (canSpawn)
    {
      int itemIndex = std::rand() % 2;
      std::unique_ptr<Item> item;

      switch (itemIndex)
      {
      case 0:
        item = std::make_unique<Gold>();
        break;

      case 1:
        item = std::make_unique<Gem>();
        break;
      }
```

```
    item->SetPosition(sf::Vector2f(m_screenCenter.x, m_
screenCenter.y));
        m_items.push_back(std::move(item));
    }
  }
}
```

Now when we run the code, we have a bunch of items that are spawned. They are currently spawning on-top of one-another, but don't worry, we're fixing that in the next chapter!

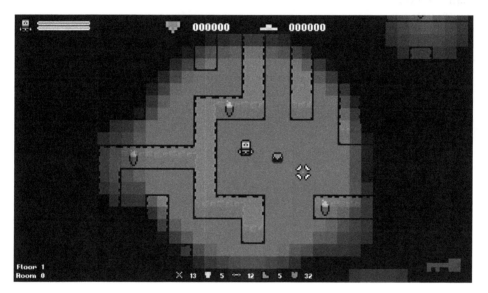

Exercises

To enable you to test your knowledge of this chapter's content, here are a few exercises that you should work through. They are not imperative to the rest of the book, but working through them will help you assess your strengths and weaknesses on the material covered.

1. Add more options to the random string generator. Try to create a generator that uses two random words.

2. Amend the random character generation program so we generate the characters A-Z uppercase, and a-z lowercase.

3. The player is currently spawned at a fixed location in the level. Create a set of possible spawn coordinates, and choose randomly between them at run-time so the spawn location varies.

Summary

In this chapter we've taken a look at a range of C++ data types, and incorporated RNG with their use. The ability to use these data types in a random, but controlled way, is key in implementing random procedural systems. Remember, procedural generation is just the creation of content as the result of a calculation. This is not random by nature, we have to induce randomness as we have in this chapter. The additions we have made to the game are small, but are the first steps in creating a procedurally generated game. Already when we run our game it will be a little different each time.

In the next chapter we're going to develop our level further by spawning our items and enemies in random locations around the map. Procedurally generated environments are a staple in procedurally generated games, and spawning our game objects in random locations is a big step towards achieving this.

4
Procedurally Populating Game Environments

Now that we're comfortable using **Random Number Generator (RNG)** with core C++ data types, let's have a look at how to create a highly randomized environment. This will include the random generation and positioning of items, enemies, and more. We'll also touch upon random map generation in this chapter before tackling it head-on toward the end of the book.

The way in which objects are spawned will largely depend on the infrastructure of your level data. With most 2D games, you'll be able to take an approach that is similar, if not identical, to the one demonstrated in this chapter. However, a 3D game requires more work because there's an extra dimension to deal with, but the principles are still valid.

In this chapter, we'll cover the following topics:

- Obstacles with procedurally populating an environment
- Defining the spawn area
- Randomly selecting a game `tile`
- Spawning items at a random location
- Procedurally generating changes to an environment

Potential obstacles

Generating game environments randomly isn't as simple as it may first appear. It's not just a case of generating a random number within the bounds of a level. Though this might technically work, there is no control there, and the environment that is generated as a result will have many flaws. Objects may overlap, be located in unreachable places, or be laid out in a poor order. In order to generate meaningful and playable levels there needs to be more control.

Keeping within the bounds of a level

I'm sure that at some point we've all played a game where an item spawned beyond our reach. It's infuriating to have that shiny new item just out of reach, but this can easily happen when spawning objects randomly around a map. Therefore, it's important to establish accurate bounds within which the objects can be spawned.

As you can imagine, the complexity of this task will match the complexity of your environment. Thankfully for us, our level is described as a simple 2D array. Hence, it's fairly easy to calculate the bounds.

Avoiding overlapping objects

Even if you define your level bounds perfectly, you are still not home and dry. Environments are generally not empty, and are mostly filled with scenery and other game objects. It's important to take these objects into account when choosing random spawn coordinates as to not spawn object within them, again pushing items out of the reach of the player.

Again, we're not going to have to worry too much about this as we will have simple levels with no scenery.

Creating meaningful levels

After all is said and done, the level has to make sense. Even if we avoid spawning items that are beyond the reach of the player, and which don't overlap one another, it's no good if they all spawn in one far corner.

We need to create suitable parameters within which our RNG operates so we retain a suitable level of control over the results. It's one of the major pitfalls of procedurally generated games. Time and time again, you will see a level that just doesn't make much sense because the algorithm has produced an odd result.

Level tiles

Before we start working with a `level` grid, we need to know how it is set up!
Our `level` is described as a 2D array of a custom type `Tile`, a `struct` defined in
`Level.h`:

```
// A struct that defines the data values our tiles need.
struct Tile
{
TILE type;          // The type of tile this is.
int columnIndex;    // The column index of the tile.
int rowIndex;       // The row index of the tile.
sf::Sprite sprite;  // The tile sprite.
int H;              // Heuristic / movement cost to goal.
int G;              // Movement cost. (Total of entire path)
int F;              // Estimated cost for full path. (G + H)
Tile* parentNode;   // Node to reach this node.
};
```

Don't worry about the final four values at this point; we'll use them later when we
get to the section on path finding! For now, we just need to know that each `tile`
struct stores its type, position in the 2D array, and its sprite. All the possible `tile`
types are defined in an enumerator in `Util.h`, as follows:

```
// All possible tiles.
enum class TILE {
  WALL_SINGLE,
  WALL_TOP_END,
  WALL_SIDE_RIGHT_END,
  WALL_BOTTOM_LEFT,
  WALL_BOTTOM_END,
  WALL_SIDE,
  WALL_TOP_LEFT,
  WALL_SIDE_LEFT_T,
  WALL_SIDE_LEFT_END,
  WALL_BOTTOM_RIGHT,
  WALL_TOP,
  WALL_BOTTOM_T,
  WALL_TOP_RIGHT,
  WALL_SIDE_RIGHT_T,
  WALL_TOP_T,
  WALL_INTERSECTION,
  WALL_DOOR_LOCKED,
  WALL_DOOR_UNLOCKED,
  WALL_ENTRANCE,
  FLOOR,
```

```
        FLOOR_ALT,
        EMPTY,
        COUNT
};
```

This gives every `tile` type a string constant. So, instead of working with vague numbers, we can work with these values instead. With this sorted, let's get started.

Defining the spawn area

Now we know what obstacles lie ahead, and how the level data is stored, let's take a look at how we can spawn items at random locations in our `roguelike` object.

Calculating the level bounds

The first step is to calculate the level bounds. Since we're making a 2D `roguelike` object, described in a 2D array, we need to identify the tiles that are suitable to spawn items on. If this was done for a 3D game, you would also have to take into account the third axis. Though we could just find the top left point of the map and calculate the distance to the bottom right, this would almost certainly cause problems.

We mentioned earlier that it's important that items are spawned within valid level areas. If we take this simple approach, we run the risk of spawning items in the walls. The following pseudocode shows how this can be achieved:

```
for (int i = 0; i < GRID_WIDTH; ++i)
{
  for (int j = 0; j < GRID_HEIGHT; ++j)
  {
    m_grid[i][j].markAsSpawnable();
  }
}
```

The following screenshot shows the spawn area if we use this simple approach in the game:

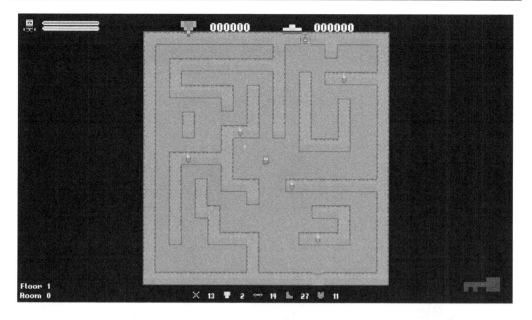

As we can see, the spawn area that was created exceeds the playable level area, even though it is technically within the level bounds.

Checking the underlying game grid

The easiest way to do this in our case is by checking the underlying game grid. Since each floor tile in the level grid has a unique tile type that denotes what kind of tile it is, we can iterate over the level grid and only mark the tiles with a valid type as possible spawn locations. The previous pseudocode has been modified and updated in the following way to make this check:

```
for (int i = 0; i < GRID_WIDTH; ++i)
{
    for (int j = 0; j < GRID_HEIGHT; ++j)
    {
        if (m_grid[i][j].type == TILE::FLOOR || m_grid[i][j].type ==
TILE::FLOOR_ALT)
        {
            m_grid[i][j].markAsSpawnable();
        }
    }
}
```

If we ran a check like this, we would end up with the following possible spawn area:

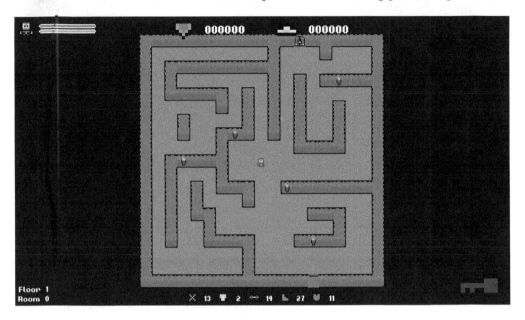

As you can see, this is a much better area to spawn items. The next step is to choose a point within this area as the spawn location.

Selecting a suitable game tile

Now, to find suitable tiles, we will generate random spawn coordinates. We know that all tiles with the TILE::FLOOR or TILE::FLOOR_ALT type are floor tiles. Therefore, we can select a tile at random and deduce if it's suitable for the spawning of an item.

To avoid having to do these checks ourselves, the project provides the Level::IsFloor function. It is quite self-explanatory; you can pass it a tile, or the indices of one, and it will return true if it's a floor tile. We'll use that from now on to check whether the tiles are valid for spawning an item.

Randomly selecting a tile

The first function that we'll look at is choosing a value from an underlying grid. In our case, the level data is described in a 2D array. Therefore, we simply need to generate a random column and a row index.

 Remember that this range is the number of rows and columns - 1 as all indices start from 0. If we have a grid with 10 rows and columns, then they are numbered 0 to 9, and the total is 10.

Here is some pseudocode to generate a random index for a 2D array with 10 rows and 10 columns:

```
// Generate random indices.
int randomColumn = std::rand() % 10;
int randomRow = std::rand() % 10;

// Get the tile of the random tile.
Tile* tile = m_level.GetTile(randomColumn, randomRow);
```

To get the `Tile` object from the level, we just need to call the `Level::GetTile` function and pass the randomly generated indices.

Checking whether a tile is suitable

To check whether a `tile` is valid, we can use the `Level::IsFloor` function that we had a look at earlier. The following pseudocode will achieve this:

```
// Get the type of the random tile.
Tile* tile = m_level.GetTile(1, 1);

// Check if the tile is a floor tile.
if (m_level.IsFloor(*tile))
{
  // tile is valid
}
```

Converting to absolute position

Now that we can choose a valid `tile` in the game grid, we need to convert that position to an absolute screen position. To convert indices into a position that is relative to the grid, we simply need to multiply them by the width of a tile in the game. In our case, the tiles have a size of 50 square pixels. For example, if we're at location `[1] [6]` in the grid, the position relative to the grid will be 50*300.

Now we just need to add the location of the grid to these values, making them absolute coordinated relative to our window. The practice of converting a grid position to an absolute position will come in handy. So let's encapsulate the behavior in its own function.

In `Level.h`, add the following code:

```
/**
 * Returns the position of a tile on the screen.
 */
sf::Vector2f GetActualTileLocation(int columnIndex, int rowIndex);
```

In `Level.cpp`, add the following definition of a function:

```
sf::Vector2f Level::GetActualTileLocation(int columnIndex, int
rowIndex)
{
    sf::Vector2f location;

    location.x = m_origin.x + (columnIndex * TILE_SIZE) + (TILE_SIZE /
2);
    location.y = m_origin.y + (rowIndex * TILE_SIZE) + (TILE_SIZE /
2);

    return location;
}
```

Spawning items at a random location

Now, let's tie all of this together to spawn items randomly in the map. Here is a quick overview of the steps that we'll take:

1. Select a random `tile` from the **level** data.
2. Check whether this tile is a `floor` tile. If not, go to step 1.
3. Convert the tile location to the absolute position and give it to the item.

The first step is to select a random tile in the **level** data. Earlier in this chapter, we covered how we'll achieve this:

```
// Declare the variables we need.
int columnIndex(0), rowIndex(0);
Tile tileType;

// Generate a random index for the row and column.
columnIndex = std::rand() % GRID_WIDTH;
rowIndex = std::rand() % GRID_HEIGHT;

// Get the tile type.
tileType = m_level.GetTileType(columnIndex, rowIndex);
```

We now need to check whether the randomly selected tile is suitable for the spawning of an item. We know that we can do this by checking the type of the tile, but we need to incorporate this into some kind of loop, so that if the randomly selected tile is unsuitable, it will try again. To accomplish this, we'll wrap the random tile selection code inside a `while` statement, as follows:

```
// Declare the variables we need.
int columnIndex(0), rowIndex(0);

// Loop until we select a floor tile.
while (!m_level.IsFloor(columnIndex, rowIndex))
{
    // Generate a random index for the row and column.
    columnIndex = std::rand() % GRID_WIDTH;
    rowIndex = std::rand() % GRID_HEIGHT;
}
```

It's worth noting that having a while loop here will not be suitable for all game types. In our game, there is more area where an item can be spawned as compared to the area where it can't be spawned. Therefore, a valid location can be easily found. If this is not the case and a suitable spawn location is scarce, then a while loop may hold the game up indefinitely, as it is looped to find the area. Use the `while` statements with extreme caution.

This code now loops until it finds a suitable, but still random, `tile` where we can spawn items. This is very useful and will most likely be reused multiple times. Therefore, we will create a dedicated function for the code named `Level::GetRandomSpawnLocation`, as follows:

```
/**
 * Returns a valid spawn location from the currently loaded level
 */
sf::Vector2f GetRandomSpawnLocation();
```

Now, add the following code to the body of the new function:

```
// Returns a valid spawn location from the currently loaded level.
sf::Vector2f Level::GetRandomSpawnLocation()
{
    // Declare the variables we need.
    int rowIndex(0), columnIndex(0);

    // Loop until we select a floor tile.
    while (!m_level.IsFloor(columnIndex, rowIndex))
    {
        // Generate a random index for the row and column.
        columnIndex = std::rand() % GRID_WIDTH;
        rowIndex = std::rand() % GRID_HEIGHT;
    }

    // Convert the tile position to absolute position.
    sf::Vector2f tileLocation(m_level.GetActualTileLocation(columnInd
ex, rowIndex));

    // Create a random offset.
    tileLocation.x += std::rand() % 21 - 10;
    tileLocation.y += std::rand() % 21 - 10;

    return tileLocation;
}
```

Note that at the end of the function we've added a `return` statement. When a suitable `tile` is found, we fetch the absolute position using the function that we added earlier, and then return the value. We also add a random offset to the coordinates of our items so they aren't all fixed to the dead center of the `tile` that they lie on.

We now have a function that will return absolute coordinates for a suitable spawn location in the level. Very handy indeed! The final step is to incorporate this function in the `Game::PopulateLevel` spawn function.

Currently, we've set the position of the items manually. To make use of the new function, simply replace the fixed values with the results of a call to the `Level::GetRandomSpawnLocation()` function:

```
    item->SetPosition(sf::Vector2f(m_screenCenter.x, m_
screenCenter.y));
    item->SetPosition(m_level.GetRandomSpawnLocation());
    m_items.push_back(std::move(item));
}
```

Now, every time we create an item, its location will be generated randomly. If we run the game now, we will see that the items are spread through the level randomly, but only on the tiles that are valid and which the player can reach:

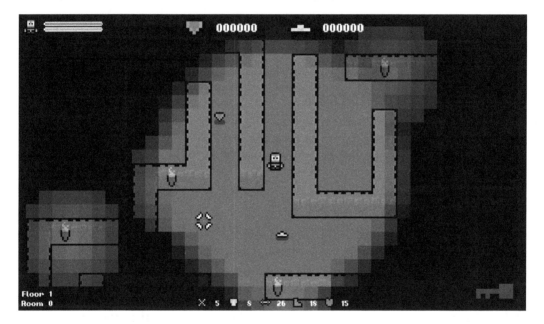

Expanding the spawning system

In the last chapter, we covered the use of enumerators; we're going to put that to good use here. We're going to break the item `spawn` code into its own dedicated function. This will give us greater control over how we populate the level. We'll also expand this system to include all items and enemies!

Using enumerators to denote an object type

The first step in constructing this system is to look at the items. In Util.h, all the item types are described in the following enumerator:

```
// Spawnable items.
enum class ITEM {
    HEART,
    GEM,
    GOLD,
    POTION,
    KEY,
    COUNT
};
```

When deciding what items need to be spawned, we will select random values from these enumerator values.

Optional parameters

Another technique that we'll utilize in this system is the use of optional parameters. By default the function will spawn an item at a random location, but we may sometimes wish to override this behavior with a set location. This is achieved by using optional parameters.

Consider the following function declaration:

```
void TestFunction(OBJECT object, sf::Vector2f position);
```

The TestFunction() function created from this declaration requires spawn coordinates that need to be passed. We could just pass an sf::Vector value that is equal to {0.f, 0.f} and ignore these values, but that's a bit messy.

Optional parameters are those that are given a default value in the function declaration. If these parameters aren't provided in the function call, the default values are used. Let's rewrite this same function declaration, this time utilizing optional parameters in the following way:

```
void TestFunction(OBJECT object, sf::Vector2f position = { -1.f, -1.f
} );
```

 Another approach to this is to create two distinct functions. One function takes parameters and the other one doesn't; you can give them different names to highlight the difference.

Now, the `position` variable has a default value of $\{-1.f, -1.f\}$. So, if no values are passed with the function call, these defaults will be used. This is the behavior that we're going to need from the spawning functions. So, with this in mind, let's declare a new function named `Game::SpawnItem`, as follows:

```
/**
 * Spawns a given item in the level.
 */
void SpawnItem(ITEM itemType, sf::Vector2f position = { -1.f, -1.f });
```

With the default values set, we now need to determine whether they should be used or not. To check this, we can just evaluate the *x* and *y* values of the `position` variable. If *x* and *y* remain at `-1.f`, then we know that the user has not overridden them and wants to generate a value randomly. However, if *x* and *y* are not `-1.f`, then they have been overridden and we should use them.

 I've used `-1.f` as my default parameter as it's an invalid spawn coordinate. The default parameter should allow you to easily determine whether they have been overwritten.

The following lines of code will choose a random spawn location:

```
// Choose a random, unused spawn location if not overridden.
sf::Vector2f spawnLocation;
if ((position.x >= 0.f) || (position.y >= 0.f))
{
    spawnLocation = position;
}
else
{
    spawnLocation = m_level.GetRandomSpawnLocation();
}
```

As the `position` variable is optional, both the following function calls are now valid:

```
SpawnITem(GOLD);
SpawnITem(GOLD, 100.f, 100.f);
```

The complete spawn functions

Now, let's put all of this together and create the `SpawnItem()` function, as follows:

```
// Spawns a given object type at a random location within the map. Has
the option to explicitly set a spawn location.
void Game::SpawnItem(ITEM itemType, sf::Vector2f position)
{
    std::unique_ptr<Item> item;
```

```
        int objectIndex = 0;

        // Choose a random, unused spawn location.
        sf::Vector2f spawnLocation;

        if ((position.x >= 0.f) || (position.y >= 0.f))
        {
            spawnLocation = position;
        }
        else
        {
            spawnLocation = m_level.GetRandomSpawnLocation();
        }

        // Check which type of object is being spawned.
        switch (itemType)
        {
            case ITEM::POTION:
                item = std::make_unique<Potion>();
            break;

            case ITEM::GEM:
                item = std::make_unique<Gem>();
            break;

            case ITEM::GOLD:
                item = std::make_unique<Gold>();
            break;

            case ITEM::KEY:
                item = std::make_unique<Key>();
            break;

            case ITEM::HEART:
                item = std::make_unique<Heart>();
            break;
        }

        // Set the item position.
        item->SetPosition(spawnLocation);

        // Add the item to the list of all items.
        m_items.push_back(std::move(item));
    }
```

To test the new function, we can update the `Game::PopulateLevel` function in the following way:

```
if (canSpawn)
{
  int itemIndex = std::rand() % 2;
  SpawnItem(static_cast<ITEM>(itemIndex));
  std::unique_ptr<Item> item;

  switch (itemIndex)
  {
  case 0:
    item = std::make_unique<Gold>();
    break;

  case 1:
    item = std::make_unique<Gem>();
    break;
  }

  item->SetPosition(sf::Vector2f(m_screenCenter.x, m_screenCenter.y));
  item->SetPosition(m_level.GetRandomSpawnLocation());
  m_items.push_back(std::move(item));
}
```

This may seem like a lot of work for a seemingly small change that does not affect the gameplay, but it's an important one. Software should be built in such a way that it is easily maintainable and scalable. Now that this system is in place, we can spawn an item with a single function call. Spot on!

A quick run of the game confirms that the code is working as intended, and we've taken a big step towards an entirely procedurally populated environment, as shown in the following screenshot:

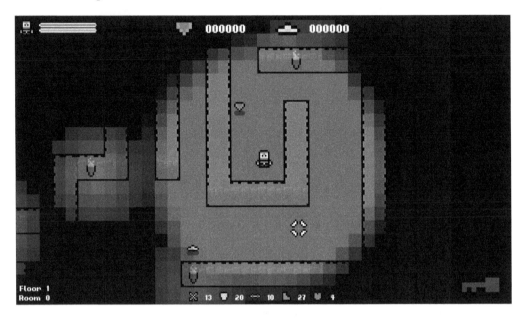

Updating the spawn code

Now that the Game::SpawnItem function is up and running, let's refactor the Game::PopulatelLevel function a little. In Game.h, let's declare the following static const:

```
static int const MAX_ITEM_SPAWN_COUNT = 50;
```

Instead of hard-coding the limit of the for loop, we can instead use this constant. The purpose of this is to remove all hard-coded values from the code. If we hard-code a value here instead of using a const, every time we want to change the value we will have to do so manually. This is both time-consuming and prone to errors. With a const, we can simply change its value, and this will affect every instance in which it's used.

We can also tidy up some variables now that we're comfortable with what the function is doing, as follows:

```cpp
// Populate the level with items.
void Game::PopulateLevel()
{
    // Spawn items.
    for (int i = 0; i < MAX_ITEM_SPAWN_COUNT; i++)
    {
        if (std::rand() % 2)
        {
            SpawnItem(static_cast<ITEM>(std::rand() % 2));
        }
    }
}
```

With this tidied up, we can now extend this approach to spawning enemies into the level!

Randomly spawning enemies

Now that we can spawn items into the game, let's take this same system and use it to spawn in enemies! We'll start by defining a `Game::SpawnEnemy` function, as follows:

```cpp
/**
 * Spawns a given enemy in the level.
 */
void SpawnEnemy(ENEMY enemyType, sf::Vector2f position = { -1.f, -1.f
});
```

Also, declare another static `const` to cap the maximum number of enemies that we can spawn:

```cpp
static int const MAX_ENEMY_SPAWN_COUNT = 20;
```

With this declared, we can now add the function's definition. It will be much like the `Game::SpawnItem` function, only instead of switching through the values in the item enumerator, we'll create enemies that are defined in the following enumerator:

```cpp
// Enemy types.
enum class ENEMY {
    SLIME,
    HUMANOID,
    COUNT
};
```

Let's add this definition:

```cpp
// Spawns a given number of enemies in the level.
void Game::SpawnEnemy(ENEMY enemyType, sf::Vector2f position)
{
    // Spawn location of enemy.
    sf::Vector2f spawnLocation;

    // Choose a random, unused spawn location.
    if ((position.x >= 0.f) || (position.y >= 0.f))
    {
        spawnLocation = position;
    }
    else
    {
        spawnLocation = m_level.GetRandomSpawnLocation();
    }

    // Create the enemy.
    std::unique_ptr<Enemy> enemy;

    switch (enemyType)
    {
        case ENEMY::SLIME:
            enemy = std::make_unique<Slime>();
        break;
        case ENEMY::HUMANOID:
            enemy = std::make_unique<Humanoid>();
        break;
    }

    // Set spawn location.
    enemy->SetPosition(spawnLocation);

    // Add to list of all enemies.
    m_enemies.push_back(std::move(enemy));
}
```

Now, to call this function, we need to jump back to the `Game::Populate` level function and add another loop to create enemies in a way that is similar to how we created items:

```cpp
// Populate the level with items.
void Game::PopulateLevel()
{
    // Spawn items.
    for (int i = 0; i < MAX_ITEM_SPAWN_COUNT; i++)
    {
```

```
        if (std::rand() % 2)
        {
            SpawnItem(static_cast<ITEM>(std::rand() % 2));
        }
    }

    // Spawn enemies.
    for (int i = 0; i < MAX_ENEMY_SPAWN_COUNT; i++)
    {
        if (std::rand() % 2)
        {
            SpawnEnemy(static_cast<ENEMY>(std::rand() % static_
cast<int>(ENEMY::COUNT)));
        }
    }
}
```

With this in place, items and enemies will be spawned randomly across the level. This system is very flexible and easy. To add another item or enemy, we just need to add it to the relevant enumerator and add a corresponding `switch` statement. This is the kind of flexible approach that is needed when generating procedural content and systems.

Let's run the game and have a look at the populated level:

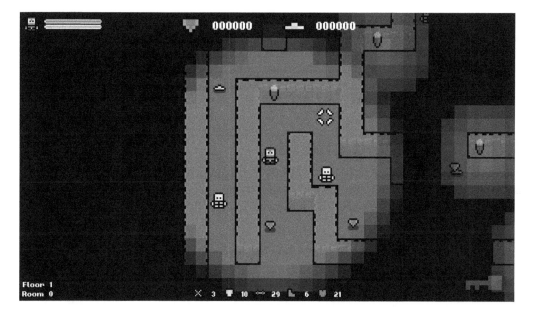

Spawning random tiles

The spawning of environmental features will be covered briefly here as there's a whole chapter toward the end of the book that is dedicated to procedurally generating the game map. This is our end goal. So, to get started, we'll generate some superficial environmental features that will be ready for the random level generation later.

Adding a new `tile` to the game will greatly increase the diversity of levels. One of the problems with procedural generation is that environments can feel too unnatural and generic. So this will help avoid that.

Let's add the following declaration to `Game.h`:

```
/**
 * Spawns a given number of a certain tile at random locations in the
 level.
 */
void SpawnRandomTiles(TILE tileType, int count);
```

We have two parameters in this function. One allows us to specify a `tile` index that we would like to spawn, and the second allows us to specify how many. We could have skipped the creation of a function and just hard-coded the behavior in the `Game::PopulateLevel` function, which would have worked, but couldn't have been used for anything else.

However, with our approach, we can easily reuse the code, specifying the `tile` that needs to be used, and the number of tiles that we wish to spawn. If we use RNG to determine these values, we gain even more procedural generation and randomness in the system. When writing procedural systems, always bear this in mind, and avoid using hard-coded values as much as possible. Always create options, even if they end up not being used.

Adding a new game tile

The next step is to add the new `tile` assets in the level object, and the `Level::AddTile()` function does just that. In `Game::Initialize`, we'll make a call to this function and add a new `tile`, as follows:

```
// Add the new tile type to level.
m_level.AddTile("../resources/tiles/spr_tile_floor_alt.png",
TILE::FLOOR_ALT);
```

This function takes two parameters, namely a `path` to a `resource` and the `ID` parameter value that the `tile` should have. In this case, we're using the `TILE::FLOOR_ALT` value.

Choosing a random tile

If we're going to spawn tiles randomly in the level, we need to first choose a random floor tile in the game grid. Luckily, we've already written the code to do this; it's in the `Level::GetRandomSpawnLocation()` function. Therefore, we can use the code and add it to the new function. We also created a parameter for the number of tiles that need to be created. So, we'll wrap up everything inside a `for` loop to repeat the process the correct number of times.

Let's give the function a definition, as follows:

```
// Spawns a given number of a given tile randomly in the level.
void Game::SpawnRandomTiles(TILE tileType, int count)
{
    // Declare the variables we need.
    int rowIndex(0), columnIndex(0), tileIndex(0);

    // Loop the number of tiles we need.
    for (int i = 0; i < count; i++)
    {
        // Declare the variables we need.
        int columnIndex(0), rowIndex(0);

        // Loop until we select a floor tile.
        while (!m_level.IsFloor(columnIndex, rowIndex))
        {
            // Generate a random index for the row and column.
            columnIndex = std::rand() % GRID_WIDTH;
            rowIndex = std::rand() % GRID_HEIGHT;
        }

        // Now we change the selected tile.
        m_level.SetTile(columnIndex, rowIndex, tileType);
    }
}
```

Once we find a `tile` that is a valid `floor` tile, we can update its type to that passed in the parameter.

Implementing the SpawnRandomTiles function

The very last step is to make a call to Game::SpawnRandomTiles. This function relies on the level grid that has already been in place. So, we'll call it at the end of the Game::Initialize function, as follows:

```
// Change a selection of random tiles to the cracked tile sprite.
SpawnRandomTiles(TILE::FLOOR_ALT, 15);
```

 I've hard-coded the parameters here, but to make it even more random, you can generate random numbers that can be used in their place. I've left this as one of the exercises in this chapter!

All that's left is to now run the game and see our work in action in the following screenshot. We can see that where the floor used to be a single tile, there are now randomly distributed broken tiles, and we can control both the sprite and their amount thanks to the way we architected the function:

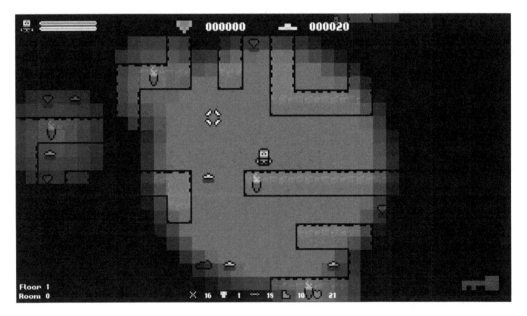

Exercises

To help you test your knowledge of this chapter's content, here are a few exercises that you should work on. They are not imperative to the rest of the book, but working on them will help you access your strengths and weaknesses in the material covered:

1. Add a new item to the game. Then, hook it up to the spawn system so that it can be randomly spawned with the existing items.

2. Add your own `tile` to the game. Hook this up to the spawn code and change the underlying level grid so that the player cannot move through it.

3. Check whether the number of tiles that we created when calling `Game::SpawnRandomTiles()` are hard-coded:

   ```
   // change a selection of random tiles to the cracked tile sprite
   this->SpawnRandomTiles(tileIndex, 15);
   ```

   Use RNG to generate a count during the runtime instead.

4. Now we have our Game::SpawnItem function, update our enemy item drops to use it.

5. Since we now have a function to calculate actual tile location, update our torch spawn code so we don't do the position calculations ourselves.

Summary

In this chapter, we implemented RNG to procedurally generate a suitable spawn location in the levels, and we encapsulated this behavior in its own function. We then used this to spawn items and enemies around the map at random locations.

In the next chapter, we're going to look at creating unique, randomized game objects. Certain items will be procedurally generated during runtime, meaning there will be an almost infinite number of possible combinations. We covered the skills and techniques that are used to achieve this in the earlier chapters, so it's time to pull it together and build our own procedural system!

5

Creating Unique and Randomized Game Objects

In this chapter, we're going to make our classes more random. We touched on a similar subject matter in *Chapter 3*, *Using RNG with C++ Data Types*, by giving the player random stats, so we'll continue further down that path and build bigger, more versatile procedural classes.

Having game items generated randomly is a great way to bring versatility and replayability to a game. For example, all the weapons in Borderlands are generated randomly; each chest and loot drop will contain a unique item. It brings an element of unknown to the game, and each time you find an item there's no knowing what it could be.

In this chapter, we'll cover the following topics:

- Giving objects random sprites
- Generating random traits for our player
- Assigning stats randomly
- Procedurally generating a range of game items

Creating a random player character

In *Chapter 3*, *Using RNG with C++ Data Types*, we gave our player random stats. Let's continue and develop the `player` object further. We'll give our `player` a random class, and use this to set an appropriate sprite and stats. We'll also give the player random traits that will buff certain stats.

Choosing a player class

Let's start by assigning the player a random class. The first step is to define an enumerator that will define the possible classes. We'll place this with the rest of the enumerators in `Util.h`:

```
// Player classes.
enum class PLAYER_CLASS {
    WARRIOR,
    MAGE,
    ARCHER,
    THIEF,
    COUNT
};
```

Now, in the constructor of the `player` class, we'll select one of these classes at random. To do this, we need to generate a number from 0 to 3, and use it as an index in the enumerator. We'll also create a variable to hold the selection in case we wish to use it later.

We'll start by declaring the variable in `Player.h`, as follows:

```
/**
 * The player's class.
 */
PLAYER_CLASS m_class;
```

> We couldn't call this variable just 'class', as it's a keyword in C++. Keep keywords in mind when naming variables to avoid such clashes

In the constructor, let's generate the random index and set the class as follows:

```
// Generate a random class.
m_class = static_cast<PLAYER_CLASS>(std::rand() % stat-ic_
cast<int>(PLAYER_CLASS::COUNT));
```

It's as simple as that. Every time a player is now created, a random class will be selected, which can be used to implement different behavior and looks.

An overview of sprites and textures

Before we start working with objects' sprites, let's just take a moment to look at how sprites and textures are handled in our game. As you may already know, to draw objects in SFML we need a sprite and a texture resource. When we want to change the sprite, we actually just need to change the sf::Texture object to which sf::sprite is holding a reference. Given this, sprites are stored in the object that they belong to, and textures are stored in a single, static texture manager class.

Textures are an expensive and heavy resource, so keeping them in all in a single object, and interacting with them only via references, is ideal. It means that we don't have to worry about moving them or them making objects heavy. The TextureManager class is used in the following way:

- To add a texture to a game, we statically call TextureManager::AddTexture and pass the path to the sprite that we want to load, and the function returns the index of the texture in the manager class.

- To get a texture out of the manager, we statically call TextureManager::GetTexture, passing the ID of the texture that we want as the only parameter. In return, we get a reference to the texture if it exists.

What this all means for our game is that instead of storing textures in objects, we instead store their texture manager IDs. Whenever we want the actual texture, we just call the TextureManager::GetTexture function, as previously described.

 The texture resource manager class does some other clever stuff such as avoiding the loading of the same textures twice. I advise you to take a look at the class and employ the same approach in your own games to ensure resources are handled correctly.

Setting an appropriate sprite

Now that the player class has a random class generated, let's update the sprite to reflect this. The player is animated, and therefore has a collection of eight texture IDs that are defined in an array.

As it currently stands, the player loads the same fixed set of textures:

```
// Load textures.
m_textureIDs[static_cast<int>(ANIMATION_STATE::WALK_UP)] =
TextureManager::AddTexture("../resources/players/warrior/spr_warrior_
walk_up.png");
m_textureIDs[static_cast<int>(ANIMATION_STATE::WALK_DOWN)] =
TextureManager::AddTexture("../resources/players/warrior/spr_warrior_
walk_down.png");
m_textureIDs[static_cast<int>(ANIMATION_STATE::WALK_RIGHT)] =
TextureManager::AddTexture("../resources/players/warrior/spr_warrior_
walk_right.png");
m_textureIDs[static_cast<int>(ANIMATION_STATE::WALK_LEFT)] =
TextureManager::AddTexture("../resources/players/warrior/spr_warrior_
walk_left.png");
m_textureIDs[static_cast<int>(ANIMATION_STATE::IDLE_UP)] =
TextureManager::AddTexture("../resources/players/warrior/spr_warrior_
idle_up.png");
m_textureIDs[static_cast<int>(ANIMATION_STATE::IDLE_DOWN)] =
TextureManager::AddTexture("../resources/players/warrior/spr_warrior_
idle_down.png");
m_textureIDs[static_cast<int>(ANIMATION_STATE::IDLE_RIGHT)] =
TextureManager::AddTexture("../resources/players/warrior/spr_warrior_
idle_right.png");
m_textureIDs[static_cast<int>(ANIMATION_STATE::IDLE_LEFT)] =
TextureManager::AddTexture("../resources/players/warrior/spr_warrior_
idle_left.png");
```

Let's update this so that if we generate a warrior we will load the warrior textures, and if we load a mage we'll load the mage textures, and so on. This could be achieved by simply using the player's class in a switch statement to load the appropriate textures.

However, this will create lots of duplicate code:

```
// Load textures.
switch (m_class)
{
    case PLAYER_CLASS::WARRIOR:
    m_textureIDs[static_cast<int>(ANIMATION_STATE::WALK_LEFT)] =
TextureManager::AddTexture("../resources/players/warrior/spr_warrior_
walk_left.png");
    m_textureIDs[static_cast<int>(ANIMATION_STATE::IDLE_UP)] =
TextureManager::AddTexture("../resources/players/warrior/spr_warrior_
idle_up.png");
    . . .
    break;

    case PLAYER_CLASS::MAGE:
```

```
. . .
    m_textureIDs[static_cast<int>(ANIMATION_STATE::WALK_LEFT)] =
TextureManag-er::AddTexture("../resources/players/mage/spr_mage_walk_
left.png");
    m_textureIDs[static_cast<int>(ANIMATION_STATE::IDLE_UP)] =
TextureManag-er::AddTexture("../resources/players/mage/spr_mage_idle_
up.png");
    . . .
```

For each class type we would have the same code repeated, with the only change being the name of the class in the resource. Taking this into consideration, we can approach this from a better angle and generate resource paths during the runtime.

 Try implementing this yourself before reading the following code. If you get stuck, the code is always here, and you may even come up with your own approach!

We'll declare a string variable that can hold the name of the class, and set this by performing a `switch` statement on the player's class once it is set. We can then load textures using this variable instead of a fixed class name:

```
std::string className;

// Set class-specific variables.
switch (m_class)
{
case PLAYER_CLASS::WARRIOR:
  className = "warrior";
  break;

case PLAYER_CLASS::MAGE:
  className = "mage";
  break;

case PLAYER_CLASS::ARCHER:
  className = "archer";
  break;

case PLAYER_CLASS::THIEF:
  className = "thief";
  break;
}

// Load textures.
m_textureIDs[static_cast<int>(ANIMATION_STATE::WALK_UP)] =
TextureManager::AddTexture("../resources/players/" + className + "/
spr_" + className + "_walk_up.png");
```

```
m_textureIDs[static_cast<int>(ANIMATION_STATE::WALK_DOWN)] =
TextureManager::AddTexture("../resources/players/" + className + "/
spr_" + className + "_walk_down.png");
m_textureIDs[static_cast<int>(ANIMATION_STATE::WALK_RIGHT)] =
TextureManager::AddTexture("../resources/players/" + className + "/
spr_" + className + "_walk_right.png");
m_textureIDs[static_cast<int>(ANIMATION_STATE::WALK_LEFT)] =
TextureManager::AddTexture("../resources/players/" + className + "/
spr_" + className + "_walk_left.png");
m_textureIDs[static_cast<int>(ANIMATION_STATE::IDLE_UP)] =
TextureManager::AddTexture("../resources/players/" + className + "/
spr_" + className + "_idle_up.png");
m_textureIDs[static_cast<int>(ANIMATION_STATE::IDLE_DOWN)] =
TextureManager::AddTexture("../resources/players/" + className + "/
spr_" + className + "_idle_down.png");
m_textureIDs[static_cast<int>(ANIMATION_STATE::IDLE_RIGHT)] =
TextureManager::AddTexture("../resources/players/" + className + "/
spr_" + className + "_idle_right.png");
m_textureIDs[static_cast<int>(ANIMATION_STATE::IDLE_LEFT)] =
TextureManager::AddTexture("../resources/players/" + className + "/
spr_" + className + "_idle_left.png");
```

Now, every time we load the game, the player will be a random class and have a matching sprite to show that, as shown in the following screenshot.

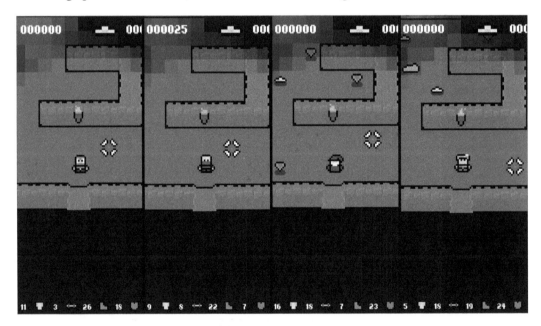

Now that the player class is set, we can update the UI and player projectile to reflect it. To do so, we'll need to get the player class from the player. So, let's first add a simple getter function to the player class. Don't forget the declaration:

```
// Returns the player's class.
PLAYER_CLASS Player::GetClass() const
{
 return m_class;
}
```

These are simple changes; instead of having fixed code, we can switch the player's class and load the correct sprites in each case. Let's start with the projectile. The sprite for this is set in Game::Initialize, and all that we have to do now is choose the right sprite for the class:

```
// Load the correct projectile texture.
//m_projectileTextureID = TextureManager::AddTexture("../resources/
projectiles/spr_sword.png");

switch (m_player.GetClass())
{
case PLAYER_CLASS::ARCHER:
 m_projectileTextureID = TextureManager::AddTexture("../resources/
projectiles/spr_arrow.png");
 break;
case PLAYER_CLASS::MAGE:
 m_projectileTextureID = TextureManager::AddTexture("../resources/
projectiles/spr_magic_ball.png");
 break;
case PLAYER_CLASS::THIEF:
 m_projectileTextureID = TextureManager::AddTexture("../resources/
projectiles/spr_dagger.png");
 break;
case PLAYER_CLASS::WARRIOR:
 m_projectileTextureID = TextureManager::AddTexture("../resources/
projectiles/spr_sword.png");
 break;
}
```

Now, let's move on to the player UI. At the top-left of the screen we have the player's stats, and one of these sprites shows the player. Since the class is dynamic, we need to update this sprite accordingly. This sprite is set in Game::LoadUI, and it will be set in a way that is similar to how we set the projectile. We'll leave this as an exercise for you to complete on your own.

Buffing the player stats

Now that the player has a class, another thing that we can do is to buff stats accordingly. We'll do this by giving certain values an initial value before we distribute the player's stat points as usual.

We already have a `switch` statement that we're using to load the appropriate textures, so we can add the code to this. As usual, we won't hard-code this value, but we will leave it to the RNG gods, as follows:

```
// Set class-specific variables.
switch (m_class)
{
case PLAYER_CLASS::WARRIOR:
  m_strength += std::rand() % 6 + 5;
  className = "warrior";
  break;

case PLAYER_CLASS::MAGE:
  m_defense = std::rand() % 6 + 5;
  className = "mage";
  break;

case PLAYER_CLASS::ARCHER:
  m_dexterity = std::rand() % 6 + 5;
  className = "archer";
  break;

case PLAYER_CLASS::THIEF:
  m_stamina = std::rand() % 6 + 5;
  className = "thief";
  break;
}
```

With this we can make certain classes more likely to have higher stat points in a given skill, and by using a random number we can induce yet more randomness and variance in the `player` objects that we can create.

Random character traits

We have five stats in the game, namely Attack, Defense, Strength, Dexterity, and Stamina. Let's create traits that affect each of these so that each character will be predisposed to certain stats and therefore certain play styles! This will mean that players have to change their gameplay to suit every character that they generate.

We need to start by defining these traits, so let's create an enumerator to do so. We'll declare the following in Util.h:

```
// Player traits.
enum class PLAYER_TRAIT {
  ATTACK,
  DEFENSE,
  STRENGTH,
  DEXTERITY,
  STAMINA,
  COUNT
};
```

Now we need to create a variable in the player class that will store the currently active traits. We'll give the player two traits, so will declare an array of that size. However, instead of hard-coding the value, we'll create a static const to define the trait count, as follows:

```
/**
 * The number of traits that the player can have.
 */
static const int PLAYER_TRAIT_COUNT = 2;
```

 We always want to make code as flexible as possible. Therefore, working with a static const with an appropriate name is preferred over a hard-coded value in this case.

Feel free to give the player more traits; simply create a larger array and amend the code as required as we move forward. Now, let's define the variable that will hold the traits:

```
/**
 * An array containing the character's traits.
 */
PLAYER_TRAIT m_traits[PLAYER_TRAIT_COUNT];
```

To assign traits randomly to a player, we now need to generate two random numbers and use them as indices from the PLAYER_TRAIT enumerator. We'll encapsulate this behavior in its own function. That way, we can change the player's traits at will while the game is running.

Let's declare the following function in the Player class:

```
/**
 * Chooses 2 random traits for the character.
 */
void SetRandomTraits();
```

We need this function to generate two indices and then use them in a switch statement to increase the appropriate stat, much like what we did when determining the player class. Let's get this added, as follows:

```
// Chooses random traits for the character.
void Player::SetRandomTraits()
{
    // Generate the traits.
    for (int i = 0; i < PLAYER_TRAIT_COUNT; ++i)
    {
        m_traits[i] = static_cast<PLAYER_TRAIT>(std::rand() % static_
cast<int>(PLAYER_TRAIT::COUNT));
    }

    // Action the traits.
    for (PLAYER_TRAIT trait : m_traits)
    {
        switch (trait)
        {
        case PLAYER_TRAIT::ATTACK: default:
            m_attack += rand() % 6 + 5;
        break;
        case PLAYER_TRAIT::ATTACK: default:
            m_attack += std::rand() % 6 + 5;
        break;
        case PLAYER_TRAIT::DEFENSE:
            m_defense += std::rand() % 6 + 5;
        break;
        case PLAYER_TRAIT::STRENGTH:
            m_strength += std::rand() % 6 + 5;
        break;
        case PLAYER_TRAIT::DEXTERITY:
            m_dexterity += std::rand() % 6 + 5;
        break;
```

```
    case PLAYER_TRAIT::STAMINA:
        m_stamina += std::rand() % 6 + 5;
    break;
    }
  }
}
```

While this approach succeeds in generating random traits, it has a big flaw; there is no check to ensure that two unique traits are generated. We could give a player five traits, and though it's quite unlikely, we could give them the same one five times. One of the exercises at the end of the chapter is to amend this, ensuring that only unique trait indices are generated. I highly suggest giving it a go.

With this function written, we now just need to make a call to it in the constructor of our player:

```
// Set random traits.
SetRandomTraits();
```

Every time a player is now created, they will have two randomly selected traits. The final step is to draw the player traits in the UI. For that, we're going to need to get the traits from the player and modify the stat sprites.

Returning the player traits array

The traits are stored in an array, and C++ does not allow us to return an entire array from a function. To get around this, we need to do some funky stuff. So, let's quickly branch off and take a look at how we can tackle this problem.

To start, the following function needs to be declared in `Player.h`, as follows:

```
/**
 * Gets the players current traits.
 * @return The players two current traits.
 */
PLAYER_TRAIT* GetTraits();
```

We'll give it the following definition:

```
// Return the players traits.
PLAYER_TRAIT* Player::GetTraits()
{
  return &m_traits[0];
}
```

Be aware that this function means that the player trait variables can be altered.

An array is simply a collection of values that are stored sequentially in the memory. The following diagram shows how this looks:

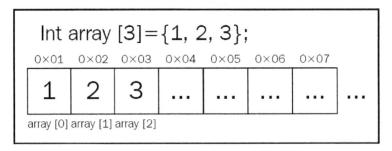

Taking this into consideration, if we return the address of the first element, we can then find the rest of the value by reading the following memory sequentially. To demonstrate this, have a look at the following two lines, which work in the same way:

```
m_traits[2] = 1;
GetTraits()[2] = 1;
```

So, while we don't return the full array, we do return the first element, and that's all we need. We can now access the array in the same way as we normally would.

Setting trait sprites

All that's left now is to draw the traits in the main `Game` class. We have already drawn the player's stats at the bottom of the window. So, to indicate the one that has been buffed by a trait, we can make the sprite bigger and switch to its alternate texture. Stat sprites are loaded and initialized in the `Game::LoadUI` function.

Before we start, we need to know how many traits the player has. So, let's add a quick `GetTraitCount()` function in the `player` object to give us this information; don't forget to add the declaration to Player.h also:

```
// Returns the number of traits the player has.
int Player::GetTraitCount()
{
    return PLAYER_TRAIT_COUNT;
}
```

Now, in `Game::LoadUI`, once we have loaded the stat sprites, we can make a call to this function and construct a loop to iterate that number of times, as follows:

```
// Set player traits.
int traitCount = m_player.GetTraitCount();

for (int i = 0; i < traitCount; ++i)
{


}
```

Now, we need to check each trait, and set its sprite scale to `1.2f` to make it slightly bigger than its neighbors. We'll also switch to its alternate texture with a white background. This has already been set up in the project, so all that we need to do is make the switch in the following way:

```
for (int i = 0; i < traitCount; ++i)
{
  switch (m_player.GetTraits()[i])
  {
  case PLAYER_TRAIT::ATTACK:
    m_attackStatSprite->setTexture(TextureManager::GetTexture(m_
attackStatTextureIDs[1]));
    m_attackStatSprite->setScale(sf::Vector2f(1.2f, 1.2f));
    break;

  case PLAYER_TRAIT::DEFENSE:
    m_defenseStatSprite->setTexture(TextureManager::GetTexture(m_
defenseStatTextureIDs[1]));
    m_defenseStatSprite->setScale(sf::Vector2f(1.2f, 1.2f));
    break;

  case PLAYER_TRAIT::STRENGTH:
    m_strengthStatSprite->setTexture(TextureManager::GetTexture(m_
strengthStatTextureIDs[1]));
    m_strengthStatSprite->setScale(sf::Vector2f(1.2f, 1.2f));
    break;

  case PLAYER_TRAIT::DEXTERITY:
    m_dexterityStatSprite->setTexture(TextureManager::GetTexture(m_
dexterityStatTextureIDs[1]));
```

```
        m_dexterityStatSprite->setScale(sf::Vector2f(1.2f, 1.2f));
        break;

    case PLAYER_TRAIT::STAMINA:
        m_staminaStatSprite->setTexture(TextureManager::GetTexture(m_
    staminaStatTextureIDs[1]));
        m_staminaStatSprite->setScale(sf::Vector2f(1.2f, 1.2f));
        break;
    }
}
```

Now if we run the game, we can clearly see which sprites are currently been buffed by traits, as shown in the following screenshot. We hooked up their behavior earlier. So we know that these icons are having an effect on the character's stats:

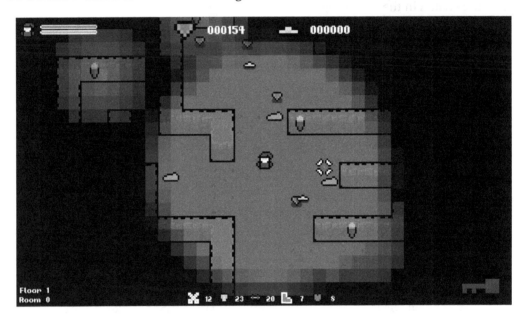

Procedurally generating an enemy class

Now that the player is well and truly generated procedurally, let's apply some of this to the enemies. We currently have two main enemy classes, namely `Slime` and `Humanoid`. `Slime` is a simple slime enemy, but our `humanoid` class is here for us to expand upon. Currently, the class loads the sprites of a skeleton, but let's make it so that it can be a number of humanoid-like enemies; in our case, it will be either a goblin or a skeleton.

We could have made individual classes for these enemies, but since most of their code will be the same, it doesn't make sense. Instead, we have this ambiguous `humanoid` class that can take the form of a humanoid enemy. All that we need to do is change the sprite, and the way we distribute stats if we want them to play differently. From this we can create a great number of different enemies from a `single` class. We'll use this same approach on potions soon!

For now, we'll start by defining an enumerator in `Util.h` to denote the different types of humanoid enemies:

```
// Enemy humanoid types.
enum class HUMANOID {
    GOBLIN,
    SKELETON,
    COUNT
};
```

Now, if we cast our minds back to the `player` constructor, we generated a class and performed a switch on that variable to perform class-dependent behavior. We'll use the exact same approach here. We'll generate a random enemy type from the enumerator that we just defined, and then set the sprites and stats accordingly.

In `Humanoid::Humanoid`, let's select a random humanoid type and create a string to hold the name of the enemy, as follows:

```
// Default constructor.
Humanoid::Humanoid()
{
    // Generate a humanoid type. (Skeleton or Goblin).
    HUMANOID humanoidType = static_cast<HUMANOID>(std::rand() %
static_cast<int>(HUMANOID::COUNT));
    std::string enemyName;
```

```
    // Set enemy specific variables.
    switch (humanoidType)
    {
        case HUMANOID::GOBLIN:
            enemyName = "goblin";
        break;

        case HUMANOID::SKELETON:
            enemyName = "skeleton";
        break;
    }
    // Load textures.
    m_textureIDs[static_cast<int>(ANIMATION_STATE::WALK_UP)] =
TextureManager::AddTexture("../resources/enemies/" + enemyName + "/
spr_" + enemyName + "_walk_up.png");
    m_textureIDs[static_cast<int>(ANIMATION_STATE::WALK_DOWN)] =
TextureManager::AddTexture("../resources/enemies/" + enemyName + "/
spr_" + enemyName + "_walk_down.png");
    m_textureIDs[static_cast<int>(ANIMATION_STATE::WALK_RIGHT)] =
TextureManager::AddTexture("../resources/enemies/" + enemyName + "/
spr_" + enemyName + "_walk_right.png");
    m_textureIDs[static_cast<int>(ANIMATION_STATE::WALK_LEFT)] =
TextureManager::AddTexture("../resources/enemies/" + enemyName + "/
spr_" + enemyName + "_walk_left.png");
    m_textureIDs[static_cast<int>(ANIMATION_STATE::IDLE_UP)] =
TextureManager::AddTexture("../resources/enemies/" + enemyName + "/
spr_" + enemyName + "_idle_up.png");
    m_textureIDs[static_cast<int>(ANIMATION_STATE::IDLE_DOWN)] =
TextureManager::AddTexture("../resources/enemies/" + enemyName + "/
spr_" + enemyName + "_idle_down.png");
    m_textureIDs[static_cast<int>(ANIMATION_STATE::IDLE_RIGHT)] =
TextureManager::AddTexture("../resources/enemies/" + enemyName + "/
spr_" + enemyName + "_idle_right.png");
    m_textureIDs[static_cast<int>(ANIMATION_STATE::IDLE_LEFT)] =
TextureManager::AddTexture("../resources/enemies/" + enemyName + "/
spr_" + enemyName + "_idle_left.png");

    // Set initial sprite.
    SetSprite(TextureManager::GetTexture(m_textureIDs[static_
cast<int>(ANIMATION_STATE::WALK_UP)]), false, 8, 12.f);
}
```

With this done, if you run the game now, you will see that there are both goblin and skeleton enemies that are spawning from a `single` class, as shown in the following screenshot:

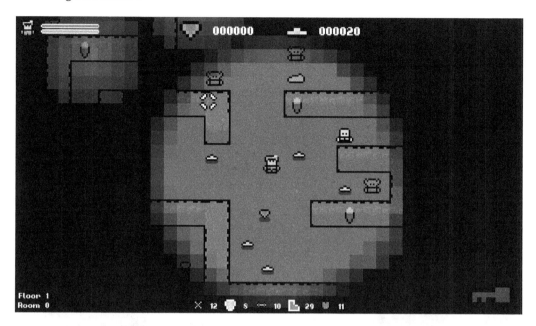

Procedural items

Now that the player and enemies have been taken care of, let's turn our attention to items. We have a number of classes that can have their member variables assigned randomly. We'll set up the `potion` class the way we set up the `humanoid` class, where we created a number of distinct objects from a `single` class.

Random Gem and Heart classes

We'll start with the smallest classes, namely `Heart` and `Gem`. These are very simple classes that have a single variable that is currently hard-coded. Let's update this so that their values are randomly generated every time they are created. Since we want this to happen each time an object is created, we'll place it in the items' constructors.

In `Gem::Gem`, we'll make the following change:

```
// Set the value of the gem.
m_scoreValue = 50;
m_scoreValue = std::rand() % 100;
```

In `Heart::Heart`, we'll make the following change:

```
// Set health value.
m_health = 15;
m_health = std::rand() % 11 + 10;
```

If we run the game now, and have a quick look around, you will see that these items provide different score and health values. Perfect!

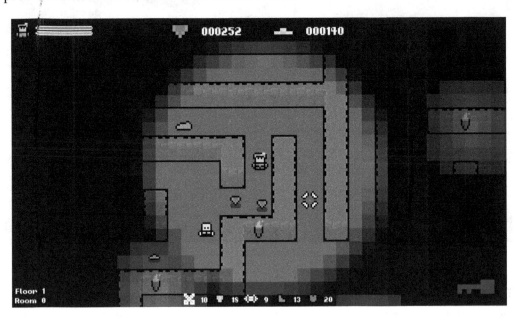

Random gold class

With the last two items, we simply generated a random value. With the gold item, we're going to take this a little further. We will use this random value to determine the sprite that the object should have.

To do so, we will split the total gold value range into three bands. We will define a lower range, an upper range, and that leaves everything else for the middle range. For example, if we were to generate a gold value between 0 and 10, we could have the following:

- Anything less than 3 is small
- Anything over 7 is large
- Anything else is medium

By doing this, we can set a sprite that matches the gold value. We'll put this code in the constructor, because it's code that should be called every time we create a gold object, and we'll never need to call its behavior manually:

```cpp
// Default constructor.
Gold::Gold()
{
    // Randomly generate the value of the pickup.
    this->goldValue = std::rand() % 21 + 5;

    // Choose a sprite based on the gold value.
    int textureID;
    if (this->goldValue < 9)
    {
        textureID = TextureManager::AddTexture("../resources/loot/
gold/spr_pickup_gold_small.png");
    }
    else if (this->goldValue >= 16)
    {
        textureID = TextureManager::AddTexture("../resources/loot/
gold/spr_pickup_gold_large.png");
    }
    else
    {
        textureID = TextureManager::AddTexture("../resources/loot/
gold/spr_pickup_gold_medium.png");
    }

    // Set the sprite.
    this->SetSprite(TextureManager::GetTexture(textureID), false, 8,
12.f);

    // Set the item type.
    m_type = ITEM::GOLD;
}
```

You can see that we generate a random gold value, then simply use a couple of `if` statements to define our ranges. Let's run the game again and check out the gold objects. You will see that their sprites vary, and with that, so does the amount of gold that they are worth when picked up:

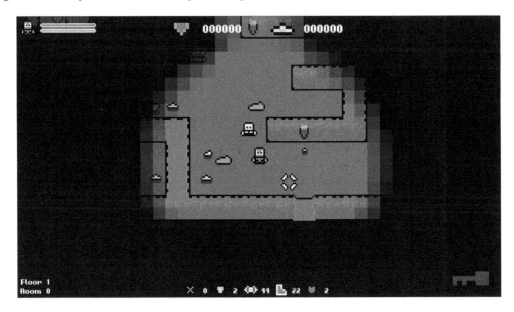

The random potion class

For the biggest class update, we'll turn our attention to the `potion` class. This class currently has a fixed sprite and doesn't give the player anything. With the `humanoid` class, we can generate a random type and essentially create two different enemies from a `single` class. We're going to use this same approach for the potions.

Creating a random potion

To start, let's define an enumerator in `Util.h` that denotes all potion types. We'll create one for each stat, as follows:

```
// Potions.
enum class POTION {
    ATTACK,
    DEFENSE,
    STRENGTH,
    DEXTERITY,
    STAMINA,
    COUNT
};
```

To save a lot of typing, the potion class already has the member variables and the `getter` functions for each possible stat, we just need to use them. One thing that we will add is a variable to hold the potion type, and a function to return it. We'll need this information when picking the object up!

Let's declare the following in `Potion.h`:

```
public:
  /**
   * Gets the potion type.
   * @return The potion type.
   */
  POTION GetPotionType() const;

private:
  /**
   * The potion type.
   */
  POTION m_potionType;
```

`GetPotionType` is a simple `getter` function, so before moving forward let's quickly give it a body:

```
// Gets the potion type.
POTION Potion::GetPotionType() const
{
    return m_potionType;
}
```

If we look at the initializer list for Potion, you'll notice it sets all of the stat variables to 0. From this point we can select a random type and set its sprite and corresponding stat, leaving the rest at their default value of 0 as we won't use them.

To start we'll generate a random value to denote its type, and create a variable that we'll use to store the sprite path. The following code needs to go in `Potion::Potion`:

```
// The string for the sprite path.
std::string spriteFilePath;

// Set the potion type.
m_potionType = static_cast<POTION>(std::rand() % static_
cast<int>(POTION::COUNT));
```

With a type selected, we can switch this value, set the appropriate stat, and give `spriteFilePath` the appropriate resource path, as follows:

```
// Set stat modifiers, sprite file path, and item name.
switch (m_potionType)
{
case POTION::ATTACK:
  m_dexterity = std::rand() % 11 + 5;
  spriteFilePath = "../resources/loot/potions/spr_potion_attack.png";
  break;

case POTION::DEFENSE:
  m_dexterity = std::rand() % 11 + 5;
  spriteFilePath = "../resources/loot/potions/spr_potion_defense.png";
  break;

case POTION::STRENGTH:
  m_strength = std::rand() % 11 + 5;
  spriteFilePath = "../resources/loot/potions/spr_potion_strength.
png";
  break;

case POTION::DEXTERITY:
  m_dexterity = std::rand() % 11 + 5;
  spriteFilePath = "../resources/loot/potions/spr_potion_dexterity.
png";
  break;

case POTION::STAMINA:
  m_stamina = std::rand() % 11 + 5;
  spriteFilePath = "../resources/loot/potions/spr_potion_stamina.png";
  break;
}
```

Finally, we just need to set the item sprite and type in the following way, and we're done. Note that this type is different from the potion type:

```
// Load and set sprite.
SetSprite(TextureManager::GetTexture(TextureManager::AddTexture(sprite
FilePath)), false, 8, 12.f);

// Set the item type.
m_type = ITEM::POTION;
```

If we run our game now, and kill a couple of enemies until we get a potion drop, we should see that the potion type changes. From a single class we've created 5 potions, created at runtime, that give buffs also generated at runtime:

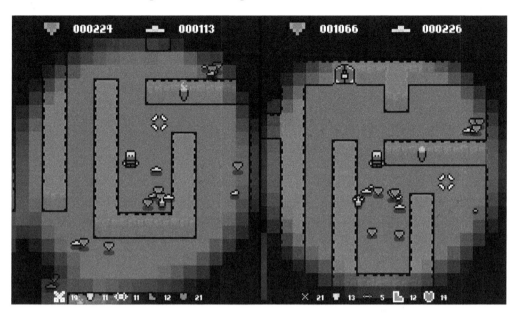

Determining potion pickups

Now that we have a `single` class that has five different potential buffs, we need to determine the potion that we're picking up. This is where the `Potion::GetType` function comes in handy. When we come in contact with a `potion` object, we can check what type of `potion` it is and use that to determine which stats getter function that we will call.

For example, if we pick up a `potion` and its type is `POTION::ATTACK`, then we know that we need to call the `Potion::GetAttack` function. The item pickup code lies in the `Game::UpdateItems` function. In this function, we check for collisions with the object and check what type of item it is.

When we have determined that we have picked up a potion, we need to call the `Potion::GetPotionType` function, but we have a problem. Since we are utilizing polymorphism to store all the items in a single collection, the type of the potion item at this point is `Item`. To get access to the `Potion::GetPotionType` function, we need to cast the item using `dynamic_cast`:

If you are unsure about why we're using `dynamic_cast` here and `static_cast` elsewhere, read up on the different types of casts.

Let's get this case added to the pickup code in `Game::UpdateItems`:

```
case ITEM::POTION:
{
  // Cast to position and get type.
  Potion& potion = dynamic_cast<Potion&>(item);
  POTION potionType = potion.GetPotionType();
}
break;
}
```

We've now identified that we've picked up a `potion` and `cast` that item to a `potion` object. Next, we can check the type of the potion and call the appropriate `getter` function to get the `potion` value. Finally, we'll update the corresponding stat in the player, as follows:

```
switch (potionType)
{
case POTION::ATTACK:
  m_player.SetAttack(m_player.GetAttack() + potion.GetAttack());
  break;

case POTION::DEFENSE:
  m_player.SetDefense(m_player.GetDefense() + potion.GetDefense());
  break;

case POTION::STRENGTH:
  m_player.SetStrength(m_player.GetStrength() + potion.GetStrength());
  break;

case POTION::DEXTERITY:
  m_player.SetDexterity(m_player.GetDexterity() + potion.
GetDexterity());
  break;

case POTION::STAMINA:
  m_player.SetStamina(m_player.GetStamina() + potion.GetStamina());
  break;
}
```

With this the potion system is complete. From a `single` class we've created five distinct potions, and all the values have been generated randomly.

Exercises

To help you test your knowledge of this chapter's content, the following are a few exercises that you should work on. They are not imperative to the rest of the book, but working on them will help you assess your strengths and weaknesses in the material covered:

1. Add your own trait to the `player` class. There is a spare trait resource included in the project that you can use.

2. When generating `player` traits, we identified that it was possible to give the player the same trait multiple times. Improve the `Player::SetRandomTraits` function so that that's no longer possible.

3. The stats that we have given to the player and enemies aren't hooked up to how much damage they deal or take. Hook these stats up so that they affect the player and enemy to a greater extent.

Summary

In this chapter, we looked at how to make game objects unique and random, giving them random properties, sprites, and variations. With this approach, the range of possible items that a game can generate is almost endless. When we have multiple classes that differ only slightly, we can design ambiguous classes that are highly flexible and greatly increase variety.

In the next chapter, we're going to step up our procedural efforts. We'll move away from the simple setting of member variables randomly, and we'll experiment with the creation of procedural art and graphics. We'll create textures procedurally for enemies, and alter the level sprites to give a unique feel to each floor of the dungeon.

6
Procedurally Generating Art

A game's art is one of its defining features. It's usually what first attracts us, and it is one of the driving forces behind keeping us hooked; great aesthetics go a long way. Given that, we want to ensure that this is an area that is as rich, diverse, and immersive as possible.

However, art is financially expensive and time-consuming to produce. Not only that, it's also expensive at the hardware level! Game textures can hit 4K in size, and creating a thousand 4K textures and storing them on traditional game media is no easy task. Thankfully, a wide range of procedural generation techniques can be employed when creating art to help combat some of these issues.

In this chapter, we'll cover the following topics:

- How procedural generation is used with art
- The benefits and drawbacks of procedurally generated art
- Using SFML sprite modifiers
- Saving modified sprites
- Programmatically creating sprites

How procedural generation is used with art

Game art is a great candidate for procedural generation. It's expensive to create manually, both in terms of developer investment and on a hardware level, and is open to be manipulated programmatically. However, like everything, it has a range of benefits and drawbacks. So, let's take a look at them before we get started.

Using sprite effects and modifiers

Perhaps the simplest way in which procedural generation can be used with game art is through the manipulation of existing sprites and models using built-in functions. For example, most game engines and frameworks will offer some functionality to edit graphics, such as the color, alpha, and scale modifiers.

Combining these functions with **Random Number Generator (RNG)** is an easy and quick way to start producing randomized game art. For example, **Simple and Fast Multimedia Library (SFML)** offers the functionality to change both the color and size of a sprite. Even if we just use these functions, we can generate a wide range of different textures during runtime. This is shown in the following screenshot:

Combining multiple textures

A step up from the simple modification of existing textures is the combining of multiple textures to create new ones. Throw in some RNG, and you can create a large number of sprites with very little effort. We'll use this technique in this chapter to give our enemies random armor!

We'll start with a base enemy sprite, randomly choose some armor, and draw it on top of the original image to create a random sprite! More on that later, but for now, here's what it will look like:

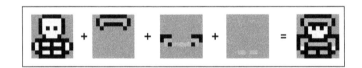

Creating textures from scratch

The most complex way of creating procedural textures is by using algorithms to create them from scratch. Algorithms such as Perlin noise can be used to create a natural looking texture base which can then be used to create a wide range of procedural textures using techniques such as image multiplication.

For example, a base Perlin noise texture, a white noise texture, and a flat color can be combined to create a procedural texture, as follows:

With this approach, changes in the algorithm that generates the first two textures will result in a different final texture. This technique can be employed to create endless unique textures for a game without creating storage problems.

 This type of procedural image creation is beyond the scope of the book. If you wish to delve into this further, read up on texture synthesis and algorithms such as Perlin noise.

Creating complex animations

The growth of computing power has also given rise to procedural animation. Traditionally, an animated game asset, such as a character, would be animated in a 3D animation package by an animator. This animation routine would then be loaded during runtime by the game engine and applied to a given model to make it move.

As computers are now able to perform more calculations that ever, procedural animation is becoming more popular. Ragdoll bodies are used in lots of game now, which is a great example of procedural animation. Instead of a set animation routine being played, information about the body, such as its weight, velocity, and rigidity, is used to calculate what position the body should be in to create realistic and dynamic movement.

The benefits of procedurally generated art

The procedural generation of game art brings with it a range of benefits to us as developers and the people who play our games. From its versatility, to being cost-effective and a time-saver, let's take a look at a few of these benefits.

Versatility

The main benefit of procedurally generating game art is **versatility**. Game art is expensive to produce, and as a result imposes limits on what can feasibly be created for a given project. It would be nice to have an artist create thousands of textures for our games, but it's not feasible. Instead, we can create a handful resources, employ procedural techniques to turn these resources into thousands of individual possible textures, and bring variety and diversity to games.

Cheap to produce

Expanding on the previous point, since we do not have to pay artists to manually create all of these textures, procedural generation saves us both time and money. In the example that we're going to work on in this chapter, we're going to provide our enemies with random armor. There will be three types of armor, each with three tiers, and the combination of which armor the enemy has will also be random. The number of possible combinations there is huge, and having an artist create them manually would be costly.

It requires little storage

Continuing with the example of giving our enemies armor, even if we could get an artist to produce all the sprites manually, how are they going to be stored? While this is less of an issue for online games, as there's usually no imposed limit on the game and download size, games that ship on traditional media, such as a disk, have to use the space wisely. Textures are an expensive resource in this regard. Therefore, creating a handful of resources and programmatically creating a texture from them alleviates these issues.

The drawbacks of procedurally generated art

With the good comes the bad, and procedurally generated art is no exception. Though it is flexible and saves space, it does come with a few drawbacks.

Lack of control

One of the first drawbacks is application agnostic, and is a drawback of procedural generation as a whole; the loss of control that comes with it. If you're generating art procedurally you lose the touch that a skilled artist can give it. The content can lack character and feel very rigid due to being the result of a deterministic process, not a creative one. A good procedural algorithm can mitigate this to a certain extent, but it's hard to generate content that feels and looks as natural as a talented artist would make it.

Repeatability

Another potential problem with procedurally generating art is that things may appear very repeated and unnatural. Content will be produced through an algorithm, and variation in the output is a result of the variance in the terms used. Given that, each algorithm has a spectrum of content that can be produced. If the operating range of the algorithm is too small, textures will be repeated and may feel unnatural and reused, despite procedural generation being used to mitigate that very thing! It's all in the quality of the algorithm and how it's used.

Performance heavy

Procedurally creating art usually involves lots of reading and copying textures, which are generally expensive operations, especially if you're working with high-resolution textures. Using the enemy armor example as a use case, if we were to create the sprites manually, we would just have to load the texture, which is a single operation. If we create a sprite procedurally, we have to load each component, edit them, and re-render them to create a new texture.

Using SFML sprite modifiers

Now that we've identified a number of strengths and weaknesses of procedurally generating art, get started! The first naïve approach that we'll look at is simply using `sprite` modifiers such as `color` and `alpha` to alter the existing sprites. With this method we'll be using the built-in sprite modifiers that SFML offers. Most engines and frameworks will have functions that are similar to these, and if not, you can just make them yourself!

How colors work in SFML

Let's start with the simplest way of procedurally generating a sprite, generating a unique color for it during runtime. A color in SFML is simply a set of four `uint8` values, with one for each color channel and one for an alpha:

```
sf::Color::Color   (
Uint8    red,
Uint8    green,
Uint8    blue,
Uint8    alpha = 255
)
```

Every `sf::Sprite` in SFML has a `sf::Color` member variable. This color value is multiplied with the color values of the pixels in the texture to arrive at the final color. The following image demonstrates this:

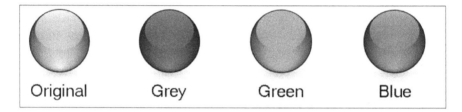

In the preceding image, we can see the original image on the far left. Also, we can see the resulting images when the sprite has various colors set.

 For the best results, it's best to start with a monochromatic gray base texture so that the color modulation arrives at the correct color.

The `sf::Color` type also has an *alpha* value, which is used to determine the opacity of the object. The lower the alpha channel, the more transparent the object. With this value, you can change how opaque an object is, as shown in the following screenshot:

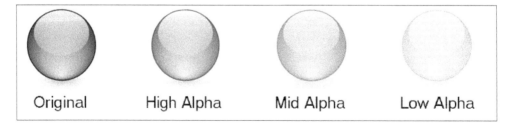

With this understanding of how SFML deals with color, let's put it into action by generating a random sprite for the slime character, setting both its color and alpha pragmatically.

 To learn more about how SFML deals with color, read the SFML documentation that is found at `http://www.sfml-dev.org/learn.php`. For more in-depth information, head to the OpenGL documentation, in the the graphics API SFML uses.

Creating sprites of a random color

In SFML, sprite objects have a member function called `setColor()`. This function takes an `sf::Color` object and sets it as the value to be multiplied with the sprite's texture when drawn. We know that `sf::Color` is essentially just four `uint8` values, with each having a range of 0 to 255. Given that, to generate a random color, we can either generate random values for these color channels, or randomly select one of the built-in pre-defined colors of SFML.

The slime enemy is a great candidate for this, as it will look great in many colors and the base sprite is a dull gray color. Multiplying a color with this sprite will work well. When we set the slime sprite, we'll give it a random color using both methods. Let's start with selecting a pre-defined color.

Selecting a preset color at random

SFML comes with the following pre-defined colors:

```
sf::Color black       = sf::Color::Black;
sf::Color white       = sf::Color::White;
sf::Color red         = sf::Color::Red;
sf::Color green       = sf::Color::Green;
sf::Color blue        = sf::Color::Blue;
sf::Color yellow      = sf::Color::Yellow;
sf::Color magenta     = sf::Color::Magenta;
sf::Color cyan        = sf::Color::Cyan;
sf::Color transparent = sf::Color::Transparent;
```

These are defined in `Color.hpp` and cover the most popular colors. The first problem is that we need some way of selecting one at random. To do this, we can create an enumerator of matching color values, generate a random index, and then use that to match the enumerator value with the matching predefined color. This will become clearer as we look at the code.

We'll start by adding the following enumerator definition to the Util.h file:

```
// Colors provided by SFML.
enum class COLOR {
  BLACK,
  WHITE,
  RED,
  GREEN,
  BLUE,
  YELLOW,
  MAGENTA,
  CYAN,
  TRANSPARENT,
  COUNT
};
```

For each of the predefined colors, we've added a corresponding value to the enum, ensuring that it ends with COUNT. With this defined, we just need to calculate a number between 0 and COLOR::COUNT and then use it in a switch statement. It's a method that we've used a few times now so we should be familiar with it.

Jumping to the constructor of the slime enemy, we'll start by generating a random index:

```
int colorIndex = std::rand() % static_cast<int>(COLOR::COUNT);
```

Now, we will simply switch the colorIndex value and set the corresponding color:

```
switch (colorIndex)
{
case static_cast<int>(COLOR::BLACK):
  m_sprite.setColor(sf::Color::Black);
  break;

case static_cast<int>(COLOR::BLUE):
  m_sprite.setColor(sf::Color::Blue);
  break;
```

This should be continued for each value of the enumerator that we defined. Now, you will see that every slime enemy that is spawned into the game has a different predefined color:

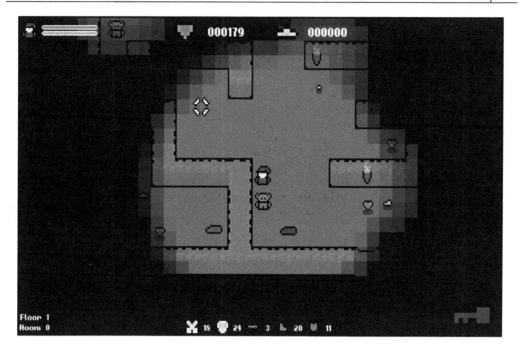

Generating a color at random

The second option, which gives us much more control, is to generate our own colors at random. This method gives us a much wider range of possibilities, as well as provides us access to the alpha channel; however, we lose some control. When selecting from predefined colors, we know that we'll always end up with a pleasant-looking color, which is something that we can't guarantee when generating our own values for each channel. Regardless of this, let's look at how we'll do it.

We know that `sf:color` has four channels (r, g, b, and a), and each value lies between 0 and 255. To generate a random color, we need to generate values for the r, g, and b channels; a is for the alpha channel, and it will allow us to alter the opacity of the sprite.

To start, we'll define the variables and generate a random value for the r, g, and b channels, as follows:

```
int r, g, b, a;

r = std::rand() % 256;
g = std::rand() % 256;
b = std::rand() % 256;
```

For the alpha channel, we want to be a bit more precise with the number generation. An alpha value of 0 would be way too low; we'd barely see the sprite. For this reason, we'll generate a number in the range of 100 to 255, as follows:

```
a = std::rand() % 156 + 100;
```

Now that we have these values, we need to create an `sf::color` object, passing the `r, g, b,` and `a` values in the `color` constructor:

```
sf::Color color(r, g, b, a);
```

The final step is to make a call to `sf::sprite::setColor()`, passing the new color. The complete code is as follows and should reside in the constructor of the slime enemy:

```
// Choose the random sprite color and set it.
int r, g, b, a;

r = std::rand() % 256;
g = std::rand() % 256;
b = std::rand() % 256;
a = std::rand() % 156 + 100;
sf::Color color(r, g, b, 255);

m_sprite.setColor(color);
```

Now, if we run the game, we should get three very different colored slimes, each with a varying degree of opacity, as shown in the following screenshot:

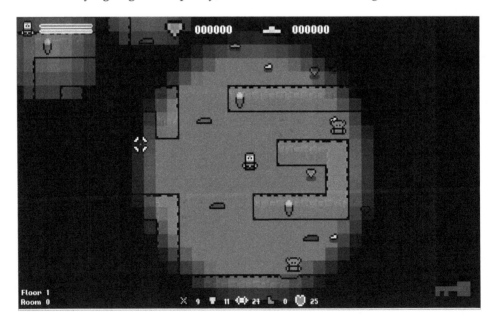

Creating sprites of a random size

The final sprite modifier that we'll play with is scale. Using the
`sf::Sprite::setScale()` function, we can set both the horizontal and vertical scale
of the sprite. The default scale is 1, so if we scale using a value of 2, the sprite will
be twice as big. Likewise, if we set a scale of 0.5, it will be half as big. Given this, we
need to generate floats that are just either side of 1. A range of 0.5 to 1.5 should give
us enough variance in size!

So, we need to generate a float, but the `std::rand()` function will only generate an
integer value. Don't worry! There is a simple trick that we can use to get a float out of
it! We simply need to generate a number between 5 and 15 and then divide it by ten
to get the float value:

```
float scale;
scale = (std::rand() % 11 + 5) / 10.f;
```

Now that the random scale value is generated, we now just need to call me
`sf::sprite::setScale()` function and use the `scale` variable as the scaling
value. The complete code is as follows:

```
// Generate a random scale between 0.5 and 1.5 and set it.
float scale;
scale = (std::rand() % 11 + 5) / 10.f;

m_sprite.setScale(sf::Vector2f(scale, scale));
```

On running the game, you will now see that the slime enemies have different colors
and they vary in size too:

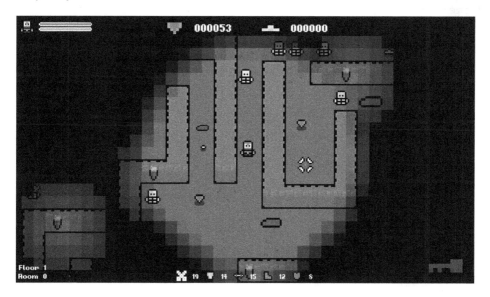

Saving modified sprites

In our game we're going to be generating new sprites each time the game is run. We want each run to be unique, so once we've generated a sprite and used it we can let it go. However sometimes, you might want to keep hold of a sprite. For example, you might want to create a randomized NPC and keep the same character throughout the entire game.

The two data types that we've used to create images so far are `sf::Sprite` and `sf::Texture`. These classes let us interact with images through a set of predefined member functions. It's great for standard drawing and simple image manipulation, but we don't get access to the raw image information. This is where `sf::Image` comes into play!

Passing a texture into an image

`Sf::Image` is a class that is used to load, manipulate, and save images. Unlike the other data types, `sf::Image` provides us with the raw image data, allowing us to interact with every pixel in the image. We'll use more of this functionality later, but for now, we're interested in the `sf::Image::saveToFile` function.

With this function, we can save an image in a file; we just need to our the texture into that image. Luckily, there's a function to do just that! The `sf::Texture` class has a function named `copyToImage` that copies the raw image data from a texture into an image. So, we should be able to copy the texture to an image and save it, right? Well, let's try it.

In `Slime::Slime`, let's add the following debug code after we've modified the sprite:

```
// Save the sprite to file.
sf::Image img = m_sprite.getTexture()->copyToImage();
img.saveToFile("../resources/test.png");
```

If you take a look at the file that we created and compare it to the original image, you will see something odd:

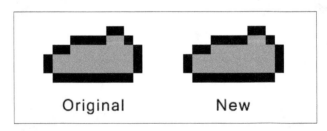

The modifications that we make to the sprite do not edit the texture. Instead, modifications are made every time we draw the object. When we output the texture like this, we simply output the same sprite that we put in! To save the changes that were made through sprite modifications, we need to utilize the `sf::RenderTexture` class as well.

Drawing to a RenderTexture class

Since sprite modifications aren't applied to the texture, we need to somehow capture the sprite once it has been rendered. Again, SFML comes to the rescue with its `sf::RenderTexture` class. This class allows us to render into a texture as opposed to the screen, solving the issue of modifications not been applied to the texture.

To start, we need to create an `sf::RenderTexture` object. For this, we need to know the size of the area that we'll be drawing to, and there's something that we need to keep in mind here. We're making changes to the size of the object. So, if we just get the size of the texture, it will either be too big or too small. Instead, we need to get the size of the texture and multiply it by the same scale value that we apply to the sprite.

Let's get some code written to make things clearer. We'll start by creating the `sf::RenderTarget` object, as follows:

```
// Create a RenderTarget.
sf::RenderTexture texture;

int textureWidth(m_sprite.getTexture()->getSize().x);
int textureHeight(m_sprite.getTexture()->getSize().y);
texture.create(textureWidth * scale, textureHeight * scale);
```

As you can see, we will get the size of the texture and multiply it by the same scale that we modified the sprite by.

Finally, we will draw the object to the render view, as follows:

```
// Draw the sprite to our RenderTexture.
texture.draw(m_sprite);
```

Saving an image to a file

From this point onwards, the code is the same as our first attempt, but with a slight modification. Because the sprite is animated, we change both its origin and the `textureRect` properties to cut it into subsections in order to animate the character. This needs reverting in order to see the entire texture. Also, when we call `sf::Texture::copyToImage`, the sprite gets flipped vertically. Before we save the file, we need to flip it back.

Here is the complete code example that is used to save the modified slime texture:

```
// Create a RenderTarget.
sf::RenderTexture texture;

int textureWidth(m_sprite.getTexture()->getSize().x);
int textureHeight(m_sprite.getTexture()->getSize().y);
texture.create(textureWidth * scale, textureHeight * scale);

// Revert changes the animation made.
m_sprite.setOrigin(sf::Vector2f(0.f, 0.f));
m_sprite.setTextureRect(sf::IntRect(0, 0, textureWidth,
textureHeight));

// Draw the sprite to our RenderTexture.
texture.draw(m_sprite);

// Copy the texture to an image and flip it.
sf::Image img = texture.getTexture().copyToImage();
img.flipVertically();

// Save the sprite to file.
img.saveToFile("../resources/test.png");
```

 Don't forget to delete this code when you're done as it is expensive to save files and it messes up the animation!

Now, if you run the game and take a look at the file, you will see the modifications that we made:

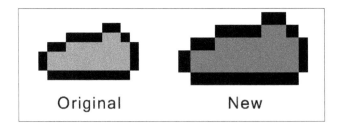

Creating enemy sprites procedurally

Having the ability to render to `sf::RenderTexture` and store the results opens up a world of possibilities. One of these is combining multiple sprites to create new, more versatile ones. We can draw to an `sf::RenderTexture` class multiple times, and the sprites will overlap. This is an incredibly useful technique that can be used to generate a vast amount of sprite variations without all the work. This is shown in the following screenshot:

Using this approach, we'll create random armor for our enemies. We'll have three pieces of armor; head, torso, and legs. For each of these, we'll also have three variations; bronze, silver, and gold. This alone gives us a large number of possible combinations. Then, let's consider that we need this for each character, of which we have two, and each character has eight sprites. That's an enormous number of textures. It's totally out of the question to create all of them manually.

Breaking sprites into components

The armor sprites that we will create are going to be laid right on top of the default enemy animations. The most important thing to consider here is that their sizes and position will line up when drawn on top of one another.

When creating an `sf::RenderTexture` class, we define a size. Everything drawn to it will then be positioned relative to the top left corner of this area. If our sprites have different sizes, when we start drawing, they will be misaligned. The following examples have had their backgrounds darkened so that we can see this. In the first example, the sprites have been cropped, and we can see that this makes them misaligned when laid over one another:

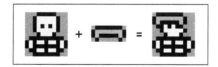

In the second example, the sprites are of the same size and are both positioned relative to the sprite over which they will be drawn. As a result, they will line up nicely:

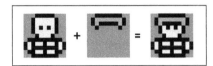

We're going to create armor for each enemy, so for each enemy animation, we need to create a matching armor sprite. This has already been done to save time, and you'll notice that there's only gray versions of these sprites. To save yet more time, we'll change the colors using the sprite modifiers.

Here's an example of an armor overlay sprite on the skeleton walking sprite strip:

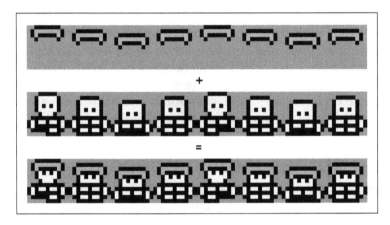

The draw setup

Before we write any code regarding generating armor, we need change the way the `Humanoid` class handles its textures. Since the textures that we'll create are unique to each instance of the class and will only be used once, there's no use filling the **Texture** manager with them. Instead, we'll create an array of our own textures and override the default draw behavior to use the new ones!

We'll start by defining an array of textures in `Humanoid.h`, as follows:

```
/**
 * An array of modified textures.
 */
sf::Texture m_textures[static_cast<int>(ANIMATION_STATE::COUNT)];
```

Now, in the `Humanoid` constructor, we need to fill this array with the default enemy textures. This is because we're going to override the default draw behavior to use the array of modified sprites over the default ones. A modified sprite is only created when armor is generated. Therefore, we need to ensure that we have the default sprites to fall back to. We will fill up the array with default sprites and then override them if we generate armor.

Add the following code to `Humanoid::Humanoid`. Then, our prep work is done and we can get started:

```
// Copy textures.
for (int i = 0; i < static_cast<int>(ANIMATION_STATE::COUNT); ++i)
{
  m_textures[i] = TextureManager::GetTexture(m_textureIDs[i]);
}
```

Randomly selecting sprite components

We have three possible pieces of armor that our enemies can have; head, torso, and legs, and we want our enemies to have a mix of these types. So, let's give each of them a 1 in 5 chance of been spawned on the enemy. This means that enemies with more gear are less likely to spawn, which is just what we want; a fully kitted out skeleton should be a rare spawn!

> Don't forget about the balance of game mechanics. When creating procedural systems, it's easy to focus on the tech and let the balance take a backseat. Always keep this in mind when designing your systems. You can visit `http://www.paranoidproductions.com/`, which contains lots of great information on this subject.

Let's get started by creating a function for all this behavior to go in. The armor is designed to fit over both the goblin and the skeleton sprites. Therefore, we can place it in the `Humanoid` class and generate armor for both variants!

Let's declare the `Humanoid::GenerateArmor` function, as follows:

```
private:
 /**
  * Generates random armor for the humanoid.
  */
void GenerateArmor();
```

The first thing that we need to do is create the `sf::RenderTexture` objects that we'll draw to. We're going to use two textures for each sprite: one for the armor and one for the final image. We'll draw the armor first and then draw that over the default enemy sprites to create the final textures.

Let's give the new function a body and set up the objects:

```cpp
// Randomly generates armor.
void Humanoid::GenerateArmor()
{
    // Create arrays of textures.
    const int textureCount = static_cast<int>(ANIMATION_STATE::COUNT);
    sf::RenderTexture armorTextures[textureCount];
    sf::RenderTexture finalTextures[textureCount];
    sf::Image renderImage;
    // Setup all render textures.
    for (int i = 0; i < static_cast<int>(ANIMATION_STATE::COUNT); ++i)
    {
        sf::Vector2u textureSize = m_textures[i].getSize();
        armorTextures[i].create(textureSize.x, textureSize.y);
        finalTextures[i].create(textureSize.x, textureSize.y);
    }
```

We can now add the code to choose which pieces of armor our enemy will have. We said we'd give each item a 20 percent chance of spawning. Hence, we need to generate a number from 0 to 4 (inclusive). There's a 20 percent chance that the result of this will be 0. Therefore, we can use this to determine whether that item of armor should spawn:

```cpp
// Create variables to determine what armor be created.
int hasHelmet(0), hasTorso(0), hasLegs(0);

hasHelmet = std::rand() % 5;
hasTorso = std::rand() % 5;
hasLegs = std::rand() % 5;

// Spawn helmet.
if (hasHelmet == 0)
{
}

// spawn torso.
if (hasTorso == 0)
{
}

// spawn legs.
if (hasLegs == 0)
{
}
```

Now that we randomly choose the pieces of armor, if any, that our enemy will have, we can turn our attention to creating different armor tiers by editing the sprites. There is a lot of code that is required to achieve this. So from this point onwards, we'll focus only on the helmet option.

Loading the default armor textures

To begin, we need to load the default armor textures. Each enemy has eight possible animation states, meaning we will need to load all the eight helmet counterparts. We'll do this in a way that is similar to how we load the default sprites in the constructor, creating an array of textures and using the enumerator of animation states as the index, as follows:

```
// Spawn helmet.
if (hasHelmet == 0)
{
  // Load the default helmet textures.
  int defaultHelmetTextureIDs[static_cast<int>(ANIMATION_
STATE::COUNT)];

  defaultHelmetTextureIDs[static_cast<int>(ANIMATION_STATE::WALK_UP)]
= TextureManager::AddTexture("../resources/armor/helmet/spr_helmet_
walk_front.png");
  defaultHelmetTextureIDs[static_cast<int>(ANIMATION_STATE::WALK_
DOWN)] = TextureManager::AddTexture("../resources/armor/helmet/spr_
helmet_walk_front.png");
  defaultHelmetTextureIDs[static_cast<int>(ANIMATION_STATE::WALK_
RIGHT)] = TextureManager::AddTexture("../resources/armor/helmet/spr_
helmet_walk_side.png");
  defaultHelmetTextureIDs[static_cast<int>(ANIMATION_STATE::WALK_
LEFT)] = TextureManager::AddTexture("../resources/armor/helmet/spr_
helmet_walk_side.png");
  defaultHelmetTextureIDs[static_cast<int>(ANIMATION_STATE::IDLE_UP)]
= TextureManager::AddTexture("../resources/armor/helmet/spr_helmet_
idle_front.png");
  defaultHelmetTextureIDs[static_cast<int>(ANIMATION_STATE::IDLE_
DOWN)] = TextureManager::AddTexture("../resources/armor/helmet/spr_
helmet_idle_front.png");
  defaultHelmetTextureIDs[static_cast<int>(ANIMATION_STATE::IDLE_
RIGHT)] = TextureManager::AddTexture("../resources/armor/helmet/spr_
helmet_idle_side.png");
  defaultHelmetTextureIDs[static_cast<int>(ANIMATION_STATE::IDLE_
LEFT)] = TextureManager::AddTexture("../resources/armor/helmet/spr_
helmet_idle_side.png");
```

With the default sprites loaded, we can now choose which armor tier they belong to, and therefore, what color we need to apply to them.

Choosing the armor tier

There will be three tiers of armor for each type, namely gold, silver, and bronze. So, we need to decide which tier to use. We could take a naive approach and generate a number from 0 and 2, but that's not ideal. Each tier would have the same chance of spawning, which is 33 percent.

Let's be a bit cannier with how we select the armor tier, making silver rarer than bronze, and gold rarer still. To do this, we'll still use the std::rand() function, but we'll be smarter in how we use the result. First, we need to decide the possibilities of each spawning. Let's say that we want 50 percent of it to be bronze, 35 percent of it to be silver, and 15 percent of it to be gold.

These percentages seem good and are nice to work with as they total 100. To replicate their chances, we need to generate a number from 1 to 100, and we can use it to get the desired percentages:

- There is a 50 percent chance that we will generate a number between 1 and 50 as it represents half of the total possible range (50/100)

- There is a 35 percent chance that we'll generate a number in the range of 51 to 85, as this range includes 35 values out of the possible 100 (35/100)

- Finally, there is a 15 percent chance that we'll generate a number in the range of 86 to 100, as this range includes 15 values out of the possible 100 (15/100)

Let's add the following code to our function, continuing from the previous code to load the default textures:

```
// Generate random number to determine tier.
sf::Color tierColor;
int tierValue = std::rand() % 100 + 1;

// Select which tier armor should be created.
if (tierValue < 51)
{
    tierColor = sf::Color(110, 55, 28, 255); // Bronze.
}
else if (tierValue < 86)
{
    tierColor = sf::Color(209, 208, 201, 255); // Silver.
}
else
{
    tierColor = sf::Color(229, 192, 21, 255); // Gold.
}
```

We used `std::rand() % 100 + 1`, and not `std::rand() % 100`. While they both technically do the same thing, the first generates a number from 1 to 100, while the later generates a number from 0 to 99. The first makes it simpler for us to work with.

We create a simple `if` statement that defines each of the ranges that we identified earlier. However, by the time we come to the `if` statement of gold, there is no need as we've already defined the other ranges. Therefore, we now know that anything that's left falls in the range of 86 to 100. We can therefore simply use an `else` statement, saving us an evaluation.

At this stage we've randomly selected a helmet, loaded the default sprites, and chosen a tier.

Rendering the armor textures

The next step is to edit the armor textures and overly them on the default enemy textures. Currently, we only have a gray sprite for each armor type. We need to use the sprite modification skills that we learned earlier in the chapter to create the bronze and gold versions. We can keep the gray as silver!

The pipeline required to do this is as follows:

- Load the default helmet texture
- Edit the color using the `tierColor` variable that we set earlier
- Draw the modified armor texture in the `armorTextures` array

We need to do this for every animation that the enemy has. So, we will encapsulate `armorTextures` array within a `for` loop, iterating over each value of the `ANIMATION_STATE` enumerator, as follows:

```
// Render helmet to armor texture.
for (int i = 0; i < static_cast<int>(ANIMATION_STATE::COUNT); ++i)
{
  // Load the default helmet texture and set its color.
  sf::Sprite tempSprite;
  tempSprite.setTexture(TextureManager::GetTexture(defaultHelmetTextu
reIDs[i]));
  tempSprite.setColor(tierColor);

  // Flip the texture vertically.
  sf::Vector2u size = armorTextures[i].getTexture().getSize();
```

```
    tempSprite.setTextureRect(sf::IntRect(0, size.y, size.x, -size.y));

    // Draw the texture.
    armorTextures[i].draw(tempSprite);
}}
```

The `armorTextures` array now contains all the helmet sprites, and their color has been set to a random tier value. We now need to do the exact same thing for the torso and legs, drawing the same `armorTextures` array again so that we can build up the armor texture. This is left as an exercise for you at the end of the chapter. For now, let's look at how to put this together to create the final texture.

Rendering the final textures

Now that the armor textures are created, we will need to render them on top of the default enemy textures to create the final images. We created copies of all the default textures in the constructor, so all that we need to do is draw our newly created armor textures on top them and save that as the final texture. One thing to remember is that the `sf::Texture::copyToImage` function flips an image vertically. Hence, right before we save the final version, we need to flip it back.

Let's add this final bit of code. This code needs to go after all the armor has been generated, so will be the final block of code in the `Humanoid::GenerateArmor` function:

```
// Create the final render texture.
for (int i = 0; i < static_cast<int>(ANIMATION_STATE::COUNT); ++i)
{
    sf::Sprite baseSprite, armorSprite;

    // Draw the default texture.
    baseSprite.setTexture(m_textures[i]);
    finalTextures[i].draw(baseSprite);

    // Draw armor on top.
    armorSprite.setTexture(armorTextures[i].getTexture());
    finalTextures[i].draw(armorSprite);

    // Flip the texture vertically.
    sf::Image img = finalTextures[i].getTexture().copyToImage();
    img.flipVertically();

    // Store the resulting texture.
    m_textures[i].loadFromImage(img);
}
```

With this function now complete, all that's left is to make a call to it at the end of our constructor:

```
    . . .
    // Copy textures.
    for (int i = 0; i < static_cast<int>(ANIMATION_STATE::COUNT); ++i)
    {
        m_textures[i] = TextureManager::GetTexture(m_textureIDs[i]);
    }

    // Generate armor.
    GenerateArmor();
}
```

Overriding the default draw behavior

The animation code for our objects lies in the base class `Object`. When the texture needs to be updated, it goes to the `m_textureIDs` variable and fetches the correct texture from the `TextureManager` class. Since we have created our own textures and stored them in the new `m_textures` array, we need to override this default behavior to provide our own textures.

To start with we need to override the update function by adding the following declaration to `Humanoid.h`:

```
/**
 * Overrides the update event of enemy.
 * @param timeDelta The time that has elapsed since the last update.
 */
void Update(float timeDelta) override;
```

We still need to call the parent's implementation, as that's where the animation logic lies. However, as soon as that's done, we need to jump in and provide our own texture before it's drawn. Luckily, that's very easy to do:

```
// Overrides the update event of enemy.
void Humanoid::Update(float timeDelta)
{
    // Call parent functionality.
    Enemy::Update(timeDelta);

    // Update the texture with our custom textures.
    m_sprite.setTexture(m_textures[m_currentTextureIndex]);
}
```

Debugging and testing

Before we run the game, let's add a little bit of debug code to see our work in action. Previously, we covered how to save textures to image files. So, let's use that here to save all the procedural sprites that we will create.

Let's update the loop that creates the final textures using the following code:

```
// Save the texture to disk.
if ((hasHelmet == 0) || (hasTorso == 0) || (hasLegs == 0))
{
  std::stringstream stream;
  stream << "../resources/test_" << i << ".png";
  img.saveToFile(stream.str());
}
```

All that this code does is save the textures to the resource folder if a piece of armor is generated. If you run the game a few times, remember that there is only a 20 percent chance that each skeleton will call this code, and head to the resources folder, you will see the following sprites:

These are the procedural sprites! In my case, it's a skeleton with a random piece of armor of a random tier that we didn't have to draw. We drew the constituent parts, did some programmatic editing, and put them together programmatically!

Well, after all that, it's time to test the code. If all is well, when you run the game, you should see some skeletons and goblins with helmets! Remember that each enemy only has a 20 percent change of having a helmet. You may have to run the game a few times to see it if you get unlucky:

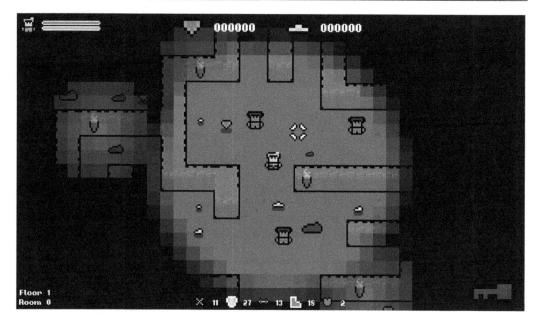

Before moving forward, you can remove the debug code that we just added to save sprites. This was purely for debugging purposes. One of the exercises at the end of this chapter is to complete the code and add the same behavior for the torso and leg armor options, but feel free to take this further. Experiment!

Editing the game tiles

The final system that we're going to look at is going to lay the groundwork for something that is coming later in the book. We're going to create a system to make each floor of the dungeon a unique environment, implementing what we know about sprite modification on the game tiles.

The goal of the game is to progress through as many floors as you can, getting the highest possible score. In *Chapter 9*, *Procedural Dungeon Generation*, we're going to look at how to generate dungeons procedurally, and after every five floors, we'll change the theme. Let's create the function that we will use later in the book to accomplish this.

The best way to solve this is to add a function to the `Level` object that sets the color of all the tile sprites. This will be a public function as we'll be calling it from the main game class.

Let's start by defining the `sf::color` function in the `Level` header, as follows:

```
public:
  /**
   * Sets the overlay color of the level tiles.
   * @param tileColor The new tile overlay color
   */
  void SetColor(sf::Color tileColor);
```

The definition for this function is very simple. It simply iterates over all the sprites in the grid, setting their color to the parameter that was passed:

```
// Sets the overlay color of the level tiles.
void Level::SetColor(sf::Color tileColor)
{
  for (int i = 0; i < GRID_WIDTH; ++i)
  {
    for (int j = 0; j < GRID_HEIGHT; ++j)
    {
      m_grid[i][j].sprite.setColor(tileColor);
    }
  }
}
```

With this in place, we're actually done. That's all there is to it! We'll use this function later in this chapter, but let's just test it while we're here. We initialize the `Level` object in `Game.cpp`, so once we've loaded the textures, we can call the `Level::SetColor` function and set the theme of the level.

Let's update the `Game::Initialize` function with the following test code:

```
// Set the color of the tiles
m_level.SetColor(sf::Color::Magenta);
```

With this, we can see what the levels will look like once we implement the function properly later.. Let's run the game and see what happens:

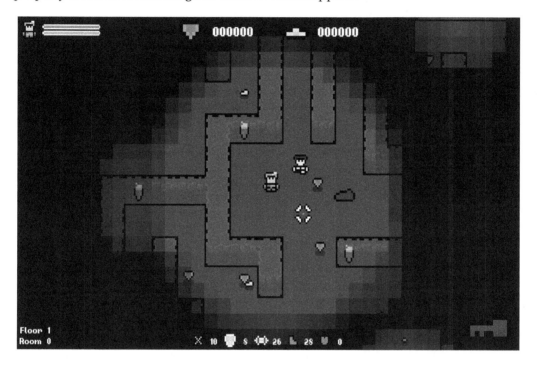

The `Level` tiles now have an ambient color applied to all the sprites that make up the environment, allowing us to create a unique look and feel for our levels. Like I previously mentioned, we'll use this system later when we generate random levels programmatically. For now, we can remove the debug code and sit tight knowing that the system is ready for use!

Exercises

To help you test your knowledge of this chapter's content, here are a few exercises that you should work through. They are not imperative to the rest of the book, but working through them will help you to assess your strengths and weaknesses in the material covered:

1. Give the goblin enemy a slightly random color and scale every time one is spawned.

2. Finish the code to generate armor procedurally for the humanoid by completing the condition for the torso and leg armor.

3. Try to generate armor in a more succinct manner. We're using two textures; maybe there's a way to use only one. See if you can improve the function.

Summary

In this chapter, we learned how to generate game art procedurally. We took a naïve approach to start, simply using RNG with built-in sprite modifiers, and moved on to algorithmically generating our own images. Generating procedural art is a vast topic, and you could write a book on the subject. Hopefully, this chapter has introduced you to the topic nicely.

In the next chapter, we're going to look at art's cousin, audio. With our art now procedurally generated we'll use similar techniques to create variance in sounds. We'll also use SFML's audio functions to create specialized 3D sound and thus bring more depth to the levels.

7
Procedurally Modifying Audio

Now that our game art has received procedural treatment, let's turn our attention to its neighbor, sound. Great sound is imperative for a good game. Think about how iconic the sound of Super Mario's jump is, or the sound of chomping ghosts in Packman! A great soundtrack and accompanying game sounds help players immerse themselves in the worlds that we create as game developers. It's an area that needs to be done correctly, and there needs to be enough diversity here so that your players don't get sick of hearing the same sound effects over and over again.

We could manually create lots of variants of sound effects, but that's not the procedural way! Instead, we'll alter sounds randomly at runtime to create a slightly different sound each time it's played. Then, we'll utilize SFML's audio functions to create spatialized 3D sounds, thus adding more depth and immersion to the game.

Procedurally generating audio from scratch is a very complex task. Our work in this area will be somewhat brief, and really limited to procedurally modifying existing sounds as opposed to their outright creation. Still, this will serve as a good introduction to taking a procedural approach toward audio.

In this chapter, we'll cover the following topics:

- SFML audio
- The difference between `sf::sound` and `sf::music`
- Altering existing sound effects
- Creating spatialized 3D sound

An introduction to SFML audio

SFML has its own module dedicated to audio, which provides a number of useful functions that we can use to modify sounds. There are two main sound types in SFML: `sf::Sound` and `sf::Music`. We'll cover the difference between these two types in detail shortly. It also provides a number of functions to edit the properties of sounds, such as pitch and volume. We'll use these to give our sound effects some variance.

sf::Sound versus sf::Music

Before we start working with audio, we need to look at the difference between `sf::Sound` and `sf::Music`:

- `Sf::Sound` is intended for shorter sound clips such as picking up an object or footsteps. The sound is loaded in its entirety into the memory, and it is ready to be played with no latency.

- `Sf::Music` is intended for longer, bigger sound files and is not loaded into the memory; it is streamed as it is used.

This might seem like a slight difference, but it's very important to use the correct type. For example, if we were to load a game's music into an `sf::Sound` object, the game would use a lot of memory!

sf::SoundBuffer

When creating a sprite in SFML, we create an `sf::Sprite` object, which contains information such as the scale and position. The texture itself is stored in an `sf::Texture` object to which the sprite object holds a reference. The `sf::Sound` class works in the same way, with an `sf::SoundBuffer` object holding the actual sound and `sf::Sound` simply holding a reference to it.

The following code shows how a sound is loaded:

```
sf::SoundBuffer buffer;
buffer.loadFromFile("sound.wav");

sf::Sound sound;
sound.setBuffer(buffer);
sound.play();
```

The sf::SoundBuffer object must remain active for the same amount of time as the sf::Sound object does. If sf::SoundBuffer goes out of scope before the sf::Sound object that holds a reference to it, we will get an error, as it will try to play a sound that no longer exists.

Also, since we only hold a reference to the sound buffer, it can be used in multiple sound objects. To play a sound, we just make a call to sf::Sound::play, and this runs the sound in a separate thread.

Selecting a random main track

Currently, the game has no sounds or music. We have been running the game frequently throughout the course of the book, and hearing the same track over and over can get very tedious. So, we've waited until now to put it in. It's a very simple process to add sounds. So, we'll cover this process in its entirety.

To start, we'll add a main music track that will underpin the game. However, instead of having a fixed track, we will add multiple possibilities and randomly choose one during startup.

Let's start by defining all the possibilities in an enumerator in the usual way. Add the following code to Util.h:

```
// Music tracks.
enum class MUSIC_TRACK {
    ALT_1,
    ALT_2,
    ALT_3,
    ALT_4,
    COUNT
};
```

As the enum shows, we're going to have four possible tracks. These are already included in the /resources/music/ folder. So, all that we have to do is select one track at random and load it at the start of the game. Since we want this music to start straightaway, we will insert the code that accomplishes this in our Game classes constructor.

We've selected a random value from an enumerator a few times now, so it should be familiar. We'll generate a number between 1 and MUSIC_TRACK_COUNT (inclusive), however, instead of casting it to the enumerator type as we normally do, we're going to leave it as an integer. The reason behind this will soon become apparent.

For now, let's add the following code to `Game::Game`:

```
// Setup the main game music.
int trackIndex = std::rand() % static_cast<int>(MUSIC_TRACK::COUNT) +
1;
```

Now, the reason why we didn't cast to the `enum` type is because we can be clever when it comes to how we load sounds. We have four music tracks to choose from, and they have the following names:

- `msc_main_track_1.wav`
- `msc_main_track_2.wav`
- `msc_main_track_3.wav`
- `msc_main_track_4.wav`

Note that the only thing that's different in their names is their number. We've already generated a number between 1 to 4. So, instead of creating a `switch` statement, we can simply use this index to load the correct track, as follows:

```
// Load the music track.
m_music.openFromFile("../resources/music/msc_main_track_" + std::to_
string(trackIndex) + ".wav");
```

Now, when we call `m_music.play()`, the sound will be streamed. Let's finish by calling this function:

```
m_music.play();
```

If we run the game now, we will hear one of the four randomly selected tracks playing!

Adding sound effects

Now that we have the game's main music, let's add some sounds effects to the mix! We've covered `sf::Sound`, `sf::SoundBuffer`, and how to play sounds, so we're ready to jump right in.

We're going to have a few sound effects in our game. One for the death of an enemy, one for us being hit, one for each pickup, and one for the sound of torches that we'll be playing with later.

We'll start by defining the `sf::Sound` variables for each sound in `Game.h`:

```
/**
 * Torch sound.
 */
```

```
sf::Sound m_fireSound;

/**
 * Gem pickup sound.
 */
sf::Sound m_gemPickupSound;

/**
 * Coin pickup sound.
 */
sf::Sound m_coinPickupSound;

/**
* Key collect sound.
*/
sf::Sound m_keyPickupSound;

/**
 * Enemy die sound.
 */
sf::Sound m_enemyDieSound;

/**
 * Player hit sound.
 */
sf::Sound m_playerHitSound;
```

Now, let's initialize these sounds in `Game::Initialize`, as follows:

```
// Load all game sounds.
int soundBufferId;

// Load torch sound.
soundBufferId = SoundBufferManager::AddSoundBuffer("../resources/
sounds/snd_fire.wav");
m_fireSound.setBuffer(SoundBufferManager::GetSoundBuffer(soundBuffer
Id));
m_fireSound.setLoop(true);
m_fireSound.play();

// Load enemy die sound.
soundBufferId = SoundBufferManager::AddSoundBuffer("../resources/
sounds/snd_enemy_dead.wav");
```

```
m_enemyDieSound.setBuffer(SoundBufferManager::GetSoundBuffer(soundBuf
ferId));

// Load gem pickup sound.
soundBufferId = SoundBufferManager::AddSoundBuffer("../resources/
sounds/snd_gem_pickup.wav");
m_gemPickupSound.setBuffer(SoundBufferManager::GetSoundBuffer(soundBu
fferId));

// Load coin pickup sound.
soundBufferId = SoundBufferManager::AddSoundBuffer("../resources/
sounds/snd_coin_pickup.wav");
m_coinPickupSound.setBuffer(SoundBufferManager::GetSoundBuffer(soundB
ufferId));

// Load key pickup sound.
soundBufferId = SoundBufferManager::AddSoundBuffer("../resources/
sounds/snd_key_pickup.wav");
m_keyPickupSound.setBuffer(SoundBufferManager::GetSoundBuffer(soundBu
fferId));

// Load player hit sound.
soundBufferId = SoundBufferManager::AddSoundBuffer("../resources/
sounds/snd_player_hit.wav");
m_playerHitSound.setBuffer(SoundBufferManager::GetSoundBuffer(soundBu
fferId));
```

With the sounds initialized, we just call `sf::Sound::play` to play the sound when we need it. We handle item pickups in the `Game::UpdateItems` function. Therefore, we'll put this code there:

```
// check what type of object it was
switch (m_items[i]->GetType())
{
    case ITEM_GOLD:
    {
        // Get the amount of gold.
        int goldValue = dynamic_cast<Gold&>(item).GetGoldValue();

        // Add to the gold total.
        m_goldTotal += goldValue;

        // Check if we have an active level goal regarding gold.
        if (m_activeGoal)
        {
            m_goldGoal -= goldValue;
```

```
        }

        // Play gold collect sound effect
        m_coinPickupSound.play();
    }
    break;

    case ITEM_GEM:
    {
        // Get the score of the gem.
        int scoreValue = dynamic_cast<Gem&>(item).GetScoreValue();

        // Add to the score total
        m_scoreTotal += scoreValue;

        // Check if we have an active level goal.
        if (m_activeGoal)
        --m_gemGoal;

        // Play the gem pickup sound
        m_gemPickupSound.play();
    }
    break;
}
```

This code covers just the gold and gem pickups. The same thing needs to be done for all the other pickups and cases where we need to play sounds, such as when an enemy dies and a player takes damage.

Editing sound effects

With the sound effects added, we can now alter them to create variety. SFML offers a number of ways in which we can manipulate sounds, which includes the following:

- Pitch
- Volume
- Position

We'll start with the simplest: the pitch. Then, we'll cover both the volume and position by creating spatialized sounds. These values will be set randomly each time we play a sound effect. Before we get into it, let's create a function to encapsulate the modification and playing of sounds. This will save us from having repeated code throughout the class.

Playing a sound function

Collisions with enemies and items are processed in the main game class. So, it's here that we will place the function to play sound effects. Add the following function declaration to `Game.h`:

```
/**
 * Plays the given sound effect, with randomized parameters./
 */
void PlaySound(sf::Sound& sound, sf::Vector2f position = { 0.f, 0.f
});
```

This function takes two parameters: we take the sound that we want to play as a reference, to avoid an expensive copy, and we also include a parameter for the position where we want to play the sound. Note that we've given the position parameter a default value of { 0.f, 0.f }. Therefore, it can be ignored should we wish to do so. We'll cover exactly what this parameter does when we create spatialized sounds.

Let's give this class a basic body for now to simply play the sound passed via the parameter:

```
// Plays the given sound effect, with randomized parameters.
void Game::PlaySound(sf::Sound& sound, sf::Vector2f position)
{
    // Play the sound.
    sound.play();
}
```

Note that if the game was any bigger and we had a large range of many sounds, it would be worthwhile to encapsulate the behavior to play sounds in the same class in which we manage them. This would ensure that all the interactions with sounds happened through a common class and would keep our code organized.

The audio listener

SFML comes with a static listener class. This class acts as the ear in the level and as such, there is only one listener in a scene. Since this is a static class, we never instantiate it, and we interact with it through its static functions such as `sf::Listener::setPosition`.

By "ear in the level", I mean that all the sounds in the level are heard at this location. This is how we create 3D sounds. For example, if the source of a sound was to the right of the listener, it would be heard more in the right speaker. Take a look at the following diagram:

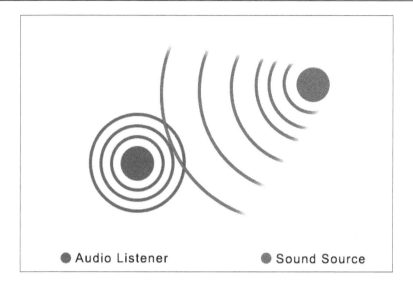

In this diagram the blue circle represents the position of the audio listener, and the red circle represents the position of the sound. You can see that since the source of the sound is to the right of the listener, we can use this to determine that the sound should be heard more from the right speaker as compared to the left one. This is how spatialized sound is created, and we'll look at this in detail later in the chapter.

For occasions where we don't want sound to be spatialized, SFML gives us the `sf::Sound::setRelativeToListener` function. This is a self-explanatory function; the position of the sound is relative to that of the listener as opposed to being absolute within the scene. We set this to `true` and give the sound a position of `{0.f, 0.f, 0.f}`, positioning it right on top of the listener.

With regards to the previous diagram, this means that the blue audio listener will be placed directly at the top of the red sound source, which means that it is not spatialized. This is the behavior that we want for the pickup sounds. For each sound, we need to make a call to this function, passing `true` as the parameter.

Let's update the code to change this:

```
// Load gem pickup sound.
soundBufferId = SoundBufferManager::AddSoundBuffer("../resources/
sounds/snd_gem_pickup.wav");
m_gemPickupSound.setBuffer(SoundBufferManager::GetSoundBuffer(soundBu
fferId));
m_gemPickupSound.setRelativeToListener(true);
// Load coin pickup sound.
soundBufferId = SoundBufferManager::AddSoundBuffer("../resources/
sounds/snd_coin_pickup.wav");
```

```
m_coinPickupSound.setBuffer(SoundBufferManager::GetSoundBuffer(soundB
ufferId));
m_coinPickupSound.setRelativeToListener(true);

// Load key pickup sound.
soundBufferId = SoundBufferManager::AddSoundBuffer("../resources/
sounds/snd_key_pickup.wav");
m_keyPickupSound.setBuffer(SoundBufferManager::GetSoundBuffer(soundBu
fferId));
m_keyPickupSound.setRelativeToListener(true);

// Load player hit sound.
soundBufferId = SoundBufferManager::AddSoundBuffer("../resources/
sounds/snd_player_hit.wav");
m_playerHitSound.setBuffer(SoundBufferManager::GetSoundBuffer(soundBu
fferId));
m_playerHitSound.setRelativeToListener(true);
```

Sounds that originate from the same location as the player require this. For example, an item is only picked up once the enemy occupies the same space. You will never pick up an item from a distance so the sound will never be spatialized.

Creating a fluctuation in a pitch

Pitch is the perceived frequency at which a sound is heard. SFML offers a way to increase or decrease the pitch of a sound, and it achieves this by increasing/ decreasing its playback speed respectively. Play it back faster, and it'll sound higher. The default value of this is 1, so generating a number that's lesser or greater than 1 will give us a fluctuation in pitch.

We'll add this behavior to our new `Game::PlaySound` function. To start, we'll generate a number between 0.95 and 1.05, set the pitch, and play the sound, as follows:

```
// Plays the given sound effect, with randomized parameters.
void Game::PlaySound(sf::Sound& sound, sf::Vector2f position)
{
    // Generate and set a random pitch.
    float pitch = (rand() % 11 + 95) / 100.f;
    sound.setPitch(pitch);

    // Play the sound.
    sound.play();
}
```

Now, whenever we want a sound to have this fluctuation in pitch, we need to play it through this function as opposed to directly playing it. This applies to all the pickup sounds. So, let's implement this change:

```
// check what type of object it was
switch (m_items[i]->GetType())
{
    case ITEM_GOLD:
    {
        // Get the amount of gold.
        int goldValue = dynamic_cast<Gold&>(item).GetGoldValue();

        // Add to the gold total.
        m_goldTotal += goldValue;

        // Check if we have an active level goal regarding gold.
        if (m_activeGoal)
        {
            m_goldGoal -= goldValue;
        }

        // Play gold collect sound effect
        PlaySound(m_coinPickupSound);
    }
    break;

    case ITEM_GEM:
    {
        // Get the score of the gem.
        int scoreValue = dynamic_cast<Gem&>(item).GetScoreValue();

        // Add to the score total
        m_scoreTotal += scoreValue;

        // Check if we have an active level goal.
        if (m_activeGoal)
        {
            --m_gemGoal;
        }

        // Play the gem pickup sound
        PlaySound(m_gemPickupSound);
    }
    break;
}
```

If we now play the game and pick up some items, we can hear that the pickup sound is slightly different each time, bringing some variance to the sound effects. If you want the sounds that are played when a key is picked up, an enemy dies, and a player is hit, to have their pitch fluctuated too, ensure that they are also played via this function as opposed to them being directly played.

3D sound – spatialization

Now let's look at ways to create some 3D audio to bring depth to a game scene. When we walk past a torch, we want to hear it move past us, and we want to be able to hear our enemies coming at us from a direction. Spatialization allows us to do this, and SFML has great features to help us achieve that.

The audio listener

We've already defined what the audio listener is and how it is used to create spatialized audio. As the first step toward achieving this, we need to set the position of the listener after each update, ensuring that all the sounds in the level are heard from the player's perspective.

At the start of each game's update, we recalculate the player's position. Right after this we can update the position of the listener class to this new location. Remember that `sf::Listener` is a static class and we don't instantiate it. All that we need to do is make a static call to `sf::Listener::setPosition`.

Let's append this to the `Game::Update` function, as follows:

```
// Update the player.
m_player.Update(timeDelta, m_level);

// Store the player position as it's used many times.
sf::Vector2f playerPosition = m_player.GetPosition();

// Move the audio listener to the players location.
sf::Listener::setPosition(playerPosition.x, playerPosition.y, 0.f);

// If the player is attacking create a projectile.
if (m_player.IsAttacking())
{
```

Moving forward, we can now be sure that the listener is in the correct position in order for us to create a 3D sound.

The minimum distance

The minimum distance is the closest the player can be to the source of a sound before it's heard at full volume. Imagine it as a circle surrounding the sound source. The radius of this circle is MinDistance, as shown in the following diagram:

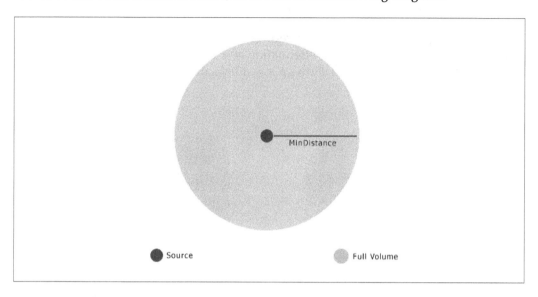

In our case, the minimum distance of the sounds will not change throughout the course of the game, which means that we can set their values once in the Game::Initialize function when we load the sounds. The value that we use here is a matter of preference, but I found a minimum distance of 80.f works well. Let's get these values set.

Make the following modifications to the Game::Initialize function:

```
// Load torch sound.
soundBufferId = SoundBufferManager::AddSoundBuffer("../resources/
sounds/snd_fire.wav");
m_fireSound.setBuffer(SoundBufferManager::GetSoundBuffer(soundBuffer
Id));
m_fireSound.setLoop(true);
m_fireSound.setMinDistance(80.f);
m_fireSound.play();

// Load enemy die sound.
soundBufferId = SoundBufferManager::AddSoundBuffer("../resources/
sounds/snd_enemy_dead.wav");
m_enemyDieSound.setBuffer(SoundBufferManager::GetSoundBuffer(soundBuf
ferId));
m_enemyDieSound.setMinDistance(80.f);
```

Attenuation

Attenuation basically means "to lessen" or "to make something smaller". In the context of audio, it's the rate at which the sound gets quieter as we move away from the source. This comes into effect when we are outside the minimum distance and is used to calculate the volume of the sound.

In the following diagram, the gradient represents the volume of the sound. The image to the left shows a high attenuation and the sound drops off very fast, while the image to the right shows a low attenuation and the sound drops off more smoothly:

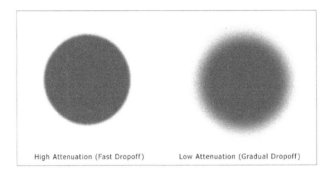

High Attenuation (Fast Dropoff)   Low Attenuation (Gradual Dropoff)

Now, let's give our two sounds an attenuation value like we did with the minimum distance. Again, the value used here is up to you, but I found out that an attenuation value of 5.f, which is just slightly above the default, created a nice fadeout.

Make the following modifications to the Game::Initialize function:

```
// Load torch sound.
soundBufferId = SoundBufferManager::AddSoundBuffer("../resources/
sounds/snd_fire.wav");
m_fireSound.setBuffer(SoundBufferManager::GetSoundBuffer(soundBuffer
Id));
m_fireSound.setLoop(true);
m_fireSound.setAttenuation(5.f);
m_fireSound.setMinDistance(80.f);
m_fireSound.play();

// Load enemy die sound.
soundBufferId = SoundBufferManager::AddSoundBuffer("../resources/
sounds/snd_enemy_dead.wav");
m_enemyDieSound.setBuffer(SoundBufferManager::GetSoundBuffer(soundBuf
ferId));
m_enemyDieSound.setAttenuation(5.f);
m_enemyDieSound.setMinDistance(80.f);
```

If we run the game now, we will see that as we approach the torches, they get louder, and as we walk away, they get quieter. However, they aren't 3D. For that, we need to update the source of the sound!

The position of the sound

The position of the sound is simply its position in the scene. It's this position, and the position of the listener, that are used to create the 3D effect and determine which speaker the sound should play out of.

 To use spatialization your sounds need to be **Mono** (have a single channel). The ones provided with this project are, but if you're adding your own, you need to keep this in mind! Sounds with more than one channel already explicitly decide how to use the speakers.

Now that we have the attenuation and minimum distance set, we can now set the correct position of the sound so that we can hear the 3D effects. We have two sounds in the game that are going to be 3D: the sound of the torches and the sound of enemies when they are killed. As we have multiple torches in the level we have a bit of work to do here. We'll start with the simpler one of the two: the sound of the enemies when they're killed.

Fixed positions

First, we need to update the `Game::PlaySound` function. Currently, it only generates a random pitch, but we need it to set the position too. You may remember that we made the position parameter optional by giving it a default value of `{0.f, 0.f }`. When we pass a position and override the default, it means that we want to utilize a 3D sound. When we leave it blank, it means that we don't want to do so and the sound will be relative to the listener. Therefore, `{0.f, 0.f, 0.f}` is just what we need.

Let's hook up the position parameter in `Game::PlaySound` and use it to set the position of the sound, as follows:

```
// Plays the given sound effect, with randomized parameters.
void Game::PlaySound(sf::Sound& sound, sf::Vector2f position)
{
    // Generate and set a random pitch.
    float pitch = (rand() % 11 + 95) / 100.f;
    sound.setPitch(pitch);
```

```
    // Set the position of the sound.
    sound.setPosition(position.x, position.y, 0.f);

    // Play the sound.
    sound.play();
}
```

The position of the sound operates in three dimensions, but since we're working with 2D sounds we can leave the Z value as `0.f`. Now, when we identify that an enemy has been killed, we simply make a call to this function and pass the correct sound and location of the enemy, as that's where the sound is coming from, as follows:

```
// 1 in 5 change of spawning potion.
else if ((std::rand() % 5) == 1)
{
    position.x += std::rand() % 31 - 15;
    position.y += std::rand() % 31 - 15;
    SpawnItem(ITEM::POTION, position);
}

// Play enemy kill sound.
PlaySound(m_enemyDieSound, enemy.GetPosition());

// Delete enemy.
enemyIterator = m_enemies.erase(enemyIterator);
```

It's time to run the game again and listen to our handiwork. As we kill the enemies, we can hear that the further away they are, the fainter the sound is. Also, if we kill an enemy to the right, we here it coming from that direction! To wrap up our work with sound, let's apply the same technique to the torches to really give the level some depth when it comes to its audio.

 The clarity of the 3D sound will depend on your setup. For example, while headphones will allow you to easily hear sounds that are created in different directions, laptop speakers might not be so clear.

Moving positions

The last area that we'll add a 3D sound to is the torches in the level. As we walk around the level, it would be great to hear torches faintly in the distance, or near us in our headphones as we walk past them. However, there's a slight problem. We know that the spatialization of sound is achieved when the sound and the listener are away from one another. But what if we have a sound that needs to come from multiple locations? We could have a sound for each torch, but that's a waste. Instead, we'll calculate which torch is closet to the player and use that as the source.

As part of our main update function, we need to look at all the torches and determine which one is the nearest to the player. As the player walks around the level, the source will switch, giving us the impression that each torch is giving off its own sound, while we have only a single source in reality.

We already have a function to find the distance between two objects, namely `Game::DistanceBetweenPoints`. Given this, we can iterate over all the torches and use this function to get the distance to the player. Let's update the `Game::Update` function to include this calculation, as follows:

```
// Update all projectiles.
UpdateProjectiles(timeDelta);

// Find which torch is nearest the player.
auto torches = m_level.GetTorches();

// If there are torches.
if (!torches->empty())
{
    // Store the first torch as the current closest.
    std::shared_ptr<Torch> nearestTorch = torches->front();
    float lowestDistanceToPlayer = DistanceBetweenPoints(playerPositi
on, nearestTorch->GetPosition());

    for (std::shared_ptr<Torch> torch : *torches)
    {
        // Get the distance to the player.
        float distanceToPlayer = DistanceBetweenPoints(playerPosition,
torch->GetPosition());
        if (distanceToPlayer < lowestDistanceToPlayer)
        {
            lowestDistanceToPlayer = distanceToPlayer;
            nearestTorch = torch;
        }
    }
}

// Check if the player has moved grid square.
Tile* playerCurrentTile = m_level.GetTile(playerPosition);
```

As you can see, for each torch in the level, we calculate how far away it is from the player. If it's closer than the last one that we checked, we mark it as the closest. When this code is finished, we end up with the nearest torch stored in the shared pointer named `nearestTorch`.

With the closest torch identified, we can use its position as the position of the fire's sound. Now, for the rest of the sounds, we've been using the new `Game::PlaySound` function, but that's not suitable here. Our fire sound is already looping, we don't need to restart it. We just need to set its position, so we'll do it directly.

Let's update that code once more:

```
// Get the distance to the player.
float distanceToPlayer = DistanceBetweenPoints(playerPosition,
torch->GetPosition());
if (distanceToPlayer < lowestDistanceToPlayer)
    {
        lowestDistanceToPlayer = distanceToPlayer;
        nearestTorch = torch;
    }
}

m_fireSound.setPosition(nearestTorch->GetPosition().x,
nearestTorch->GetPosition().y, 0.0f);
}

// Check if the player has moved grid square.
Tile* playerCurrentTile = m_level.GetTile(playerPosition);
```

Let's run the project for the last time! We should now hear a random music track, some of our sound effects will be played with a fluctuating pitch, and the sounds of the torches and the enemies dying will be spatialized.

Exercises

To help you test your understanding of this chapter's content, here are a few exercises that you should work on. They are not imperative to the rest of the book, but working on them will help you assess your strengths and weaknesses in the material covered:

1. Add more tracks to the list of main tracks.
2. Add a sound that is spatialized for the door when it opens in the `level`. When a player collects the key for the `level`, hearing the door sliding open in the background will help them find it.
3. Add some atmospheric sound effects to the `level`; the sound effects should be spatialized and must play at random intervals. We have not covered anything like that so far so it should be a challenge.

Summary

In this chapter, we used SFML's built-in audio modifiers to make alterations to our sound effects. We also utilized the modifiers to create spatialized 3D sounds, bringing more depth to our game scene.

In the next chapter, we're going to use everything that we learned so far to create complex procedural behavior and mechanics in the form of pathfinding and unique level goals. We'll give our enemies the intelligence to traverse levels and chase the player, and we'll create a unique level goal with unique rewards for the player.

8
Procedural Behavior and Mechanics

Until now, the focus of our efforts has been the procedural creation of resources. Let's branch out using what we've learned and procedurally create behavior and game mechanics. While the creation of *procedural game behavior* may sound exotic, you run into it in every game that you play; **artificial intelligence (AI)**. AI in games is calculating behavior at runtime based on current factors. This definitely counts as procedural generation! Previously, when approaching large topics, I've commented that a whole book could be dedicated to the subject. Well, with AI, you'd need an entire library. For our project, we're going to have a look at pathfinding; allowing enemies to intelligently chase the player around our levels.

Another aspect that we'll look at is the procedural generation of mechanics, specifically the generation of unique game goals. A great example of where this can be applied is game quests. How many times have you come across a quest that said, *Kill X of this animal and bring me Y of its fur?* Probably around a thousand! We can use procedural generation to add some variety here. We can generate random goals for each room/floor of our dungeon that aren't so static.

In this chapter, we'll cover the following topics:

- The A* pathfinding algorithm
- Generating unique game tasks

An introduction to pathfinding

We're going to start by tackling the biggest job: implementing a pathfinding algorithm so that the enemies can move intelligently around the map. Before we do so, let's take a look at pathfinding algorithms as a whole, what they do, and how they do it! This context will help you make the task ahead clearer and show you the wealth of choices that we have.

What is a pathfinding algorithm?

A **pathfinding algorithm** is an algorithm that calculates the best path from one position to another. A good algorithm will take into account the terrain and several other factors to ensure that the movement is intelligent and won't result in any weird behavior. Remember the last time you were playing a game and an NPC kept walking into the wall? This is the weird behavior that pathfinding errors produce. Every time an enemy runs around an object to get you in a game, it's the result of such an algorithm, and they're essential in the creation of a gameplay that's challenging and which feels natural.

For example, in the following diagram, the green circle is an NPC that has to get the red circle:

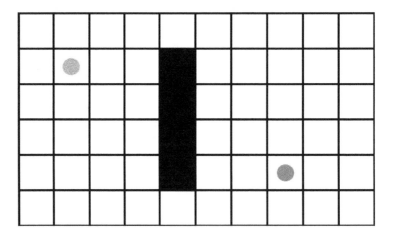

In this example, the NPC can't go directly towards the goal point as it would get stuck walking into the wall. Instead, we need to take the wall into account and move around it, as shown in the following diagram:

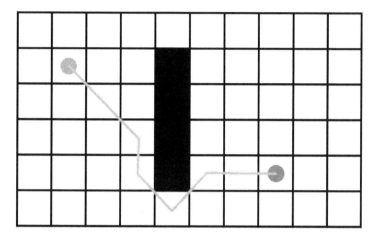

You can see that the NPC here intelligently avoided the wall while still reaching the goal as efficiently as possible. This is the essence of pathfinding, and it is what we'll implement in our game in the first part of this chapter. Let's take a look at what's going on behind the arrows.

Dijkstra's algorithm

As with anything, there are a number of ways in which pathfinding can be implemented, and a number of common algorithms can be used to do so. Different algorithms have different characteristics, and while their finished product may appear similar, they achieve it in different ways. The most common pathfinding algorithm in games is **A***, an extension of Dijkstra's algorithm.

Dijkstra's algorithm was created by Edsger Dijkstra in 1959. It is a best-first search algorithm, that is, it visits the node with the least value first in an effort to produce the shortest path possible. From its starting point, it radiates out, checking every node in turn until it finds its goal. As you can imagine, this is both expensive and it can take a long time to find the end node.

The following diagram shows how, to find the end node, Dijkstra's algorithm has to search most of the available nodes:

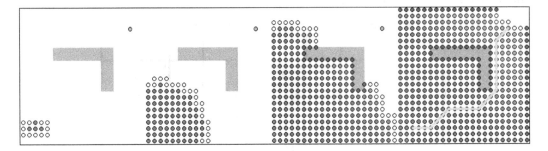

The A* algorithm

A* is an extension of Dijkstra's algorithm. Its aim is to decrease the time it takes to find the end node by introducing a heuristic to help guide the search. A **heuristic** (or heuristic technique) is simply a way of approaching a problem using a practical method that isn't perfect, but it's sufficient. For example, trial and error is a fundamental heuristic. While it's not perfect, you'll reach the solution to a problem using trial and error.

In terms of A*, our heuristic is taking into account the distance that has already been travelled to guide the search towards the end node. Take another look at the preceding diagram that shows Dijkstra's algorithm. Now, look at the same pathfinding problem that's solved by A* in the following diagram:

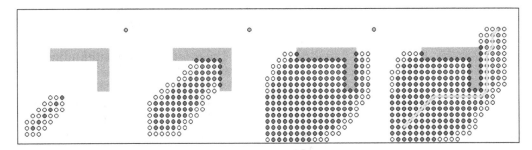

It's clear that the A* implementation tended towards the target location and thus found the goal node quickly. Also, look at how many nodes each algorithm had to look at to find the goal. Dijkstra's algorithm practically visited every node, while in A*, thanks to the heuristic, significantly fewer nodes were visited.

A breakdown of A*

Before we start coding our own A* implementation, it will do us good to break down the algorithm into its key areas and take an isolated look at each.

Representing a level as nodes

Perhaps the most important area of understanding when we look at A* is how the algorithm will view our level. While we see tiles, the pathfinding algorithm sees only nodes. In this context, a node just represents a valid location that an entity can move to within the level.

How nodes are defined differs from game to game. For example, in our game, the level is already described as a 2D array of tiles. Therefore, each tile in that grid will act as a node. In 3D games however, we don't have this grid so navigation meshes are used to create a surface that can be represented as nodes.

 Valve has a great article on their developer wiki page regarding navigation meshes. So head to `https://developer.valvesoftware.com/wiki/Navigation_Meshes` if you want to learn more about this subject.

The following image shows how the level is split into the 2D array of tiles that it is at heart. Each of these tiles will be used as a node in the A* algorithm. The tiles that are valid locations for players to move to (floor tiles) are marked in green, and the tiles that should be avoided (walls, obstacles, and so on) are marked in orange.

The resulting green is the valid region of nodes that the algorithm will try and find a path through.

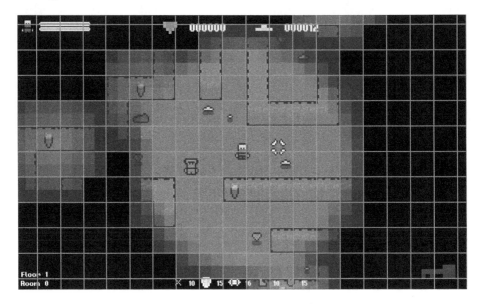

The open and closed list

Once the nodes have been identified, they are stored into the following two lists:

- **The open list**: This list contains all the nodes that are waiting to be the subject of the algorithm. This will make more sense when we get into some code, but the algorithm operates on one node a time, and the open list is the queue for this.

- **The closed list**: This list simply contains all the nodes that have already been through the algorithm. Once a node gets added to this list, it's ignored until the algorithm is complete.

The H, G, and F costs

When reading about the A* pathfinding algorithm, there are 3 letters that you're going to come across: H, G, and F. These are crucial values in the algorithm, but they aren't very descriptive. So let's take a moment to look at what each value is and the role that it plays in calculating a path.

The H value

The H value, often referred to as the heuristic, is the estimated cost to reach the goal node from the current position. Every node in the level has an H value, which is calculated at the start of the pathfinding algorithm, and then used in later calculations. This value helps guide the search towards the target node instead of equally spreading out in all directions. How this value is calculated is up to the specific implementation, but a common method is called the **Manhattan distance**. We'll cover what this exactly is shortly.

The G value

The G value is the current movement cost from the start node to this node. The way this is calculated is again implementation-specific. However, as with the H value, a common method and the one that we'll be using is the Manhattan distance. As the algorithm iterates, every time a link between two nodes is made, the movement cost of that individual movement is added to that of the entire path so far. In this way, as the paths build, each node knows how long the entire path before it is.

The F value

The F value is simply the sum of the H and G values. This value is used to determine which node the algorithm uses next. The lower this value, the lower the estimated complete path is. Thus, the algorithm prioritizes these nodes. This behavior is what makes Dijkstra's algorithm, and therefore A*, a best-first search algorithm.

The Manhattan distance

At the heart of a pathfinding algorithm lies calculating the distance between two points. As mentioned previously, exactly how this is done is implementation-specific, but there is a common and cheap method known as Manhattan distance (also known as taxicab geometry), which is what we'll be using.

It's formally defined as the distance between two points calculated by taking the sum of the absolute difference of their Cartesian coordinates.

That's quite a mouthful, but it's actually pretty simple. Cartesian coordinates are simply a way of expressing a position relative to two fixed perpendicular axes (even if this seems unfamiliar, we've all covered this at school), and absolute simply means that we ignore the sign of a number.

Take a look at the following graph:

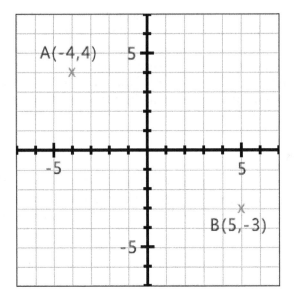

We have two points on the graph: **A(-4,4)** and **B(5,-3)**. The following pseudocode calculates the Manhattan distance between the two:

```
// Calculate the absolute difference in X.
diffX = abs(-4 - 5) = 9;

// Calculate the absolute difference in Y.
diffY = abs(4 - -3) = 7;

// Add them to get the Manhattan distance.
manhattenDistance = 9 + 7 = 16;
```

It's as simple as that!

Parenting nodes

Another crucial aspect of pathfinding is the idea of parenting nodes. A* works by building up a chain of nodes. Once the goal node is found, we work back through this chain to get the final path. When the shortest path between two nodes is identified, node A will be assigned as the parent of node B.

For example, the following screenshot shows a situation where the skeleton enemy has found a valid path to the player:

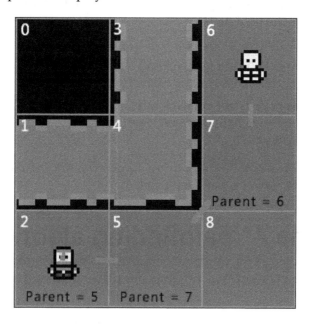

Let's imagine a situation where a path between two nodes is found. For example, the path between nodes **6** and **7**. Then, the first node is set as the parent of the second node, in this case, node **6** is set as the parent of node **7**. In this way, each node knows where it came from. When the algorithm finds the goal node (in our example, it's node **2**), we can use this parent hierarchy to work our way from the goal node to the start node, giving us the final shortest path. In this case, the shortest path between the skeleton and the player is **6, 7, 5, 2**.

The pseudo-algorithm

To wrap up the breakdown of the algorithm, let's look at a pseudo-implementation:

1. Compute the H values beforehand, if possible.
2. Add the start node to the open list.
3. Find the node with the lowest F value in the open list.
4. Remove that node from the open list and add it to the closed list.

5. For all adjacent nodes, perform the following steps:

- If the node is the goal node, set its parent to the current node and store the final path.

- If the node is in the closed list, ignore it and go to step 3.

- If the node is not in the closed list and the open list, set its parent to the current node and calculate its G and F value.

- If the node is not in the closed list but is in the open list, check whether the path between it and the current node is quicker than its current path.

This is a simplified look at the A* algorithm. Hopefully, this breakdown has given context to some of these steps. Let's get it coded!

Coding the A* pathfinding algorithm

With an understanding of the fundamentals of A*, let's start implementing it in our game. This will allow the enemies to follow our player around the level regardless of its topology.

With a complex algorithm such as this, having a visual representation of what's happening is really helpful. Wherever it's appropriate, we will take a look at a visual representation of what's happening using the following example:

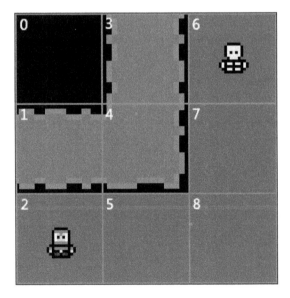

The Tile datatype

Let's start by taking a quick look at the `Tile` struct that was defined in `Level.h`. As we've seen, a node contains quite a few values. In the implementation, it's the level tiles that will act as nodes. As such, all the information that's required by a node is defined in its type:

```
// The level tile/node type.
struct Tile {
    TILE type;         // The type of tile this is.
    int columnIndex;   // The column index of the tile.
    int rowIndex;      // The row index of the tile.
    sf::Sprite sprite; // The tile sprite.
    int H;             // Heuristic / movement cost to goal.
    int G;             // Movement cost. (Total of entire path).
    int F;             // Estimated cost for full path. (G + H).
    Tile* parentNode;  // Node to reach this node.
};
```

For the rest of the chapter, a node is synonymous with a tile. So don't worry if they're used interchangeably. However, remember that this will not be the case in every A* implementation, as what you use as nodes will depend on the game.

Creating supporting functions

Before we implement the algorithm itself, we need to create some supporting functions and variables that the algorithm will require. Note that these are specific to the implementation and are not a part of the A* algorithm.

The Level class

The first class that we need to do some groundwork in is the `Level` class. We're going to need a function that resets all the variables in the nodes/tiles, as we need these values to be reset back to their defaults every time we run the algorithm.

Add the following function declaration to `Level.h`:

```
public:
/**
* Resets the A* data of all level tiles.
*/
void ResetNodes();
```

Also, add the following definition in `Level.cpp`:

```cpp
// Resets the A* data of all tiles.
void Level::ResetNodes()
{
    for (int i = 0; i < GRID_WIDTH; ++i)
    {
        for (int j = 0; j < GRID_HEIGHT; ++j)
        {
            m_grid[i][j].parentNode = nullptr;
            m_grid[i][j].H = 0;
            m_grid[i][j].G = 0;
            m_grid[i][j].F = 0;
        }
    }
}
```

You can see that all that we're doing here is iterating over each tile in the level grid and resetting all the variables that we'll use in the A* calculations.

The Enemy class

Next, we need to create a function that will run the algorithm in the `Enemy` class. Add the following function declaration in `Enemy.h`:

```cpp
public:
/**
 * Recalculates the target position of the enemy.
 */
void UpdatePathfinding(Level& level, sf::Vector2fplayerPosition);
```

You can see that this function takes a reference to the level, the main player position, and is public. We need the function to be public so that we can call it from the main game class. This is for efficiency and it will become clearer why later. We will pass a reference to the level object, as the enemy will need to access the level information, and the player location is needed to calculate the target position.

We also need to add the following variables in `Enemy.h`:

```cpp
private:
/**
 * The target positions of the enemy.
```

```
*/
std::vector<sf::Vector2f> m_targetPositions;

/**
 * The current target of the enemy.
 */
sf::Vector2f m_currentTarget;
```

With this work done, we can add the empty function definition for
Enemy::UpdatePathFinding in Enemy.cpp:

```
// Updates the target position of the enemy.
void Enemy::UpdatePathfinding(Level& level, sf::Vector2f
  playerPosition)
{
    // . . .
```

All code from this point onwards will be appended to this function.
There's quite a bit to it!

Variable declarations

The first step in the function is going to be the declarations of all the variables
that we'll use:

```
// Create all variables.
std::vector<Tile*> openList;
std::vector<Tile*> closedList;
std::vector<Tile*> pathList;
std::vector<Tile*>::iterator position;
Tile* currentNode;
```

The openList and closedList variables are used to manage the nodes. Nodes
in the openList variable are waiting to be checked, and nodes in the closedList
variable have already been checked and should be ignored from now on. This will be
explained in detail when we come across them in the implementation. The pathList
variable will store all the nodes in the final path.

The position variable is an iterator that will be used to find and remove values from
our vectors. Finally, the currentNode variable is used to keep track of the node that
we're currently working with.

The next step is to reset all the nodes. Every time we run the function, we need the nodes to have their default values. To achieve this we'll make a call to the `Level::ResetNodes` function that we just created, as follows:

```
// Reset all nodes.
level.ResetNodes();
```

The final step in the setup will be to identify the start and end nodes, marking the start and end of the path that we're looking for. The start node is going to be the position of the enemy. The end node, which is our goal, is the position of the player:

```
// Store the start and goal nodes.
Tile* startNode = level.GetTile(m_position);
Tile* goalNode = level.GetTile(playerPosition);
```

The `Level::GetTile` function returns the tile at a given location, so we can use this to get the nodes. Once we've identified these, we're going to perform a quick check to ensure that they are not the same nodes. If they are, there is no valid path between them and we can simply clear the current path and exit the function, as follows:

```
// Check we have a valid path to find. If not we can just end the
    function as there's no path to find.
if (startNode == goalNode)
{
    // Clear the vector of target positions.
    m_targetPositions.clear();

    // Exit the function.
    return;
}
```

At this point, we have declared all the variables that we'll be using, reset all the nodes to their default values, and identified that we're working with a valid path. It's time to jump into the bulk of the algorithm!

Precalculating the H values

The next step in our A* algorithm implementation is to calculate the H value for every node in the level. Remember that the H value is the estimated cost of the path from the start node to the goal node.

We're going to use the Manhattan distance for this. So, for every tile in the level, we need to calculate this distance to the goal node, as follows:

```
// Pre-compute our H cost (estimated cost to goal) for each node.
for (int i = 0; i < level.GetSize().x; ++i)
{
    for (int j = 0; j < level.GetSize().y; ++j)
    {
        int rowOffset, heightOffset;
        Tile* node = level.GetTile(i, j);

        heightOffset = abs(node->rowIndex - goalNode->rowIndex);
        rowOffset = abs(node->columnIndex - goalNode->
          columnIndex);

        node->H = heightOffset + rowOffset;
    }
}
```

Defining the main loop

We're now going to define the main loop in which the algorithm actually takes place, but before we do so, we need to quickly add the start node to the list of open nodes, as follows:

```
// Add the start node to the open list.
openList.push_back(startNode);
```

The open list is a list of all the nodes that the algorithm has left to check. While this list has values in it, the algorithm should run. Therefore, we'll define this behavior to create the main loop, as follows:

```
// While we have values to check in the open list.
while (!openList.empty())
{
```

The next step in the algorithm is to decide which node we're going to operate on next. You may remember that the F value is used for this purpose. The open list contains all the nodes that are waiting to be checked. So we need to iterate over this vector and find the node with the lowest F (the estimated cost of the complete path) value:

```
// Find the node in the open list with the lowest F value and mark
  it as current.
```

```
int lowestF = INT_MAX;

for (Tile* tile : openList)
{
    if (tile->F < lowestF)
    {
        lowestF = tile->F;
        currentNode = tile;
    }
}
```

This code is pretty straightforward. We initially set `lowestF` to `INT_MAX`, a macro that contains the maximum value of an `int`, as we can be sure that no F value will come anywhere near that. When we identify a node with a smaller F value, we update the `lowestF` value and mark that node as the node that needs to be operated on next.

Once we have identified the node with the lowest F value, we remove it from `openList` and add it to the `closedList` vector to ensure that we don't operate on the same node again, as follows:

```
// Remove the current node from the open list and add it to the
   closed list.
position = std::find(openList.begin(), openList.end(),
   currentNode);
if (position != openList.end())
    openList.erase(position);

closedList.push_back(currentNode);
```

This is where the iterator variable comes into play. An iterator is simply an object with the ability to iterate through a range of elements. To remove an item from a vector, we make a call to `std::find()`, passing the start of the vector, the end, and the value that we are looking for. If the value is found, `std::find()` will return an iterator to that element. If the value is not found, it returns an iterator that refers to an imaginary element, which will follow the last element in the vector. Then, we call erase in `openList`, passing this iterator value to get to the right element.

Finding the adjacent nodes

Now that the next node is selected and assigned to the `currentNode` variable, it's time to identify all the adjacent nodes. This is another area that will differ depending on each specific implementation.

In our case, the level is defined as a 2D grid. Therefore, it's easy for us to get the surrounding nodes:

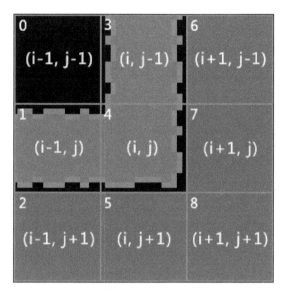

You can see from the preceding diagram how the column and row indices, i and j respectively, range from -1 to 1 surrounding the middle tile. We can use this to get the nodes around us that we want to check. We're only interested in valid floor nodes, so while we're fetching them, we can perform these checks.

Let's implement this in the function, as follows:

```
// Find all valid adjacent nodes.
std::vector<Tile*> adjacentTiles;

Tile* node;

// Top.
node = level.GetTile(currentNode->columnIndex, currentNode->
  rowIndex - 1);
if ((node != nullptr) && (level.IsFloor(*node)))
{
    adjacentTiles.push_back(level.GetTile(currentNode->
  columnIndex, currentNode->rowIndex - 1));
}
```

```
// Right.
node = level.GetTile(currentNode->columnIndex + 1, currentNode->
  rowIndex);
if ((node != nullptr) && (level.IsFloor(*node)))
{
    adjacentTiles.push_back(level.GetTile(currentNode->columnIndex
      + 1, currentNode->rowIndex));
}

// Bottom.
node = level.GetTile(currentNode->columnIndex, currentNode->
  rowIndex + 1);
if ((node != nullptr) && (level.IsFloor(*node)))
{
    adjacentTiles.push_back(level.GetTile(currentNode->
      columnIndex, currentNode->rowIndex + 1));
}

// Left.
node = level.GetTile(currentNode->columnIndex - 1, currentNode->
  rowIndex);
if ((node != nullptr) && (level.IsFloor(*node)))
{
    adjacentTiles.push_back(level.GetTile(currentNode->columnIndex
      - 1, currentNode->rowIndex));
}
```

In this code, we got the 4 nodes around us, ensuring that they're both valid and are floor tiles. Only then are they added to the list of adjacent nodes that need to be checked. With these identified, we now need to loop over each node. A `for` loop will allow us to do this:

```
// For all adjacent nodes.
for (Tile* node : adjacentTiles)
{
```

The algorithm is over when we reach the goal node. Therefore, every time we select an adjacent node, we can check whether we've done so. With the goal node stored in a variable, this is a simple check:

```
// If the node is our goal node.
if (node == goalNode)
{
```

Since we select nodes by the lowest F value, the first time we reach the goal node, we know that we will have travelled the shortest possible path. Before we move on to finding this path, we first need to make the parent of the goal node the current node:

```
// Parent the goal node to current.
node->parentNode = currentNode;
```

Next we have to construct a list of all the nodes that made up the path, from the start node to the goal node. There is no set way to do this, but we'll use a `while` statement. While the node has a parent, add the node to the list and then set the node to its parent. Let's add the code for this:

```
// Store the current path.
while (node->parentNode != nullptr)
{
    pathList.push_back(node);
    node = node->parentNode;
}
```

In this way, we build a complete path from the goal node to the start node. Note that the resulting path is backwards, but we'll sort this out later!

Now, the final step is to exit the main loop. We're currently nested within a `while` loop and a `for` loop. To exit this, we need to empty the open list and call `break`. The `break` component kicks us out of the `for` loop, and with the open list now empty, we exit the `while` loop too:

```
        // Empty the open list and break out of our for loop.
        openList.clear();
        break;
    }
    else
    {
```

Now that this is done, we have found the goal node, stored the path of nodes from the start to the goal, and exited the main loop. This was all the result of finding the goal node. We now need to turn our attention to the case where we didn't find the goal node.

Calculating the G and F costs

If a node is in the closed list then it's already been the subject of the algorithm. All the adjacent nodes have been checked and had their G and F values calculated. If this is the case, we can simply ignore the node:

```
// If the node is not in the closed list.
position = std::find(closedList.begin(), closedList.end(), node);
if (position == closedList.end())
{
```

After insuring that the node is not in the closed list, we next check the open list:

```
// If the node is not in the open list.
position = std::find(openList.begin(), openList.end(), node);
if (position == openList.end())
{
```

Unlike the previous check, if our node is in the open list, we do not ignore it. If the node is not in the open list, then it's the first time that the algorithm has encountered it. If this is the case, we need to perform the following actions:

1. Add the node to the open list.
2. Set `parent` to `currentNode` (it's the last node when checking the F values).
3. Calculate its G value.
4. Calculate its F value.

We'll start by adding it to the open list and setting its parent node; these are quick and easy tasks:

```
// Add the node to the open list.
openList.push_back(node);

// Set the parent of the node to the current node.
node->parentNode = currentNode;
```

Calculating the G and F cost

You may remember that the G cost is the total cost of movement from the start node to this node. In our grid, we can move in all the four directions, we don't move diagonally, so each movement costs 10. This value is specific to the implementation and not the algorithm. It's the cost of movement between two nodes, and 10 is simply a nice value to work with.

 We are not using diagonals only for the sake of an easier presentation. One of the exercises at the end of the chapter is to add diagonal movement and I highly suggest that you give it a go!

Since we know that the movement cost between the nodes is 10, we now need to add the G cost of currenNode to it to arrive at the final value. The G cost of currentNode is the cost of that path far, so adding the last movement cost to it gives the new node the total cost of the path from the start node to itself:

```
// Calculate G (total movement cost so far) cost.
node->G = currentNode->G + 10;
```

Finally, we need to calculate the F cost of the node, which is simply the sum of its G and H costs. We just calculated the G cost, and we precalculated the H costs at the start of the algorithm. All that is needed is a simple addition:

```
// Calculate the F (total movement cost + heuristic) cost.
node->F = node->G + node->H;
```

Checking for superior paths

The final step of the algorithm is the condition where we check whether the node is already in the open list, and it is. If this is the case, we've already generated its G and F values. We now however need to check whether they are the lowest possible values.

In the following image, node **7** is the parent to node **8**, and node **8** is the parent to node **5**:

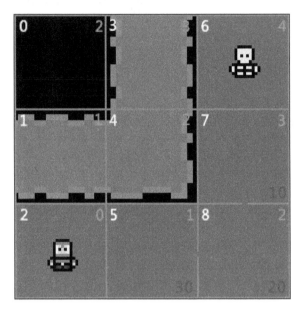

This has resulted in a movement cost of 30 from node **7 – 8 – 5**. However, this is not the shortest path. The movement cost from **7** to **5**, assuming that we allowed diagonal movement, is 14. If we drop **8** from the path, the total movement cost is 24, which is lower than its current value of 30. When this is the case, we make 7 the parent of **5** instead of **8**. Since we don't use diagonal movements, this exact example won't apply unless you add them yourself.

Hopefully however, it demonstrates that we're looking for superior paths as shown the following image:

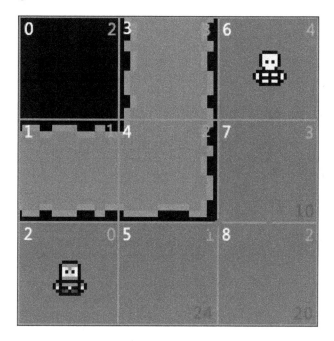

We can see here that the movement cost of node **5** is lower and it is parented to **7**. This has created a diagonal path that is shorter than the previous one.

Let's append some code to the function to include this behavior:

```
}
else
{
    // Check if this path is quicker that the other.
    int tempG = currentNode->G + 10;

    // Check if tempG is faster than the other. I.e, whether it's
      faster to go A->C->B that A->C.
    if (tempG < node->G)
    {
        // Re-parent node to this one.
        node->parentNode = currentNode;
    }
}}}}}
```

Creating the final path

The final part of the A* implementation is to turn the list of nodes into a valid path that the enemy can follow. In the work that we did to prepare for the A* implementation, we added the following variable to the Enemy class:

```
/**
 * The target positions of the enemy.
 */
std::vector<sf::Vector2f> m_targetPositions;
```

This vector is going to hold a list of target locations that we'll get from the nodes in the final path. However, before we do so, we need to ensure that we clear it. This is done so that every time the pathfinding algorithm is run, the player has a fresh set of coordinates to move to. Let's clear the vector. Again, this code is just appended to the Enemy::UpdatePathFinding function, as follows:

```
// Clear the vector of target positions.
m_targetPositions.clear();
```

Now, to convert the tiles into target locations we will iterate over the vector of the final nodes, get their actual positions, and add them to the m_targetPositions vector, as follows:

```
// Store the node locations as the enemies target locations.
for (Tile* tile : pathList)
{
    m_targetPositions.push_back(level.GetActualTileLocation(tile->
        columnIndex, tile->rowIndex));
}
```

There's one last thing that we need to do and which is easy to overlook. When we find the goal node and create the final path list, we store them from the goal node back to the start node. This means that the final path is backwards. The final step in the Enemy::UpdatePathFinding function is to reverse the m_targetPositions vector to correct this and add the final closing brackets:

```
// Store the node locations as the enemies target locations.
for (Tile* tile : pathList)
{
    m_targetPositions.push_back(level.GetActualTileLocation(tile->
        columnIndex, tile->rowIndex));
}
```

```
// Reverse the target position as we read them from goal to origin and
we need them the other way around.
std::reverse(m_targetPositions.begin(), m_targetPositions.end());
```

That's it! We're done. The A* algorithm is complete. The base enemy class has a function that will create a vector of target locations and take the enemy to the player in the quickest path possible. The next step is to enable the enemy to follow this path!

 If you want to explore pathfinding further, head over to `https://qiao.github.io/PathFinding.js/visual/`. It's a fantastic app that visualizes a range of popular pathfinding algorithms.

Implementing A* in the game

Now that we have the function that can calculate the shortest path, we need to incorporate this behavior into the game.

Enabling the enemy to follow a path

We now need to make the enemies follow the vector of target locations that the pathfinding algorithm generates. We need the enemy to constantly follow this path, so we'll override its base classes' `Update` function, as it's called during every game's tick. The code that will do this is fairly simple; if there is a location in the vector, move towards it at a fixed pace. When the position is reached, we simply remove it from the vector. When the vector is empty, we know that the enemy has reached its goal.

We'll start by adding the function declaration to `Enemy.h`:

```
public:
/**
 * Overrides the default Update function in Enemy
 */
void Update(float timeDelta) override;
```

Now we can add the code to follow the path. Like we just said, if there is a value in the vector of the target positions, move towards it at a fixed pace. We do this by creating and normalizing a movement vector.

We won't cover the mathematics behind this movement. So, if you want to read more about it, check out http://www.fundza.com/vectors/normalize/ for an overview.

The following code is used for the creation and normalization of a movement vector:

```
// Updates the enemy.
void Enemy::Update(float timeDelta)
{
    // Move towards current target location.
    if (!m_targetPositions.empty())
    {
        sf::Vector2f targetLocation = m_targetPositions.front();
        m_velocity = sf::Vector2f(targetLocation.x - m_position.x,
            targetLocation.y - m_position.y);

        if (abs(m_velocity.x) < 10.f && abs(m_velocity.y) < 10.f)
        {
            m_targetPositions.erase(m_targetPositions.begin());
        }
        else
        {
            float length = sqrt(m_velocity.x * m_velocity.x +
                m_velocity.y * m_velocity.y);
            m_velocity.x /= length;
            m_velocity.y /= length;

            m_position.x += m_velocity.x * (m_speed * timeDelta);
            m_position.y += m_velocity.y * (m_speed * timeDelta);

            m_sprite.setPosition(m_position);
        }
    }

    // Call character update.
    Entity::Update(timeDelta);
}
```

You can also see that at the end of the function we call `Entity::Update`. The animation code lies in this function. We need to ensure that it still gets called!

Calling the pathfinding behavior

The final step in incorporating pathfinding into the game is to call the `Enemy::UpdatePathFinding` function when we want to generate a new path. The enemies are updated with each game update, but we don't want to update the path that frequently.

Although A* is an efficient algorithm, we still want to call it as seldom as possible. The path will only change when the player moves to a new tile, so there's no point in updating the pathfinding until this happens. In order to achieve this, we need to be able to tell which tile the player was on during the last update, and which tile the player is on this update. Let's add the following variable to `Game.h` and ensure that we give it a default value in the class initializer:

```
/**
 * The last tile that the player was on.
 */
Tile* m_playerPreviousTile;
```

In the `Game::Update` function, we can now check whether the player has moved to a tile, and if that's the case, call the `Enemy::UpdatePathFinding` function of all the enemies in the level, as follows:

```
// Check if the player has moved grid square.
Tile* playerCurrentTile = m_level.GetTile(playerPosition);

if (m_playerPreviousTile != playerCurrentTile)
{
    // Store the new tile.
    m_playerPreviousTile = playerCurrentTile;

    // Update path finding for all enemies if within range of the
      player.
    for (const auto& enemy : m_enemies)
    {
        if (DistanceBetweenPoints(enemy->GetPosition(),
          playerPosition) < 300.f)
            enemy->UpdatePathfinding(m_level, playerPosition);
    }
}
```

That's it! We can now test the game. We should see the enemies following us around the level instead of standing like stationary objects as shown in the following screenshot:

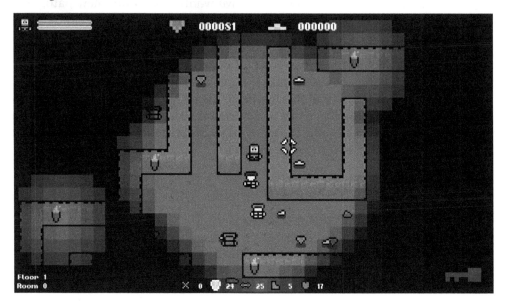

Viewing our path

We have the code working, which is great, but let's add some debug code so that we can see the path that the enemy is generating. I'm not going to cover this code in detail, as it's just for the purpose of demonstration. It basically just draws a sprite at each point in the target location's vector.

In `Enemy.h`, we'll declare the following variables and function:

```
public:
/**
 * Override the default draw function.
 */
void Draw(sf::RenderWindow& window, float timeDelta) override;

private:
/**
 * Debug sprite for path
 */
sf::Sprite m_pathSprite;

/**
 * Debug font for the path
 */
```

```
sf::Font m_font;

/**
 * Debug text for the path
 */
sf::Text m_text;
```

In `Enemy::Enemy`, we'll set up the debug sprites and font, as follows:

```
// Set the sprite.
int textureID = TextureManager::AddTexture("../resources/spr_path.
png");
m_pathSprite.setTexture(TextureManager::GetTexture(textureID));

// Set the sprite origin.
sf::Vector2u spriteSize = m_pathSprite.getTexture()->getSize();
m_pathSprite.setOrigin(sf::Vector2f(static_cast<float>(spriteSize.
  x / 2), static_cast<float>(spriteSize.y / 2)));

// Set the font.
m_font.loadFromFile("../resources/fonts/04B_03__.TTF");

// Set the text.
m_text.setFont(m_font);
m_text.setCharacterSize(12);
```

Also, we'll add a body for the new draw function named `Enemy::Draw`:

```
// Override the default draw function.
void Enemy::Draw(sf::RenderWindow& window, float timeDelta)
{
    Object::Draw(window, timeDelta);

    // DEBUG Draw the current path
    for (int i = 0; i < m_targetPositions.size(); i++)
    {
        // draw the path sprite
        m_pathSprite.setPosition(m_targetPositions[i]);
        window.draw(m_pathSprite);

        // set the path index
        std::ostringstream ss;
        ss << i;
        std::string str(ss.str());
        m_text.setString(str);
        m_text.setPosition(m_targetPositions[i]);
        window.draw(m_text);
    }
}
```

This code will show us the paths that the enemies' A* algorithm find, helping us visualize what the A* algorithm is doing. Let's run the game and take a look. Remember that you need to delete this debug code when you're done as it's going to have an impact on the performance. The following screenshot shows our enemies' paths:

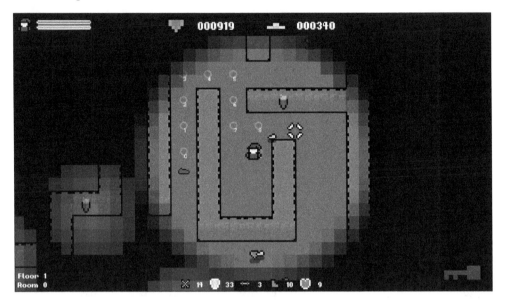

Procedurally generated level goals

The final system that we're going to build in this chapter is one that will generate randomized level goals. In each level, we have to find the key, find the exit, and kill all enemies that get in our way. Let's add more gameplay and challenge by adding random goals that the player can also complete. Every time a level is entered, we'll potentially give the player an optional task that, if completed, will yield a random reward.

The variable and function declarations

The first step in creating this system is to declare the variables and functions that we're going to need. We'll encapsulate the behavior to generate a goal in its own function. For starters, we need to declare the following `private` function in `Game.h`:

```
private:
/**
 * Generates a level goal.
 */
void GenerateLevelGoal();
```

Given the type of goals that we want to generate (killing enemies, collecting gold, and collecting gems), we need variables to hold these values. Let's also declare the following `private` variables in `Game.h`:

```
private:
/**
 * The value of gold remaining for the current goal.
 */
int m_goldGoal;

/**
 * The value of gems remaining for the current goal.
 */
int m_gemGoal;

/**
 * The number of kills remaining for the current goal.
 */
int m_killGoal;
```

Finally, we're going to want to be able to tell whether we have an active goal or not and draw the goal to the screen. We'll declare a Boolean value to track whether we have a goal, and a string object to store the description of the current goal:

```
/**
 * A string describing the current level goal.
 */
sf::String m_goalString;

/**
 * A boolean denoting if a goal is currently active.
 */
bool m_activeGoal;
```

Generating a random goal

Now we can generate the random goal. We have three types available, namely gold, gems, and enemies. So for a start, we need to choose which of these goals we're going to create.

Let's give `Game::GenerateLevelGoal` a body in `Game.cpp` by adding the following code:

```
// Generates a random level goal.
void Game::GenerateLevelGoal()
{
    std::ostringstream ss;

    // Reset our goal variables.
    m_killGoal = 0;
    m_goldGoal = 0;
    m_gemGoal = 0;

    // Choose which type of goal is to be generated.
    int goalType = rand() % 3;

    switch (goalType)
    {
        case 0:     // Kill X Enemies
        break;

        case 1:     // Collect X Gold
        break;

        case 2:     // Collect X Gems
        break;
    }
}
```

We started by defining a stream object that we'll use later, and resetting the goal variables to 0. This is done to ensure that the goals start fresh every time this function is called. Then, we generate a number between 0 and 2 and use it in a `switch` statement.

For each case we need to generate a random number as the goal value and set it to the appropriate variable. We also need to construct a string that describes the goal and store it in the `m_goalString` variable, as follows:

```
switch (goalType)
{
case 0:         // Kill X Enemies
    m_killGoal = rand() % 6 + 5;
```

```
        // Create the string describing the goal.
        ss << "Current Goal: Kill " << m_killGoal << " enemies" << "!"
          << std::endl;
        break;

    case 1:         // Collect X Gold
        m_goldGoal = rand() % 51 + 50;

        // Create the string describing the goal.
        ss << "Current Goal: Collect " << m_goldGoal << " gold" << "!"
          << std::endl;
        break;

    case 2:         // Collect X Gems
        m_gemGoal = rand() % 6 + 5;

        // Create the string describing the goal.
        ss << "Current Goal: Collect " << m_gemGoal << " gems" << "!"
          << std::endl;
        break;
    }

    // Store our string.
    m_goalString = ss.str();
```

With this complete, our goals are essentially created. We now need to activate the goal by setting the m_activeGoal variable to true:

```
        // Set the goal as active.
        m_activeGoal = true;
    }
```

The complete function looks like this:

```
    // Generates a random level goal.
    void Game::GenerateLevelGoal()
    {
        std::ostringstream ss;

        // Choose which type of goal is to be generated.
        int goalType = rand() % 3;
```

```
switch (goalType)
{
case 0:          // Kill X Enemies
    m_killGoal = rand() % 6 + 5;

    // Create the string describing the goal.
    ss << "Current Goal: Kill " << m_killGoal << " enemies" <<
        "!" << std::endl;
    break;

case 1:          // Collect X Gold
    m_goldGoal = rand() % 51 + 50;

    // Create the string describing the goal.
    ss << "Current Goal: Collect " << m_goldGoal << " gold" <<
        "!" << std::endl;
    break;

case 2:          // Collect X Gems
    m_gemGoal = rand() % 6 + 5;

    // Create the string describing the goal.
    ss << "Current Goal: Collect " << m_gemGoal << " gems" <<
        "!" << std::endl;
    break;
}

// Store our string.
m_goalString = ss.str();

    // Set the goal as active.
    m_activeGoal = true;
}
```

We'll hook up this function properly in the next chapter when we turn our attention to the level, but for now, we can test it by making a call to it in Game::Game. Add the following debug code so that we can test the function:

```
// DEBUG: Generate a level goal.
GenerateLevelGoal();
```

Checking whether a goal is complete

We can now generate a random level goal at the call of a function. We now need to hook gameplay into these goals so that we can tell when one of them has been accomplished. Whenever we process an action that is related to a goal, we need to check whether we have an active goal and respond accordingly.

Starting with the kill count, when we determine that an enemy has been killed, we check whether we have an active goal, and if this is the case, we decrement the m_killGoal variable, as follows:

```
// If the enemy is dead remove it.
if (enemy.IsDead())
{
    enemyIterator = m_enemies.erase(enemyIterator);

    // If we have an active goal decrement killGoal.
    if (m_activeGoal)
    {
        --m_killGoal;
    }
}
```

The same approach is taken for other level goals. In the object pickup code, when we have picked up either gold or a gem, we'll check whether we have an active level goal, and if this is the case, we decrement the appropriate values, as follows:

```
switch (m_items[i]->GetType())
{
case GAME_OBJECT::GOLD:
{
    // cast the item to a gold type
    Gold& gold = dynamic_cast<Gold&>(*m_items[i]);

    . . .

    // Check if we have an active level goal.
    if (m_activeGoal)
    {
        m_goldGoal -= gold.GetGoldValue();
    }
}
break;
```

```
case GAME_OBJECT::GEM:
{
    // cast the item to a gem type
    Gem& gem = dynamic_cast<Gem&>(*m_items[i]);

    . . .

    // Check if we have an active level goal.
    if (m_activeGoal)
    {
        --m_gemGoal;
    }
}
break;

. . .
```

With this complete, the actions in the game are now hooked up to the goal counters. Next, we need to actually check whether we've achieved the goal. We'll put this code right at the end of Game::Update so that we can ensure that all the other actions have been executed.

Checking whether we've achieved our goal is simple. First, we check whether we have an active goal. Then, we check whether all the counter variables are less than or equal to 0. If that's the case then we know that we've decremented the appropriate counter to 0. With this approach the other values will dip to negative values, but we won't be collecting enough loot for that to be a problem. Let's add this code at the end of Game::Update:

```
// Check if we have completed an active goal.
if (m_activeGoal)
{
    if ((m_gemGoal <= 0) &&
        (m_goldGoal <= 0) &&
        (m_killGoal <= 0))
    {
        m_scoreTotal += std::rand() % 1001 + 1000;
        m_activeGoal = false;
    }
}
```

With this complete, the majority of the goal system is set up. You can see that if we determine that a goal is active, and all counters are 0 or lower, we reward the player. We also set the m_activeGoal variable to false to show that the goal has now been achieved.

Drawing the goal on the screen

The final step now is to draw our goal on screen! We have a `bool` variable that denotes when we have an active goal, and when we generate that goal, we store its descriptor in a string variable. Drawing it is as simple as making a call to `Game::DrawText` and passing the description, but we'll only do this when the `m_activeGoal` variable is `true`.

It's time to finish this system by adding the following to `Game::Draw`:

```
// Draw the level goal if active.
if (m_activeGoal)
{
    DrawString(m_goalString, sf::Vector2f(m_window.getSize().x /
        2, m_window.getSize().y - 75), 30);
}
```

Now, if you run the game, you will see that a unique goal is shown every time:

We could call it a day here, but we can do better! Since the string that defines the level goal is stored only once, when we create it, it doesn't update itself as we work towards achieving it. Let's fix this! If we jump back to `Game::Update` and find where we check whether we achieved our goal, we can make some modifications here to achieve this.

Currently, we check whether we've achieved the active goal, but we only do something if we have achieved it. This is our opportunity to update the string. All we have to do it determine which type of goal is set, which we can do by checking the values of our goal variables, and rebuild the string in the same way we do in Game::GenerateLevelGoal:

```cpp
// Check if we have completed an active goal.
if (m_activeGoal)
{
    if ((m_gemGoal <= 0) &&
        (m_goldGoal <= 0) &&
        (m_killGoal <= 0))
    {
        m_scoreTotal += std::rand() % 1001 + 1000;
        m_activeGoal = false;
    }
    else
    {
        std::ostringstream ss;

        if (m_goldGoal > 0)
            ss << "Current Goal: Collect " << m_goldGoal << "
              gold" << "!" << std::endl;
        else if (m_gemGoal > 0)
            ss << "Current Goal: Collect " << m_gemGoal << " gem"
              << "!" << std::endl;
        else if (m_killGoal > 0)
            ss << "Current Goal: Kill " << m_killGoal << "
              enemies" << "!" << std::endl;

        m_goalString = ss.str();
    }
}
```

Now, when we have an active goal, the string on the screen is updated as we work towards it!

Exercises

To help you test your knowledge of this chapter's content, here are a few exercises that you should work on. They are not imperative to the rest of the book, but working on them will help you assess your strengths and weaknesses in the material covered:

1. When calculating pathfinding, we currently do not allow diagonal movement. Update the algorithm so that this is now allowed. To get you started, when calculating the G cost, you'll need to determine whether we moved diagonally or straight.

2. Currently, the enemies will chase us throughout the entire level. Amend the function so that the enemy will only chase the player if they are within a certain distance.

3. Currently our enemies move at a fixed speed and don't take into account the speed variable that we generated in an earlier chapter. Incorporate the speed variable in the game so that the enemies move at their correct speeds.

Summary

In this chapter, we extended our efforts to procedural behavior and mechanics as opposed to just resources. Specifically, we implemented A* pathfinding algorithm to give the enemies some intelligence and natural movement around our levels and created random level goals. Hopefully, this has been a good demonstration of the fact that procedural generation isn't limited to just resources; it can be put to use for every aspect of a game.

In the next chapter, we're going to implement what is perhaps the most iconic feature of roguelike games: procedurally generated levels. Up until now we've been working with the same fixed level, so it's about time we started generating them procedurally! We'll also create some variance between the levels and implement the goal generator that we just created!

9
Procedural Dungeon Generation

Perhaps the most iconic and defining feature of roguelike games is their procedurally generated levels. This is one of the main features that contributes to the replayability that the genre is renowned for having. It keeps the game fresh and challenging and the players on their toes.

Throughout the course of this book, we've progressed from the simple generation of single numbers to the implementation of complex procedural behavior, such as path finding. It's time for our pièce de résistance: procedurally generating our levels. In addition to this, we'll also work on making levels more distinct using the functions that we created in *Chapter 6, Procedurally Generating Art*.

In this chapter, we'll cover the following topics:

- The benefits of procedurally designing levels
- Maze generation
- Room generation
- Tile mapping

The benefits of procedural level design

The procedural generation of game levels and environments brings with it a myriad of benefits, not only for players but also for developers. It's always good to understand the positives and negatives of a technology before we use it. So, let's take a look at some of the biggest benefits that it brings to games before we implement it.

Replayability

The most obvious benefit of procedurally generated levels is their variety and the replayability that they bring to a game. With each run, the environment changes. This means that players cannot learn the locations of items, enemies, and this keeps the challenge alive and fresh, giving players reasons to play the game again and again.

A reduction in development time

Another benefit that is common in all implementations of procedural generation is the time that it saves in development. In our roguelike game, we're going to have an endless number of unique levels. If we were creating our levels manually this would simply not be possible. We would be limited to perhaps a hundred levels at the most.

Utilizing procedural generation like this takes this workload off the developers, saving both time and money, and increases the scope of what's possible.

Larger game worlds

Remember that procedural generation in itself is in no way random. We induce randomness by using random values and terms in our algorithms and calculations. Given that, we can use procedural generation within a level design to share levels without actually having to store them.

Lots of games that generate worlds randomly will allow you to input a world seed. With this value, two people on two different machines can generate the same level. With this approach, you can generate a theoretically never-ending level, ensuring that all players generate the same one. Also, you'll only have to store the world seed instead of potentially hundreds of megabytes of world data.

Considerations

As with everything, there are two sides of the same coin. Therefore, despite the benefits that procedural level generation brings, there are some considerations and compromises that need to be made.

A lack of control

A lack of control is a common pitfall of procedural generation in general, but it's perhaps never more prevalent than when generating levels. Game levels are the arena in which our stories are told and our game mechanics are experimented with. Given that, they are usually handcrafted by dedicated level designers. Leaving this job to an algorithm results in a significant loss of control.

Games with simple mechanics and stories will generally fair okay, but if you have complex mechanics or a story that you want to tell in a particular way, procedural level generation may require you to relinquish more control than you can afford. An algorithm can never replicate the little touches that a seasoned professional brings.

Required computing power

Another consideration that needs to be taken into account is the computing power that is required. In our case, it's not that bad. We only have a 2D array of a small size that needs to be generated. However, if you're generating 3D terrain on a large scale, this cost becomes more significant and needs to be factored.

Imagine a situation where we are required to work with a level grid of 1000 by 1000. Every time we generate a level there will be a significant number of calculations that will need to be performed, and we need to ensure that all our players' hardware can cope! With steady increases in the computing power this is becoming less of an issue. In fact, this is the reason why games are becoming very complex and dynamic. We have the hardware that is required to achieve it, but we still need to be conscious of the limits.

Suitability

The final consideration is simply whether your game will benefit from procedural generation. Just because it might be technically possible to implement it in a title, it doesn't mean that it belongs there. If you don't require lots of levels and you have complex mechanics and systems, then it's probably not worth implementing it. You're better off spending this time in handcrafting a selection of levels that you know will work really well.

This is a good point to bear in mind in general. Don't get carried away with the technicalities of the game and how amazing the code is. The bottom line is that your game needs to be fun and engaging. Always prioritize gameplay.

An overview of dungeon generation overview

Dungeon generation is a vast topic with a wide range of possible implementations, with each implementation having its own characteristics. However, underneath the nuances of different algorithms, dungeon generation generally involves the generation of rooms and a maze and the integration of the two, as shown in the following diagram:

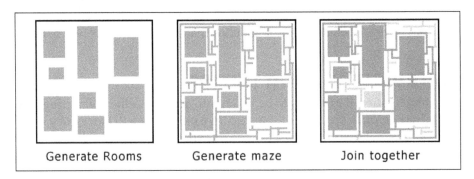

Generate Rooms   Generate maze   Join together

Procedurally generating dungeons is not that different from the work that we did on path finding. It's all about viewing a level as nodes and manipulating them. Before we implement it we'll break it down into the three main stages that were identified previously, namely the generation of rooms, the generation of a maze, and the integration of all together.

Generating rooms

Dungeons are a series of interconnected rooms, and their generation is the first step in many systems. There is no complex algorithm behind this; we simply choose a room size and place a number of them in the level. The characteristics of this level will be determined by factors such as the number of rooms, their size, and how they are placed, as shown in the following diagram:

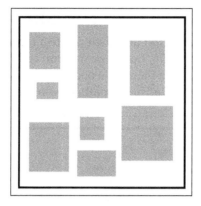

Generating a maze

Another important step in dungeon generation is to generate a maze throughout the playable area, turning the level into a series of connected hallways. These can then either join the existing rooms, or have rooms carved into them to create open areas. There are a number of algorithms that are used to generated mazes like this, and we'll use the popular **recursive backtracker** algorithm. Don't worry, we'll have a look at this algorithm in detail shortly! The following screenshot shows an example of such a maze:

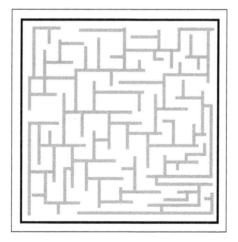

Connecting rooms and mazes

If you choose to generate rooms first and then create a maze to connect them, the final step is to integrate them. Currently, the maze will run right past all the rooms, but thankfully, it's an easy task to join them. We need to just look around each room and add a connecting block to a valid adjacent path, as shown in the following diagram:

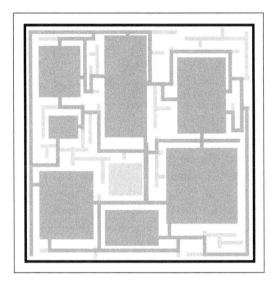

In our implementation, we're actually going to do this the other way around. We'll generate a maze and then carve open areas into it. This method creates more open and maze-like areas, whereas the first method creates interconnected closed rooms.

The recursive backtracker

The recursive backtracker, as the name suggests, involves recursively calling a function that carves passages between two tiles in the game grid. By choosing random directions to carve this path, the algorithm carves its way through the level as far as possible before resolving its recursions, working back to the start node.

The following is pseudocode for one such algorithm:

1. Choose random direction and make a connection to the adjacent node if it has not yet been visited. This node becomes the current node (a recursive call).

2. If all the adjacent cells in each direction have already been visited, go back to the last cell (return from the previous recursive call).

3. If you're back at the start node, the algorithm is complete.

As we can see, there's really not much to it! The only pitfall is that you need to have the entire maze in memory. For large mazes this method can be inefficient or maybe not possible at all! However, for our implementation, it will work perfectly.

Procedurally generating a dungeon

It's time to put this theory into practice and implement procedural dungeon generation in our game for real. We'll move the `Level` class from loading its data from a text file to generating it at runtime, and we'll also cover the application of the correct sprites to the tiles in the random level.

As we identified, one way of approaching this is to generate a maze over the entire play area and then generate rooms to carve out some larger open areas. This method not only generates tighter, more intertwined levels, but also saves us the step of having to connect mazes to rooms, leaving us with just two steps to generate great levels:

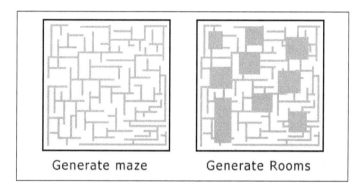

Generate maze   Generate Rooms

Changing how we view the maze

Before we write any code, we're going to make a change to the project so that we can easily see the entire level. Currently, the view is zoomed, and we have the light blocking the level. We want to be able to see the entire maze as we work on the algorithm. So let's make some changes.

The first thing that we'll do is disable the main game view and instead draw everything using the **UI** view. The **Game** view draws draws everything twice as large as the original size, while the UI view draws things with a scale of 1:1. By disabling the change to the **Game** view, we'll see more of the level.

Update the following code:

```
case GAME_STATE::PLAYING:
{
  // Set the main game view.
  //m_window.setView(m_views[static_cast<int>(VIEW::MAIN)]);
```

All that we've done here is comment out the line that sets the main game's view. Let's now do the same for the code responsible for drawing the light in the level:

```
// Draw level light.
//for (const sf::Sprite& sprite : m_lightGrid)
//{
//   m_window.draw(sprite);
//}
```

These two changes drastically change how the level now appears and will help us see the maze as we work:

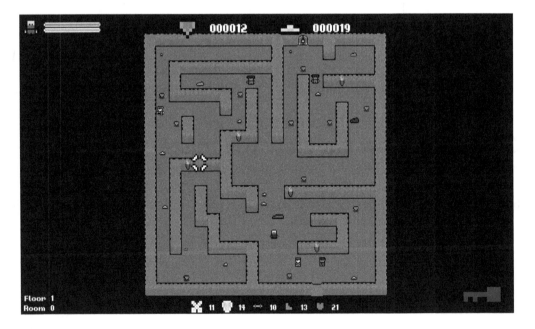

Updating the Game and Level classes

Before we start implementing the maze generator, we need to define some functions that we'll be using. For starters, our level is currently loaded from the `Level::LoadLevelFromFile` function. We need to create an appropriate function for the new code. Let's remove the `Level::LoadLevelFromFile` function and add the following code in its place in `Level.h`:

```
public:
/**
 * Generates a random level.
 */
void GenerateLevel();
```

We're going to need a similar function in the `Game` class, which will encapsulate all the code to generate a random level, so ensure that you add the same function declaration to `Game.h` also. We have a couple of functions that are related to generating a level, and all of these can be encapsulated in this function. We need to add the following:

- A call to `Level::GenerateLevel`: This enables the placement of key in the level
- A call to `Game::PopulateLevel`: This helps in the generation of a random level goal

Notice one of these items is to add a key to the level. The item already exists in our solution, as does all supporting code, and as we'll soon be able to generate levels at random we can now spawn one in the level.

Let's add this function to `Game.cpp`:

```
// Generates a new level.
void Game::GenerateLevel()
{
  // Generate a new level.
  m_level.GenerateLevel();

  // Add a key to the level.
  SpawnItem(ITEM::KEY);

  // Populate the level with items.
  PopulateLevel();

  // 1 in 3 change of creating a level goal.
  if (((std::rand() % 3) == 0) && (!m_activeGoal))
  {
    GenerateLevelGoal();
  }
}
```

We created the `Goal::GenerateLevelGoal` function in *Chapter 8, Procedural Behavior and Mechanics*. So, this is where we actually implement it. Each time a new level is generated, we create a 1 in 3 chance that a goal will be generated if there isn't one that's currently active.

Since we now have the function that will generate our levels at random, and have added the key, let's quickly add the code to generate a new level when the player reaches the door. We already have the if statement ready, we just need to add the behavior:

```
    .  .  .

if (playerTile.type == TILE::WALL_DOOR_UNLOCKED)
{
    // Clear all current items.
    m_items.clear();

    // Clear all current enemies.
    m_enemies.clear();

    // Generate a new room.
    GenerateLevel();

    // Set the key as not collected.
    m_keyUiSprite->setColor(sf::Color(255, 255, 255, 60));
}


    .  .  .
```

Now that this is completed, all we have left to do is call our `Game::GenerateLevel` function instead of our depreciated `Level::LoadLevelFromFile`, and remove the code to set the players location and the call to `Game::PopulateLevel`. Our new `Game::GenerateLevel` function will take care of all of that. Let's update the following code in `Game::Initialize`:

```
// Load the level.
//m_level.LoadLevelFromFile("../resources/data/level_data.txt");

// Set the position of the player.
//m_player.SetPosition(sf::Vector2f(1155.f, 940.f));

// Populate level.
//PopulateLevel();
```

```
// Generate a level.
GenerateLevel();
```

Now that the code is updated, we can now turn our attention towards the dungeon generation algorithm.

Generating a maze

The first stage of creating a random dungeon is to generate a maze throughout the entire play area. We've covered the recursive backtracker method that we're going to use. However, we need to do some preparation beforehand.

Preparing before the generation of a maze

The recursive backtracking algorithm works by forging passages between two nodes. Given this, we need the maze to be in a position where all the nodes in the grid are surrounded by walls, that is, something that looks like this:

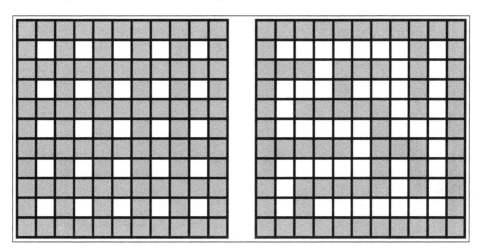

The shaded squares represent wall tiles, and the blank squares represent floor space. You will see in the left grid that each floor tile is surrounded on all sides by a wall. The right tile shows what the grid would look like once the algorithm is run, breaking through these walls to create paths. Our task is to make the grid look like the one on the left!

When you look at the grid to the left, you will see that all the shaded tiles have odd indices; only the tiles that have an even column and a row index are blank. This makes it easy to create this grid. We need to loop through all the tiles, and if both the indices are even, we leave it blank. Otherwise, we convert it into a wall tile.

Let's start defining the `Level::GenerateLevel` function by implementing this:

```
// Generates a random level.
void Level::GenerateLevel()
{
    // Create the initial grid pattern.
    for (int i = 0; i < GRID_WIDTH; ++i)
    {
        for (int j = 0; j < GRID_HEIGHT; ++j)
        {
            if ((i % 2 != 0) && (j % 2 != 0))
            {
                // Odd tiles, nothing.
                m_grid[i][j].type = TILE::EMPTY;
            }
            else
            {
                m_grid[i][j].type = TILE::WALL_TOP;
                m_grid[i][j].sprite.setTexture(TextureManager::GetText
ure(m_textureIDs[static_cast<int>(TILE::WALL_TOP)]));
            }
            // Set the position.
            m_grid[i][j].sprite.setPosition(m_origin.x + (TILE_SIZE *
i), m_origin.y + (TILE_SIZE * j));
        }
    }
}
```

Before we run our game we need to quickly disable any code that uses the level grid. This includes our call to `Game::PopulateLevel` and the placement of the key in `Game::GenerateLevel`. It also includes the call to `Game::SpawnRandomTiles` in `Game::Initialize`. These functions rely on the level grid been setup, and it isn't yet! Without disabling these the game will hang as it looks for floor tiles! We'll turn them back on when we're done.

If you run the game now, you will see that we have a grid that looks like the image to the left. The first step is complete!

The following screenshot shows the result when we run the game now:

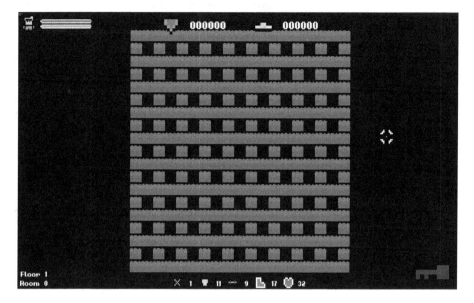

Carving passages

Now that the checkerboard pattern is created, it's time to implement the main body of the algorithm. Here's a reminder of how the recursive backtracker algorithm works:

1. Choose a random direction and make a connection to the adjacent node if it has not yet been visited. This node becomes the current node (a recursive call).

2. If all adjacent cells in each direction have already been visited, go back to the last cell (return from the previous recursive call).

3. If you're back at the start node, the algorithm is complete.

We know that this algorithm is recursive, so let's start by declaring the function that will contain the algorithm. Since this function will create paths between two nodes, we'll call it `CreatePath`:

```
private:
/**
 * Creates a path between two nodes in the recursive backtracker
algorithm.
 */
void CreatePath(int columnIndex, int rowIndex);
```

Starting with the first point in the algorithm breakdown, we need to identify the node that we're working with and choose a random direction. Getting the correct node is easy, and to choose a random direction, we'll use an array. We can define an array of `sf::vector2i` that defines all the possible directions. For example, `{-2, 0}` will indicate a movement to the tile to the left, as we'll decrement the column index by 2.

Remember, we have to move two tiles at a time due to the checkerboard pattern. The tile that is directly adjacent to us is a wall so we need to move one step further to reach the tile that we want to work on. We then need to shuffle the array of directions so that the algorithm doesn't tend towards any one in particular. If we didn't do this for example, it would always check north first, resulting in lots of north-running passages!

Let's start defining the `Level::CreatePath` function by adding the following to `Level.cpp`:

```
// Create a path between two tiles in the level grid.
void Level::CreatePath(int columnIndex, int rowIndex)
{
  // Store the current tile.
  Tile* currentTile = &m_grid[columnIndex][rowIndex];

  // Create a list of possible directions and sort randomly.
  sf::Vector2i directions[] = { { 0, -2 }, { 2, 0 }, { 0, 2 }, { -2, 0
} };
  std::random_shuffle(std::begin(directions), std::end(directions));
```

Next, we iterate over these directions and check whether we can find any valid tiles that have not yet been visited. A tile is valid if it exists in the grid, and you can tell whether it's been visited yet or not depending on whether it's empty.

Let's add this functionality by appending the following code to the open function's definition:

```
// For each direction.
for (int i = 0; i < 4; ++i)
{
  // Get the new tile position.
  int dx = currentTile->columnIndex + directions[i].x;
  int dy = currentTile->rowIndex + directions[i].y;

  // If the tile is valid.
  if (TileIsValid(dx, dy))
  {
```

```
    // Store the tile.
    Tile* tile = &m_grid[dx][dy];

    // If the tile has not yet been visited.
    if (tile->type == TILE::EMPTY)
    {
```

If the code reaches this point we know that we're looking at a new tile as it's both valid and currently empty. To create a path to it we need to knock down the wall between us and change both the wall and our new tile with floor tiles. We now call `Level::CreatPath` once more, passing the indices of the new tile as the parameters. It's here that the recursion happens and the algorithm progresses forward.

Let's finish the function's definition with the following bit of code to achieve this:

```
    // Mark the tile as floor.
    tile->type = TILE::FLOOR;
    tile->sprite.setTexture(TextureManager::GetTexture(m_
    textureIDs[static_cast<int>(TILE::FLOOR)]));

    // Knock that wall down.
    int ddx = currentTile->columnIndex + (directions[i].x / 2);
    int ddy = currentTile->rowIndex + (directions[i].y / 2);

    Tile* wall = &m_grid[ddx][ddy];
    wall->type = TILE::FLOOR;
    wall->sprite.setTexture(TextureManager::GetTexture(m_
    textureIDs[static_cast<int>(TILE::FLOOR)]));

    // Recursively call the function with the new tile.
    CreatePath(dx, dy);
}}}}
```

Let's clarify exactly what's happening here. Every time an empty tile is identified, a recursive call to `Level::CarvePath` is made, and that tile's indices are passed. As it does this, it works its way through the level, nesting deeper and deeper into recursion.

When all the directions have been checked and there is no valid tile, the current call from `Level::CreatePath` will return, allowing the previous call to check its remaining directions. As this process continues the algorithm works its way back through the path until it reaches the start node, at which point nodes have been visited.

Hopefully, the comments in the function make it clear which part is doing what. Now that this is complete we can now call it from the `Level::GenerateLevel` function right after we set up the grid:

```
// Generates a random level.
void Level::GenerateLevel()
{
  // Create the initial grid pattern.
  for (int i = 0; i < GRID_WIDTH; ++i)
  {

  // Make the first call to CarvePassage, starting the recursive
  backtracker algorithm.
    CreatePath(1, 1);
}
```

Let's compile the project once again and see what we have:

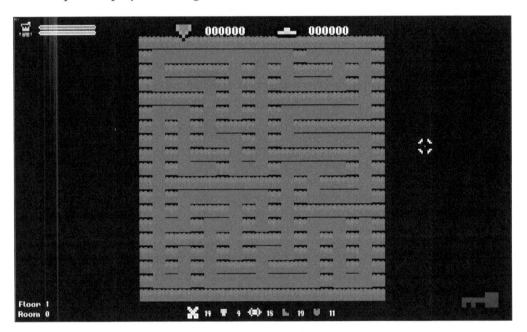

We have the maze! For some games, this will be enough, but we don't want all the single tile paths. We're want more open areas so that we can fight the enemies! You'll also see that the tile sprites are looking very weird. Don't worry about it now; we'll fix it as soon as we add the rooms!

Adding rooms

Previously, we learned that adding rooms was a simple task. We now get to see this firsthand. Our goal is to add some open areas, and the simplest way to do this is to pick some random locations and convert the surrounding tiles to floor tiles. To keep the `Level` class neat, we'll encompass this behavior in its own function. Add the following function declaration to `Level.h`:

```
private:

    /**
     * Adds a given number of randomly sized rooms to the level to create
    some open space.
     */
    void CreateRooms(int roomCount);
```

In our ongoing efforts to write versatile and scalable code, we added a parameter to denote how many rooms we want to create so that we can vary it at will.

Let's jump right into defining the function. To start, we're going to need a loop to iterate once for each room that we wish to add. Add the following method definition in `Level.cpp`:

```
// Adds a given number of randomly sized rooms to the level to create
some open space.
void Level::CreateRooms(int roomCount)
{
    for (int i = 0; i < roomCount; ++i)
    {
```

Now we can create our rooms. The first task is to decide how big we want them to be. After playing with the algorithm I found that having a greater number of smaller rooms works well. As always, we'll throw in some RNG here by having the rooms' size fall within a random range:

```
// Generate a room size.
int roomWidth = std::rand() % 2 + 1;
int roomHeight = std::rand() % 2 + 1;
```

This will generate rooms with a width and height of either 1 or 2. I know that this sounds small, but trust me. It works really well!

Next we need to choose a place in the level for this room to be placed. We'll pick a random point and build the room around it. For this we need to generate a random tile index and then create nested `for` loops to iterate over the 2D array, thus describing the room:

```
// Choose a random starting location.
int startI = std::rand() % (GRID_WIDTH - 2) + 1;
int startY = std::rand() % (GRID_HEIGHT - 2) + 1;

for (int j = -1; j < roomWidth; ++j)
{
  for (int z = -1; z < roomHeight; ++z)
  {
```

When generating the start position, you can see that we've been careful not to include the outer edge in either direction. These are the level's retaining walls and should be left alone.

The last part of the function now simply involves turning the room tiles into floor tiles. First, we check whether we haven't gone out of bounds by making a call to `Level::TileIsValid`. We then ensure that the new title does not lie on the outer edge of the grid; the outer rows/columns should all be walls to contain the level. If both of these criteria are met, we can make it a floor block by using the following code:

```
int newI = startI + j;
int newY = startY + z;

// Check if the tile is valid.
if (TileIsValid(newI, newY))
{
  // Check if the tile is not on an outer wall.
  if ((newI != 0) && (newI != (GRID_WIDTH - 1)) && (newY != 0) &&
(newY != (GRID_HEIGHT - 1)))
  {
    m_grid[newI][newY].type = TILE::FLOOR;
    m_grid[newI][newY].sprite.setTexture(TextureManager::GetTexture
(m_textureIDs[static_cast<int>(TILE::FLOOR)]));
  }
}}}}}
```

It's time to make a call to this function. Currently in `Level::GenerateLevel` we set our grid up and then make the first call to `Level::CreatePath` to start the recursive algorithm. When this first initial call is returned, we know that the maze has been fully generated. It's at this stage that we'll create the rooms.

Let's append a call to the new `Level::CreateRooms` function right after the first call to `Level::CreatePath`:

. . .

```
// Make the first call to CarvePassage, starting the recursive
backtracker algorithm.
CreatePath(1, 1);

// Add some rooms to the level to create some open space.
CreateRooms(10);
```

It's time for another build so that we can see our work. Hopefully now we have a random maze running through the level as well as a number of larger open areas where we can allow players to fight more freely:

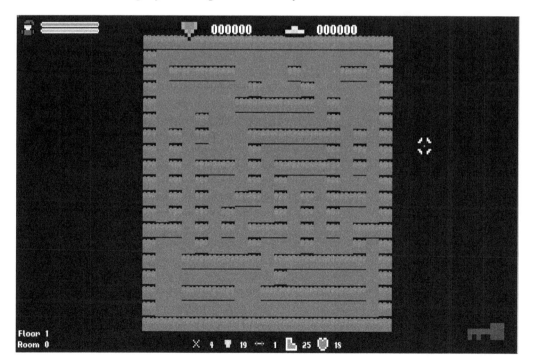

Choosing the tile textures

Until now we've been loading a prebuilt level from a text file. This level file already knew which textures needed to be used and where they should be used, but since we're now generating them procedurally, that's not the case. We need to decide which tiles should have which sprites.

The if/else approach

A common way of approaching this is simply to create a monstrous `if/else` statement. In principle, it's a simple task; define each tile through a series of `if` statements and set the right tile. However, in reality, you end up with a complex mess of code that is very difficult to read.

Imagine a situation where you have a tile set of fifty possible variants. The amount of code required to choose which tile goes where would be crazy. Thankfully, there's a much simpler solution to the problem, and it is one of my favorite examples of an elegant solution to a problem.

Bitwise tile maps

In our game, we concern ourselves with four directions, namely up, down, left, and right. Given that, when we need to calculate tile textures we only need to check in these four directions:

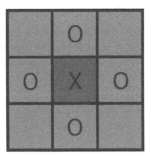

In the preceding diagram, you can see that the tiles marked with 0s are those that are used to determine the texture given to tile X. This is where the elegant solution comes into play. If we read the tiles into a binary number, starting from the top tile and counting from the least significant digit, we get the 4 digit binary number, 0000. If the tile is a wall we set the corresponding bit to 1. If the tile is floor we leave it as 0.

If we apply this to the four possible tile locations that surround the tile X, we can calculate values for each tile:

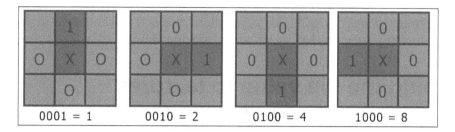

Hopefully, this diagram makes things clearer. Starting from the top tile and reading clockwise, we feed the values of the tiles into a bit integer from the least significant digit to the most. This gives each tile surrounding the main tile a distinct value, and we can visualize this through the following image:

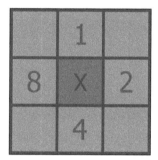

Calculating the tile values

When deciding upon the tile texture that we need, we evaluate which tiles surround the target tile, and where we have a wall we store its value that we identified in the previous image. A real example will help you visualize this process. Let's suppose that we need to find the correct texture for tile X:

In this scenario, the tile value will be calculated in the following way:

1 + 4 = 5

Using this method, each possible tile orientation for X is represented through a unique value ranging from 0 to 15. It's so elegant and simple!

Mapping the tile value to textures

The final piece of this puzzle is mapping these values to textures. In `Util.h`, you will see that the following enumerator defines the all types:

```
// Tiles.
enum class TILE {
  WALL_SINGLE,
  WALL_TOP_END,
  WALL_SIDE_RIGHT_END,
  WALL_BOTTOM_LEFT,
  WALL_BOTTOM_END,
  WALL_SIDE,
  WALL_TOP_LEFT,
  WALL_SIDE_LEFT_T,
  WALL_SIDE_LEFT_END,
  WALL_BOTTOM_RIGHT,
  WALL_TOP,
  WALL_BOTTOM_T,
  WALL_TOP_RIGHT,
  WALL_SIDE_RIGHT_T,
  WALL_TOP_T,
  WALL_INTERSECTION,
  WALL_DOOR_LOCKED,
  WALL_DOOR_UNLOCKED,
  WALL_ENTRANCE,
  FLOOR,
  FLOOR_ALT,
  EMPTY,
  COUNT
};
```

While the order of these tiles may seem somewhat random, they are actually in a very specific order. Enumerators start counting from 0. Therefore, we can see that the first value, WALL_SINGLE, has a value of 0. Going back to our chart, we can see that this is correct, as that's the texture that we'll need when there is nothing surrounding the tile.

Taking another random example, the WALL_TOP value has a value of 10. If we look at the grid, this will mean that the tiles only to the right and left of the target tile are walls. 2 + 8 = 10. That's correct! For all possible tiles, I worked out their bitmask values and ensured that their enumerator values matched up.

Calculating tile textures

Let's get this implemented in the project. First, we'll declare a function that we can encapsulate this behavior in our Level header:

```
/**
 * Calculates the correct texture for each tile in the level.
 */
void CalculateTextures();
```

For the function's body, we want to start by iterating over all the tiles, identifying which of them are walls. It's these tiles that need their sprites calculating correct texture:

```
// Calculates the correct texture for each tile in the level.
void Level::CalculateTextures()
{
  // For each tile in the grid.
  for (int i = 0; i < GRID_WIDTH; ++i)
  {
    for (int j = 0; j < GRID_HEIGHT; ++j)
    {
      // Check that the tile is a wall block.
      if (IsWall(i, j))
      {
        // Calculate bit mask.
```

```
        int value = 0;

        // Store the current type as default.
        TILE type = m_grid[i][j].type;
```

Now we look at those tiles around us, using the values we calculated earlier, to come up with a final value for the tile. We check each tile in procession, again starting from the top, going clockwise, and increasing the value by the appropriate amount if there is a wall there:

```
// Top.
if (IsWall(i, j - 1))
{
  value += 1;
}

// Right.
if (IsWall(i + 1, j))
{
  value += 2;
}

// Bottom.
if (IsWall(i, j + 1))
{
  value += 4;
}

// Left.
if (IsWall(i - 1, j))
{
  value += 8;
}
```

All that's left at this stage is to assign the correct texture and ID to the tile. We previously covered how we set up the enumerator, denoting the tile types to line up directly with this value, so we can simply use the texture value as the tile type and the index of the texture:

```
// Set the new type.
m_grid[i][j].type = static_cast<TILE>(value);
m_grid[i][j].sprite.setTexture(TextureManager::GetTexture(m_
textureIDs[value]));
}}}}
```

With this the function is complete. The final step is to ensure that we add a call to it in the `Level::GenerateLevel` function right after we've generated the rooms, as follows:

```
    . . .
    // Add some rooms to the level to create some open space.
    CreateRooms(10);

    // Finally, give each tile the correct texture.
    CalculateTextures();
}
```

Let's not waste any time and get our game built:

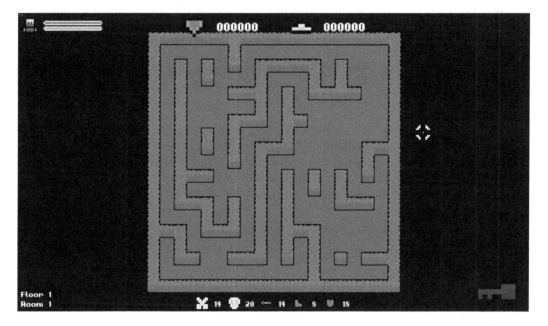

How great does that look! Run it a few times and see all the different mazes that are generated. We generate a maze, carve some larger areas, and resolve the textures. Procedurally generated dungeons. While this is great, we can do better. Our mazes lack character and individuality. So let's introduce some aesthetic variance to the environment.

Creating unique floor themes

In *Chapter 6, Procedurally Generating Art,* we spent some time looking at procedurally generating sprites. We also created a function named `Level::SetColor`, which allows us to set an overlay color for all the tiles in the level. Let's put this to use and create a unique feel for each floor of the dungeon.

Let's create distinct floors that each have a unique aesthetic. Every 5 levels we can generate a new random color and apply it to our level. Our `Level` class already has the following variables:

```
/**
 * The floor number that the player is currently on.
 */
int m_floorNumber;

/**
 * The room number that the player is currently in.
 */
int m_roomNumber;
```

We can use these to track how many rooms we have generated and when we should change the effect. To start, we have to keep track of which floor and room we're on. At the end of the `Level::GenerateLevel` function, we'll start by incrementing the `m_roomNumber` variable. When it's 5, we can increment `m_floorNumber` and generate a new color overlay; don't forget to reset the room counter:

```
    . . .

    // Calculate the correct texture for each tile.
    CalculateTextures();

    // Increment our room/floor count and generate new effect if
necessary.
    m_roomNumber++;

    // Move to next floor.
    if (m_roomNumber == 5)
    {
        m_roomNumber = 0;
        m_floorNumber++;
    }
}
```

As we learned in *Chapter 6, Procedurally Generating Art*, to generate a new color we need to generate three random values that lie between 0 and 255. These values are the red, green, and blue channels that make up the color. The fourth value is alpha and denotes the transparency of the sprite.

It's important to bear in mind that if we generate color values that are closer to 0, we'll get a white color, and if we go too far on the other end, the color will be too dark. For this reason, we aren't going to generate a number anywhere in the range of 0 to 255, but cap this slightly so that we always get a workable color. The alpha value will be set to 255 every time, as we don't want any of the tiles to be transparent.

We'll generate a random color and then make a call to `Level::SetColor`, passing the newly generated value to it. This will give the level a unique aesthetics:

```
// Increment our room/floor count and generate new effect if
necessary.
m_roomNumber++;

if (m_roomNumber == 5)
{
  // Move to next floor.
  m_roomNumber = 0;
  m_floorNumber++;

  // Generate a random color and apply it to the level tiles.
  sf::Uint8 r = std::rand() % 101 + 100;
  sf::Uint8 g = std::rand() % 101 + 100;
  sf::Uint8 b = std::rand() % 101 + 100;

  SetColor(sf::Color(r, g, b, 255));
}
```

This is the second time we wanted to generate a random color. Given this, it might be a good candidate to receive its own function. As a short exercise, abstract this code into its own function and update the game code accordingly.

Before we can run our game and see the results, we need to make one more change. Currently, a random level color will only be set when we move the floors for the first time. We need to execute the same code when our level is first generated. We can do this in the constructor of the level. Let's simply append the following code to `Level::Level`, as follows:

```
    . . .

    // Store the column and row information for each node.
    for (int i = 0; i < GRID_WIDTH; ++i)
    {
        for (int j = 0; j < GRID_HEIGHT; ++j)
        {
            auto cell = &m_grid[i][j];
            cell->columnIndex = i;
            cell->rowIndex = j;
        }
    }

    // Generate a random color and apply it to the level tiles.
    sf::Uint8 r = std::rand() % 101 + 100;
    sf::Uint8 g = std::rand() % 101 + 100;
    sf::Uint8 b = std::rand() % 101 + 100;

    SetColor(sf::Color(r, g, b, 255));
```

Now we're ready to run the game once more. We can see that when our level is a random color, and when we make our way through 5 levels we know this color will change!

Let's run the game and see this in action:

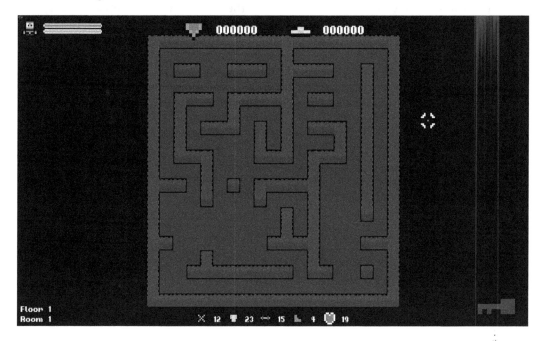

Adding entry and exit points

Since we're no longer loading our level from pre-defined level data, we need to calculate a valid entry and exit point for each room. Since the whole level is a maze, we can generate an entry point right at the bottom of maze and make it the player's goal to find the exit at the top of the level. The multiple passages and dead ends will keep the player searching!

We already have these tiles defined in our wall enumerator, so it's a simple case of finding locations for them in the level. As always, we'll start by declaring a function in which this behavior will lie. It's always a good idea to encapsulate chunks of code that perform a single task in a function. This not only makes behavior and responsibility clear, but also makes code more reusable.

Let's declare the following function in `Level.h`:

```
private:
/**
 * Generates an entry and exit point for the given level.
 */
void GenerateEntryExit();
```

Now, for the method body, we want to start by identifying suitable indices for the start and end tiles. Since we'll place the tiles on the top and bottom rows, we only have to generate a single index, namely the column. The rows' indices will be 0 and GRID_HEIGHT-1 respectively.

To do this, we'll select a column index at random and check whether the location is suitable for entry node. For the entry node, we need to ensure that there's no tile above. Likewise, for the exit node, we need to ensure that there's nothing below us:

```cpp
// Generates an entry and exit point for the given level.
void Level::GenerateEntryExit()
{
  // Calculates new start and end locations within the level.
  int startI, endI;
  startI = endI = -1;

  while (startI == -1)
  {
    int index = std::rand() % GRID_WIDTH;

    if (m_grid[index][GRID_HEIGHT - 1].type == TILE::WALL_TOP)
    {
      startI = index;
    }
  }

  while (endI == -1)
  {
    int index = std::rand() % GRID_HEIGHT;

    if (m_grid[index][0].type == TILE::WALL_TOP)
    {
      endI = index;
    }
  }
}
```

Using the while loops like this needs to be approached with extreme caution. If a valid tile did not exist, the program will hang and crash. In this case, we can be sure that there's always a valid tile due to the way the algorithm works.

Now that we have the start and end nodes identified, all that's left is to set the nodes as the correct type of tiles. The entry node needs to be set to TILE::WALL_ENTRANCE, and the exit node has to be set to TILE::WALL_DOOR_LOCKED, as follows:

```
    // Set the tile textures for the entrance and exit tiles.
    SetTile(startI, GRID_HEIGHT - 1, TILE::WALL_ENTRANCE);
    SetTile(endI, 0, TILE::WALL_DOOR_LOCKED);
}
```

Now that this function is finished, we just need to make a call to it once a level is generated. We'll do this at the end of the Level::GenreateLevel function right after we calculate the textures:

```
        . . .

        // Generate a random color and apply it to the level tiles.
        sf::Uint8 r = std::rand() % 101 + 100;
        sf::Uint8 g = std::rand() % 101 + 100;
        sf::Uint8 b = std::rand() % 101 + 100;

        SetColor(sf::Color(r, g, b, 255));
    }

    // Add entrance and exit tiles to the level.
    GenerateEntryExit();
}
```

Setting a player's spawn location

Now we have identified the entrance and exit nodes, we need to move our player accordingly. The code to generate a start node lies in the level class, so we're going to need to add a function that will return this start location. We could just generate the entrance and exit nodes in the game class, but this would be poor design. It's much better to place the code where it belongs and create getter and setter methods to access it.

However, before we can return the spawn location we actually have to calculate it! To do so, we need to know where the entry node is. Once the Level::GenerateEntryExit function has returned that information is lost. We could iterate over the bottom row of the tiles to find it, but that would be inefficient. Instead, we'll create a variable in Level class to hold this information and calculate the spawn location in Level::GenerateEntryExit.

Let's start by declaring these variables in `Level.h`, as follows:

```
/**
 * The spawn location for the current level.
 */
sf::Vector2f m_spawnLocation;
```

Now, we know that the entrance to each level is going to be somewhere in the bottom row. This means that to calculate the spawn location we simply need to find the absolute position of the tile immediately above that. The `Level` class already has a function to get the absolute location of a tile, so it's as simple as making a single call to that function and passing the correct tile.

While we're here we need to sneak in a little bit of similar code. We need to store the location of the new exit so that the `Level::UnlockDoor` function knows which tile to change. The Level class already has a variable for this information, so it's a simple one-liner code that we'll sneak in.

Let's append this behavior to the end of the `Level::GenerateEntryExit` function, as follows:

```
// Set the tile textures for the entrance and exit tiles.
SetTile(startI, GRID_HEIGHT - 1, TILE::WALL_ENTRANCE);
SetTile(endI, 0, TILE::WALL_DOOR_LOCKED);

// Save the location of the exit door.
m_doorTileIndices = sf::Vector2i(endI, 0);

// Calculate the spawn location.
m_spawnLocation = GetActualTileLocation(startI, GRID_HEIGHT - 2);
}
```

Now all that we need is a dead simple `getter` function to return the spawn location of the player, don't forget the declaration:

```
// Returns the spawn location for the current level.
sf::Vector2f Level::SpawnLocation()
{
  return m_spawnLocation;
}
```

Now it's time to apply this spawn location to a player. `Game::GenerateLevel` is the function where we generate a level so we'll set the player's location here. After the call to `Level::GenerateLevel` we can fetch the spawn location, knowing that it will be updated, and use this value as the position for the player.

We can also now uncomment the code to spawn a key, our call to `Game::PopulateLevel`, and our call to `Game::SpawnRandomTiles`. With our level now setup these function will work as intended. Let's get that code uncommented, and update `Game::GenerateLevel` with the following:

```cpp
// Generates a new level.
void Game::GenerateLevel()
{
  // Generate a new level.
  m_level.GenerateLevel();

  // Add a key to the level.
  SpawnItem(ITEM::KEY);

  // Populate the level with items.
  PopulateLevel();

  // 1 in 3 change of creating a level goal.
  if (((std::rand() % 3) == 0) && (!m_activeGoal))
  {
    GenerateLevelGoal();
  }

  // Moves the player to the start.
  m_player.SetPosition(m_level.SpawnLocation());
}
```

Time to test the code. Now when we run the game, we should see not only a great looking maze, but also an entrance at the bottom with our player directly above it, and an exit at the top of the level:

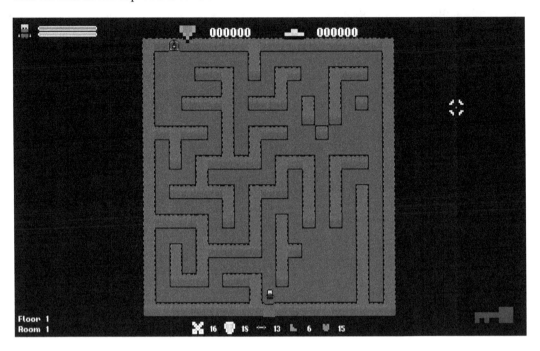

Undoing the debug changes

The work on our dungeon generation is now complete! Let's quickly revert the debug changes that we made to the code. We need to uncomment the line that enables the game view and the lighting code; both of these lines are in the `Game::Draw` function:

```
. . .

case GAME_STATE::Playing:
{
  // Set the main game view.
  //m_window.setView(m_views[static_cast<int>(VIEW::MAIN)]);

  // Set the main game view.
  m_window.setView(m_views[static_cast<int>(VIEW::MAIN)]);
```

```
// Draw level light.
//for (const sf::Sprite& sprite : m_lightGrid)
//{
//   m_window.draw(sprite);
//}

// Draw level light.
for (const sf::Sprite& sprite : m_lightGrid)
{
  m_window.draw(sprite);
}
```

 Instead of adding or removing the debug code like this, you could create a dev mode that can be toggled and is available in the DEBUG mode.

Exercises

To help you test your knowledge of this chapter's content, here are a few exercises that you should work on. They are not imperative to the rest of the book, but working on them will help you assess your strengths and weaknesses in the material covered:

1. There are many different algorithms available that could be used to generate mazes, such as the randomized **Prim**'s algorithm and **Kruskal**'s algorithm. Choose one of these algorithms and have a go at replacing the recursive backtracking implementation with your own implementation.

2. We worked with quite a small level size. Try increasing it and varying the characteristics of the levels that are generated. Increase the number of rooms, their size, and so on.

3. You may have noticed that our torches are missing! Since we no longer load the level from a level file, we need to add them ourselves. Torches should be placed on tiles of the TILE::WALL_TOP type. Have a go at creating this function yourself. If you get stuck, you can always look at the next chapter's code for a hint on where to start.

Summary

In this chapter we learned how our game, which previously loaded predefined level data from a text file, can generate its own level data during runtime. This brings a great level of replayability to the game, ensuring gameplay stays fresh and challenging. We also used a function that we defined in the earlier chapters to bring more character to our levels; we used sprite effects to create a distinct feeling for each floor. Practically all aspects of our game are procedurally generated now, and we have a fully-fledged roguelike project under our belt.

Now that our work on the template project is complete, we'll be using the final chapter to take a look at component-based design. Procedural generation is all about flexibility. Therefore, it makes sense that we'd want to work with the most flexible architecture. Component-based architecture can achieve this. Having a good understanding of this design approach will help you progress and build larger, more flexible systems.

10
Component-Based Architecture

Procedural game systems are incredibly versatile by nature. Therefore, the frameworks and infrastructures that they're implemented into need to share the same properties. Component-based systems, such as the Unity game engine, excel at this, and typically offer more versatility over traditional inheritance-based systems.

When building a large, dynamic system such as a game engine, a tradition inheritance-based approach will present problems. Inheritance structures become messy and objects become larger as they are required to do more. As a result, behavior becomes less encapsulated. A component-based approach solves these issues, so to finish our work we'll branch off a little to take a look at what a component-based system is, why it works hand in hand with procedural generation, and how we can improve the existing engine to benefit from it.

In this chapter, we'll cover the following topics:

- Problems with a traditional inheritance approach
- The pros and cons of a component-based approach
- Understanding component-based architecture
- Implementing a component-based system

 If you are unfamiliar with the Unity engine, head to `https://unity3d.com/` and check it out. It's one of the industry's leading game engines and uses a component-based approach. The best part is that it's completely free!

Understanding component-based architecture

Component-based architecture, also known as component-based design and modular programming, is an approach to software design that aims to break down behavior into succinct, reusable components. We already do this to a certain extent with object-orientated design, but component-based architecture takes this further. For example, if an object such as a sprite or a 3D model needs a certain behavior, it will be defined through a component that the object will own, as opposed to being inherited from a `base` class.

Problems with a traditional inheritance-based approach

Before we get into the pros and cons of a component-based approach, let's look at the problems that a traditional inheritance-based approach brings. It's these problems that we'll aim to fix.

Convoluted inheritance structures

Let's suppose that we have a simple `player` object that requires a 3D model and to be effected by our game physics. Let's look at an inheritance structure that may be needed to create this object:

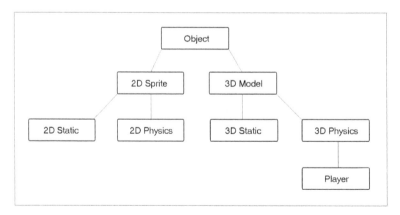

You can see from this diagram that even this simple scenario can result in a complex inheritance structure. If you now replace this simple example with an entire game engine, you can imagine how complex and unmanageable the inheritance structure would be.

This is a major downfall of traditional inheritance-based design; as your system grows larger, objects get more convoluted and entangled in the inheritance tree. This complexity does not help us when we're trying to create a procedural system. We want a system that is as flexible as possible.

Circular dependencies

Another problem that can arise with complex inheritance structures is that of circular dependencies. This is where class A depends on class B, which in turn depends on class A, and so on. The following diagram should make this clearer:

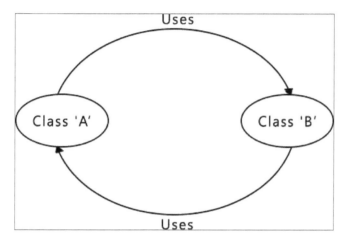

While circular dependencies can be avoided through proper program structure, it becomes increasingly harder as the system grows larger. As the inheritance tree grows, so do the dependencies, and it can cause real problems within a system. By removing complex inheritance, we also remove the risk of messy dependencies.

Benefits of component-based architecture

As developers, we're always making trade-offs. It's imperative to know both the pros and cons of an approach so that we can make informed decisions regarding whether it belongs in a solution. Since we've identified some flaws with an inheritance-based approach, and aim to solve them with a component-based approach, let's familiarize ourselves with a few of its pros and cons.

Avoiding complex inheritance structures

We identified a hypothetical game situation earlier and looked at what a typical inheritance-based approach might look like. Let's take a look at the same example if we take a component-based approach:

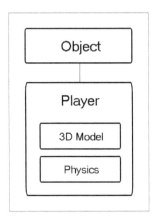

It's clear that this solution is much simpler and neater than its inheritance-based equivalent. Instead of obtaining its behavior from parents and thus creating a chain of dependencies, it's instead broken into succinct components that can simply be attached to an object.

Code is broken into highly reusable chunks

Another benefit of component-based architecture is the high reuse value of code once it's encapsulated in a component. Once encapsulated, behavior can be easily given to objects by simply attaching the component. This not only avoids duplicate code, but also makes it easy to build complex objects by combining multiple components. This is where it lends itself to procedural generation. We can procedurally put objects together like Lego with these reusable components.

Highly maintainable and scalable

As a result of the code being reusable, it also makes it very easy to maintain. If a set of objects all obtain their behavior from a single source, then only one edit is needed and it will affect them all.

Component-based systems are also easier to scale. Since our components are succinct individual modules and don't have complex dependencies, we can add them at will. If we want new behavior, we don't have to worry about questions such as *Where it will go?*, *What will it depend on?*, *What will it inherit from?*, and so on. We simply build the new component and use it where we need to.

The disadvantages of component-based architecture

Now it's time to have a look at the opposing side of the argument. Although component-based design does bring with it a range of great benefits, there are things that you need to consider.

Code can become too fragmented

To a certain extent this is the goal of component-based design: to break code into manageable chunks. But this can be taken too far. If objects and functionality are broken down too far, then we end up with the code base scattered into hundreds of tiny components, making it a mess. Always keep this in mind. Yes, we do want to break our code into manageable and reusable components; just don't go crazy with it!

Unnecessary overhead

Expanding on the previous point, if code is broken down into too many small components, then we'll see an increase in useless overhead. If a project contains many components, we'll frequently find ourselves dipping in and out of them to perform tasks. While adding a component might make code easier to manage and maintain, it also introduces overhead when it's used.

Complex to use

The final disadvantage of components is simply their use, as it can be more complex than a traditional object model. Instead of accessing a member function directly, we have to go through the component that they belong to. If we have 20 components in an object, then we have to remember where the variables are and which component we need to use. While it's not rocket science, it's certainly more complex than having a single object that directly owns all the behavior and data.

An overview

Hopefully, it's now clear how component-based design aids procedural design more than a traditional inheritance-based approach. Procedural generation is all about flexibility, and when systems grow to a certain size an inheritance-based system can struggle to provide that. By allowing us to break code into reusable objects, component-based design keeps code flexible and without dependencies so that we can move components wherever we want.

Designing the component system

A component-based system can be implemented in many ways. So, before we write any code, let's look at some possibilities. The goal is to break reusable behavior into succinct components and be able to add and remove them from the existing objects with ease. All objects share a common base class named object so we'll add the facility to add components to and remove them from this class. We can then ensure that it will be propagated to all the subsequent classes in the project.

There are a number of ways to implement a component-based approach, and there is no single right answer. For example, we could create a function to add or remove each component individually. Here's an example:

```
bool      AttachSpriteComponent(SpriteComponent spriteCompontent);
bool      AttachInputComponent(InputComponent inputComponent);
```

While this will make things straightforward, we will have a lot of duplicate code in the class. Also, every time we add a component, we will have to create two matching functions: one to get the component and one to set it. That's a bit cumbersome!

Another approach involves simply making the component values public. So, instead of interacting with the components through functions, we can directly access them through the object that they belong to:

```
Object object;
object.spriteComponent = SpriteComponent();
```

Even though this is an attractive option, as it would make life a thousand times simpler for us, it's almost never a good idea to make variables public like this. Having to make variables public to make code work usually indicates a flaw in the architecture of the system. If you ever find that this is the case, the cause of the problem should be sorted.

If we look at an existing component-based game engine such as Unity, we can see how they approach this problem. The following code demonstrates how to get a component from an object in Unity. This is taken directly from the Unity documentation:

```
// Disable the spring on the HingeJoint component.
HingeJoint hinge = GetComponent<HingeJoint>();
hinge.useSpring = false;
```

We can see that a single function named `GetComponent` is defined, and a type is supplied to return the corresponding component. We could create a similar system using enumerators to denote the type, allowing users to specify a component type via a parameter and then using that in a `switch` statement to return the correct variable.Let's assume that we created an `AttachComponent` function to add a component to an object using the following declaration:

```
void AttachComponent(COMPONENT_TYPE type, Component component);
```

In the function definition, we have something that looks like this:

```
void Object::AttachComponent(COMPONENT_TYPE type, Component component)
{
    switch (type)
    {
        case SOME_TYPE:
            m_someTypeVariable = component;
        break;
    . . .
```

This would work fine if the user passed a matching type and component, but there's nothing about this that will guarantee that. For example, a user can specify a movement component but actually pass an audio component, and that would be bad! We'll actually solve this through the use of templates!

C++ templates

C++ templates allow us to define functions and classes that work with generic types. This allows a function or a class to accept any type, and it only has to be written once. This is what we want. We want to define a single get/set function for components, and we'll template them to make them generic and flexible.

Let's take a look at a practical example of templates to get a better idea of how they actually work.

Using templates

Let's suppose that we require a function to add two numbers, and we want to support a range of types. To achieve this, we could declare a function for each type that we want to support, as follows:

```
int Add(int value1, int value2)
{
    return value1 + value2;
}
```

```
double Add(double value1, double value2)
{
    return value1, value2;
}
```

Looking at these two functions, the only thing that is different about them is their return and parameter types. How great would it be if we could say "Don't worry about the type, I'll give you it later" and just have one function? Enter templates!

Template declarations

C++ templates allow us to define functions with generic types and specify the type later as we call the function. It's an incredibly useful feature that creates flexible and reusable code instead of having multiple function definitions that are almost identical. If you use templates, the previous example requires only one function:

```
template<typename T>
T Add(T value1, T value2)
{
    T value;
    Value = value1 + value2;
    return value;
}
```

 Template parameters can use either the **typename** or the **class** keywords. Both of these keywords are entirely interchangeable and do the same thing. However, they can be used as a hint to denote the parameter type. Use **class** if a parameter is a class, and use **typename** with all the other types (int, char*, and so on).

The following syntax is used to declare a template:

```
template<template-parameters> function-declaration;
```

In the declaration, we create a template parameter named T. This gives us an ambiguous data type that can be used within the function declaration until an actual type is set later when the template is called. The generic T type can be used just like normal types: specifying the return types, creating variables, and setting the parameter types.

 The name of your template parameters can be anything that you like, although it's most commonly **TYPE** or **T**.

Templates can also have multiple types defined. For example, let's say that a function needs to take two different data types. We can use the following template:

```
template<typename T1, typename T2>
bool AreEqual(T1 value1, T2 value2)
{
    return value1==value2;
}
```

Finally, templates can also be used with normal data types and they don't have to be ambiguous:

```
template<typename T, int I>
T IntegerMultiply(T value1)
{
    return value1 / value2;
}
```

Using templates

With the templates defined, let's have a look at how to use them. We've given the templates ambiguous types, so one way to call them is to explicitly tell the template what type we want to work with. This is done by passing a type in the <> brackets after the function/class call:

```
float floatValue = Add<float>(1.f, 2.f);
bool isEqual = AreEqual<double, int>(5.0, 5);
int intValue = IntegerMultiply<float, 2>(1.f);
```

The first two are straightforward; we assigned a type for each template parameter. However, the last one is slightly different. Since the second type is fixed, there's no need to specify it in angle brackets. Instead, we can use it like a normal parameter, passing the value that we want to use. This leaves us with just one parameter in the parentheses: the generic type value.

Something important that needs to be noted is that the value of template parameters is determined at compile time. This means that for each different instantiation of a template, a unique function is created. In the last example, the value of the **int** is passed as a template function, which means that a function that is hard-coded to multiply by the value 2 is created.

Let's suppose that we called IntegerMultiple twice:

```
int intValue = IntegerMultiply<float, 2>(1.f);
int intValue = IntegerMultiply<float, 10>(1.f);
```

Even though we've called the same template, the complier will create two different versions of `IntegerMultiply`. One version will always multiply by 2, and the other version will always multiply by 10. For this reason, the second template's parameters, the integers, have to be constant expressions. The following code will result in a compilation error:

```
int a = 10;
int intValue = IntegerMultiply<float, a>(1.f);
```

These functions can also be called without the type being explicitly denoted in angle brackets when the type can be resolved by the compiler. For this to happen there needs to be no ambiguity regarding the type. For example, the following calls are fine:

```
float floatValue = Add(1.f, 2.f);
bool isEqual = AreEqual(5.0, 5);
```

In these calls, each ambiguous type in the template is given a single type. The compiler can therefore deduce the type of **T** automatically. However, consider a scenario where different parameters are passed:

```
float floatValue = Add(1.f, 2);
```

T now has two possible values, which means that the compiler cannot deduce the type and will result in an error.

Template specialization

Now that we have an understanding of how templates work in general, let's have a look at template specialization. We already know that we can define a template with generic types and define them later when we call the function. That's fine if all the possible implementations share the same behavior, but what if we want different behavior depending on the type?

Let's suppose that we want to use the `Add` function with a string type. We want to pass in two words, but we want to put in a space between them when this is the case. The default template function doesn't facilitate this so we have to specialize it for this case. To specialize a template we simply create a declaration where we replace the ambiguous type with a fixed one, which is `std::string` in our case:

```
template<>
std::string Add<std::string>(std::string value1, std::string  value2)
{
```

```
    std::string result;
    result = value1 + " " + value2;
    return result;
}
```

Now, when the `template` function is called and the `std::string` type is specified, it will use this definition and not the generic one. With this, we can still use templates but provide specific implementations for certain types. Very handy.

 If you wish to learn more about C++ templates, visit `http://www.cplusplus.com/doc/tutorial/templates/`. This is a great site in general, and it has some awesome information on this topic.

Function overloading

Somewhat similar to templates, function overloading is another way in which we can make code and classes more versatile. We've already used overloaded functions during the course of the book, but they were provided with the code base. So, let's take a quick look at them.

When we define functions, we set fixed parameter types. Here's an example:

```
void DoStuff(T parameter);
```

With this definition, we can only pass a parameter of the `T` type. What if we want a choice of parameters? What if we want to be able to pass parameters of type `T` or type `Y`. Well, we can redefine the function, setting the same return type and name, but with unique parameters:

```
void DoStuff(T parameter);
void DoStuff(Y parameter);
```

We now have two function declarations with different parameters. When we call `DoStuff`, we'll have the option of which parameter to pass. Also, with function overloading, each declaration gets its own body, just like with template specialization. While similar on the surface, function overloads and template specializations work in different ways, though that's beyond the scope of this book. For now, all that we need is a basic understanding of them and we can get started!

 As with templates, for further reading on function overloading, visit `http://www.cplusplus.com/doc/tutorial/functions2/`.

Creating a base component

With the theory covered, let's implement this into our project. The overwhelming message of this chapter has so far has been to use components to avoid messy inheritance, but we still need *some* inheritance as we need to use polymorphism!

Each object will be able to hold a range of components so we'll store them in a single `generic` container. In order for us to do this we need to make use of polymorphism, ensuring that all components inherit from a common base class. That base class is what we're going to implement now.

Let's add a new class to the project and call it `Component`. We'll leave it to you to implement the `.cpp`:

```
#ifndef COMPONENT_H
#define COMPONENT_H

class Component
{
public:

    /**
    * Default Constructor.
    */
    Component();

    /**
    * Create a virtual function so the class is polymorphic.
    */
    virtual void Update(float timeDelta) {};
};
#endif
```

Note that we've added a `virtual update` function here as a class must have at least one `virtual` function in order to be polymorphic. With the `Component` base class created, we can now add the functions to `get` and `set` components, and they will reside in the base `Object` class so that they are available to all objects.

Component functions

If we think about the behavior that we want, we need to be able to give an object a component of any given type. We also need to be able to fetch that same component later. We'll call these functions `AttachComponent` and `GetComponent`.

Earlier in the chapter, we identified how we can use templates to create a function with generic types and give them real values when we need them. We'll use templates and polymorphism to create these two functions.

Attaching a component

The first function that we're going to write will be used to attach a component of a given type to the `Object` class. Since we've already identified that we're going to store all components in a single generic container, this function will be a relatively simple template. The only thing that we need to be aware of is that we should not add the same component twice!

Let's start by defining the container, as that's where we'll store the objects. Since we need to take advantage of polymorphism, we can't store actual objects. So instead, we're going to use shared pointers so that we can pass them around with ease.

Let's start by defining the generic container in `Object.h`. Don't forget to #include our new Component class so that Object can see it:

```
private:
/**
 * A collection of all components the object has attached.
 */
std::vector<std::shared_ptr<Component>> m_components;
```

Now it's time for the actual `AttachComponent` method. We could take a naïve approach and just append the new component to the `generic` container. The problem here is that we could add multiples of the same component type, and that's not something that we want. Before we add the component to the collection, we'll first check whether a component of the same type already exists, and for that, we'll use the `std::dynamic_pointer_cast` function.

This function lets us cast between pointers and returns a null pointer if it fails. It's very handy, and when combined with templates, we can create a single function that will accept any component type, create one, check whether one of the same type already exists, and if it does, it will overwrite it. We'll define this template function inline in the header. Let's add the following code to `Object.h`:

```
/**
 * Attaches a component to the object.
 */
template <typename T>
std::shared_ptr<T> AttachComponent()
{
```

```
    // First we'll create the component.
    std::shared_ptr<T> newComponent = std::make_shared<T>();

    // Check that we don't already have a component of this type.
    for (std::shared_ptr<Component>& exisitingComponent : m_
components)
    {
        if (std::dynamic_pointer_cast<T>(exisitingComponent))
        {
            // If we do replace it.
            exisitingComponent = newComponent;
            return newComponent;
        }
    }

    // The component is the first of its type so add it.
    m_components.push_back(newComponent);

    // Return the new component.
    return newComponent;
};
```

Using templates, we can operate with the generic T type, which allows us to perform the cast to check whether the types match. If they do match, we overwrite the old component with the new one; if not, we simply add it to our collection. We also return the new component when we're done in case the user wants it straightaway.

That's all there is to it, and the beauty of using templates like this is how scalable the system is. It doesn't matter if we add 1,000 components; this function will be able to attach them to any object.

Retuning a component

The next template that we need to create is for a function that's used to return a given component. Again, let's think about where we'll need the generic type. The function will need to return the component type, so that needs to be generic, and we also need to find the correct component type. So, we'll use the generic type in the pointer cast like we did with the previous function.

Let's get this template defined in the header of `Object`:

```
/**
 * Gets a component from the object.
 */
template <typename T>
std::shared_ptr<T> GetComponent()
{
    // Check that we don't already have a component of this type.
    for (std::shared_ptr<Component> exisitingComponent : m_components)
    {
        if (std::dynamic_pointer_cast<T>(exisitingComponent))
        {
            return std::dynamic_pointer_cast<T>(exisitingComponent);
        }
    }

    return nullptr;
};
```

With this, we have the ability to add any component to any object and return the correct type. The best part is that two simple functions provide all this functionality! How awesome are templates!

If you want to test this code before we move on you can do. At the end of the `Game::Initialize` function, add the following lines:

```
m_player.AttachComponent<Component>();
m_player.AttachComponent<Component>();

std::shared_ptr<Component> component = m_player.
GetComponent<Component>();
```

If you use **breakpoints** and look at the values at runtime, you'll see that this code does the following things:

- It adds a new `Component` object to the generic container
- It tries to add a second `Component` object; so it instead overwrites the current one
- It realizes that we want the component with the type `Component`; so it returns it

Creating a transform component

With the ability to attach and return components, let's get our first component built and added. We'll start with a simple one first. Currently, all objects have a position by default that's provided by the `Object` base class. Let's break this behavior into its own component.

Encapsulating transform behavior

Since we're converting an inheritance-based approach to a component-based one, the first task is to take the transform behavior out of the `Object` class. Currently, that consists of a `single` position variable and a function to both `get` and `set` that value.

Let's create a new class named `TransformComponent` and move this behavior into it, as follows:

```cpp
#ifndef TRANSFORMCOMPONENT_H
#define TRANSFORMCOMPONENT_H

#include "Component.h"

class TransformComponent : public Component
{
public:
    TransformComponent();
    void SetPosition(sf::Vector2f position);
    sf::Vector2f& GetPosition();

private:
    sf::Vector2f m_position;
};
#endif
```

We'll also take the function definitions from `Object.cpp` file and place them in `TransformComponent.cpp`, as follows:

```cpp
#include "PCH.h"
#include "TransformComponent.h"

TransformComponent::TransformComponent() :
m_position({ 0.f, 0.f })
{
}
```

```
void TransformComponent::SetPosition(sf::Vector2f position)
{
    m_position = position;
}

sf::Vector2f& TransformComponent::GetPosition()
{
    return m_position;
}
```

We now have a component that will provide a position to an object. The last thing that we need to do is include the header for this component in the `Object` class so that all the extending classes can see it. Let's add the following code to `Object.h`:

```
    . . .

#ifndef OBJECT_H
#define OBJECT_H

#include "Component.h"
#include "TransformComponent.h"

class Object
{
public:

    . . .
```

It's time to add this component to the objects! This is a large task, and it's one that will be left for you to complete in your own time, but to demonstrate how it's done, we'll quickly add the component to the `player` class.

Adding a transform component to the player

Since we placed the two functions to attach and get components in the base `Object` class, we can call `AttachComponent` directly from within the player. We'll do this in the constructor as we'll need the component set up before we get to any logic. Let's head to `Player::Player` and add the following code to it:

```
// Add a transform component.
AttachComponent<TransformComponent>();
```

That's all there is to it! The `player` now has all the data and functionality that we added to the transform component, and when we want to use it, we can simply go through this new component. You may remember that we identified overhead as one of the potential downsides of component-based design. We can see now how moving the behavior into a component has introduced overhead.

Using the transform component

The final part to this puzzle will be looking at how we use the new component. Previously, if we wanted to get the position of the player, all we had to do was use the following code:

```
// Get the position.
sf::Vector2f playerPos = m_position;

// Set the position.
m_position = sf::Vector2f(100.f, 100.f);
```

Since these values now belong to the `transform` component, we need to make a slight change and access those values through the `component` instead, as follows:

```
// Get the transform component.
auto transformComponent = GetComponent<TransformComponent>();

// Get the position.
sf::Vector2f position = transformComponent->GetPosition();

// Set the position.
transformComponent->SetPosition(sf::Vector2f(100.f, 100.f));
```

Since these functions are public, we can call them anywhere. For example, if we were in the game class and wanted the position of the player object, we would do something like this:

```
sf::Vector2f position = m_player.GetComponent<TransformComponent>()-
>GetPosition();
```

Updating the game code

With the architecture in place, and an understanding of how the `transform` component works, it's time to update the game code to make use of the new component. This will require a number of changes. For this reason, we won't be running through them in the chapter; it's left as a task for you!

Every object that has a position will need a `transform` component adding, and the places where these position variables are used will now need to be accessed via the component. If at any point you get stuck, refer to the previous code examples. If you do run through the project and make these changes yourself, make sure that you give the project a run once you're done to ensure that everything is still running smoothly:

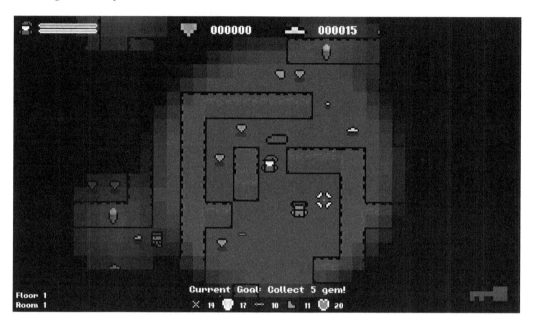

Although things may look the same, we know that the underlying system is now much more flexible, maintainable, and saleable. Let's create more components!

Creating a SpriteComponent

The next component that we're going to make is a `SpriteComponent`. This will provide an `object` with either a `static` or an `animated` sprite. It's a behavior that is commonly reused through many objects so is a great candidate to be moved into a component.

Encapsulating sprite behavior

Currently, all the animation-related behavior is inherited from the base `Object` class. The following code consists of all the sprite- and animation-related functions and variables that we'll pull from `Object` into its own class:

```
public:
    virtual void Draw(sf::RenderWindow &window, float timeDelta);
    bool SetSprite(sf::Texture& texture, bool isSmooth, int frames =
1, int frameSpeed = 0);
    sf::Sprite& GetSprite();
    int GetFrameCount() const;
    bool IsAnimated();
    void SetAnimated(bool isAnimated);

protected:

    sf::Sprite m_sprite;

private:

    void NextFrame();

private:

    int m_animationSpeed;
    bool m_isAnimated;
    int m_frameCount;
    int m_currentFrame;
    int m_frameWidth;
    int m_frameHeight;
```

Currently, every object that we create has these variables and functions but doesn't necessarily need them which is a waste. With our `component`, we can give an object this behavior without worrying about inheritance.

Let's start by creating a new class in the project and call it `SpriteComponent`, ensuring that it extends the base `Component` class.

 Keeping a clean project is important. Create folders and organize your classes into logical groups!

Now, we can add all the functions and variables that we pulled out of `Object`:

```
#ifndef SPRITECOMPONENT_H
#define SPRITECOMPONENT_H

#include <SFML/Graphics.hpp>
#include "Component.h"

class SpriteComponent : public Component
{
public:
    SpriteComponent();

    virtual void Draw(sf::RenderWindow &window, float timeDelta);
    bool SetSprite(sf::Texture& texture, bool isSmooth, int frames =
1, int frameSpeed = 0);
    sf::Sprite& GetSprite();
    int GetFrameCount() const;
    bool IsAnimated();
    void SetAnimated(bool isAnimated);

private:

    void NextFrame();

private:
sf::Sprite m_sprite;
    int m_animationSpeed;
    bool m_isAnimated;
    int m_frameCount;
    int m_currentFrame;
    int m_frameWidth;
    int m_frameHeight;
};
#endif
```

We've made some slight changes here regarding the `public/protected/private` modifiers that we use. Previously, with things being inheritance-based, a number of functions and variables were given the `protected` keyword, exposing them to child classes. Since we're moving away from inheritance, all of these have now been moved to `private`.

We now just need to initialize the variables in the initializer list of the constructor, and add the function's definitions in `SpriteComponenet.cpp`. Again, these can just be picked up from the `Object` class and moved over. Also, don't forget to include the class in `Object.h`:

```
    .  .  .

#ifndef OBJECT_H
#define OBJECT_H

#include "Component.h"
#include "TransformComponent.h"
#include "SpriteComponent.h"

class Object
{
public:

    .  .  .
```

With the class complete and the header included, we can now implement the component!

Adding a sprite component to the player class

Let's continue using the player class to demonstrate, giving the class a `sprite` component. We decided earlier that the best place for this is within the constructor. So, let's add the following code to `Player::Player` right after we create the `transform` component:

```
    .  .  .

    // Add a transform component.
    AttachComponent<TransformComponent>();

    // Add a sprite component.
    AttachComponent<SpriteComponent>();
}
```

The updated drawing pipeline

Now that our `objects` are able to receive `sprite` components, we need to update the drawing pipeline so that they can be used. Currently, we loop through all the objects in the main game loop, drawing each in turn. However, the object itself isn't responsible for drawing now, the `sprite` component is (if it has one, that is). In the `main draw` loop, instead of iterating over all the objects and calling their `Draw` function directly, we need to check whether they have a sprite component attached, and if they do, call the `Draw` function of the component. The `GetComponent` function returns a `nullprt` if no component is found making this easy to check:

```
. . .

// Draw all objects.
for (const auto& item : m_items)
{
    //item->Draw(m_window, timeDelta);

    auto spriteComponent = item->GetComponent<SpriteComponent>();

    if (spriteComponent)
    {
        spriteComponent->Draw(m_window, timeDelta);
    }
}

. . .
```

With the drawing pipeline updated, let's quickly look at how to use the `component`.

Updating the game code

Here comes the big job again! On every occasion where a sprite is used, we need to update the code to go through the `sprite` component instead. As with the last component, this brings many changes to the code so is another task for you to complete in your own time.

It's is also suggested at the end of the chapter that you try to split this component into multiple types: one for `static` sprites and another for `animated` sprites. This will keep the code even more encapsulated and efficient as currently this component provides animation even if it isn't needed.

If you do undertake this, hopefully nothing has imploded and you still are able to compile without issues. If all is well, we will see nothing new, but that's a good thing!

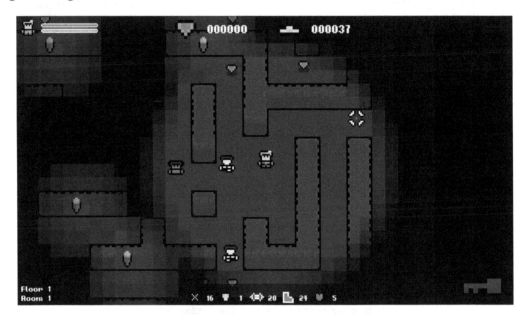

Creating an audio component

The final component that we're going to create is an `audio` component. Now, this is the first component that we'll create from scratch. However, our experience with the two previous components should make this one easy to implement.

Defining the behavior of an audio component

This is slightly different from our past components. Instead of encapsulating existing behavior, we need to define it. We're going to create a simple `audio` component, and the only behavior that we're going to have is the ability to play a single sound effect. For this, we'll require a single variable to hold the sound object, a function to set a sound buffer, and a function to play the sound.

In the function that will be used to set the sound buffer, we're going to make use of function overloading. If we think about how we may want to use this function, we might either want to pass an already created sound buffer into the component or pass a path to one and create it before we use it. We covered function overloading earlier in the chapter, and this is a textbook case of its use. We define the same function name and return type but varying parameter types.

Let's add this new `AudioComponent` class to the project, as follows:

```cpp
#ifndef AUDIOCOMPONENT_H
#define AUDIOCOMPONENT_H

#include "SFML/Audio.hpp"
#include "Component.h"

class AudioComponent
{
public:
    AudioComponent();

    void Play();
    bool SetSoundBuffer(sf::SoundBuffer& buffer);
    bool SetSoundBuffer(std::string filePath);

private:
    sf::Sound m_sound;
};
#endif
```

Again, we'll leave it as an exercise for you to complete this class and provide definitions for the functions. With the class complete let's not forget that we have to include the class in the `Object.h` file so that all the objects can see and use it:

```cpp
. . .

#ifndef OBJECT_H
#define OBJECT_H

#include "Component.h"
#include "TransformComponent.h"
#include "SpriteComponent.h"
#include "AudioComponent.h"

class Object

. . .
```

Adding an audio component to the player class

The final step is to actually hook up our components to the object. We've covered doing this before and it's simply a case of adding a call to the `AttachComponent` function, specifying `AudioComponent` as the type. To demonstrate this on the player, let's add an audio component along with the sprite and transform components:

```
    . . .

    // Add a transform component.
    AttachComponent<TransformComponent>();

    // Add a sprite component.
    AttachComponent<SpriteComponent>();

    // Add an audio component.
    AttachComponent<AudioComponent>();
}
```

Using the audio component

Using the `audio` component is very simple. We give it a sound buffer, which is either a pre-constructed one, or the path to a file that needs to be loaded, and then call the `AudioComponent::Play` function. Let's give the player their own attack sound instead of it been held in the `main` game class. After we give the player the `audio` component, let's set up the sound that it will use:

```
    . . .

    // Add an audio component.
    AttachComponent<AudioComponent>();

    // Set the player's attack sound.
    GetComponent<AudioComponent>()->SetSoundBuffer("../resources/
sounds/snd_player_hit.wav");
}
```

In the `main` class, where we detect the collision with the player, we now play the sound via this component instead directly:

```
    . . .

    // Check for collision with player.
    if (enemyTile == playerTile)
    {
```

```
    if (m_player.CanTakeDamage())
    {
        m_player.Damage(10);
        //PlaySound(m_playerHitSound);
        m_player.GetComponent<AudioComponent>()->Play();
    }
}
```

. . .

You can see just how easy it was to add this behavior to an object, and it's not much work to add it to as many objects as we want! If we want to make a change, we just need to change the `component` class, and it affects all the child classes. Brilliant!

Exercises

To help you test your knowledge of this chapter's content, here are a few exercises that you should work on. They are not imperative to the rest of the book, but working on them will help you assess your strengths and weaknesses in the material covered:

1. Move the game input from a fixed, `static` class to a component.
2. Split `SpriteComponent` into two individual components; one that provides a static sprite, and one that provides an animated sprite.
3. Create a `component` that encapsulates a certain behavior and use it in your game.

Summary

In this chapter we took a good look at component-based architecture, including the major benefits that it brings when creating procedural systems and how it can be achieved through the use of templates. The approach outlined in this chapter is just one of many possible implementations so I encourage you to experiment with different methods. Its plug-and-play nature makes it very flexible, which is an important trait that we look for when creating procedural systems.

In the next chapter, we're going to take a retrospective look at the project and the topics that we covered as we reach the end of the book. For each area of procedural generation that we've used, we'll also identify some jumping-off points should you wish to explore the topic in more depth.

11
Epilogue

With our game finished, and after a quick foray into component based design, our introduction to procedural content generation is complete. We started simply with the generation and use of random numbers, and worked our way right up to creating complex procedural behaviors and content. We've touched upon many subjects, and hopefully working through this book has helped define what procedural generation is, and given some solid examples of how to approach and implement it in your games.

Before you close the book for the final time, let's take a quick look back at the project, identifying how and where we implemented procedural generation. We'll then reiterate its pros and cons one last time before finishing our work.

Project breakdown

Our game project started as a blank roguelike template with limited functionality, but with our work, we turned it into a fully fledged procedural roguelike game. Let's run through the project to identify how we used procedural generation to do so.

We'll also identify some further possible exercises for each chapter if you wish to explore the topic in detail. The goal of this book was to introduce you to the fundamentals of the topic, so hopefully you can hit the ground running as you take this further.

Procedurally populating environments

We started by spawning game items randomly around the level. This involved the generation of random numbers within a given range and using those as tile indices and enumerator values. This was the first time we used random numbers and enumerators to select random values and items, which is a technique that we relied heavily on throughout the course of the book.

If you wished to take this further, you could have a look at how to bias the spawn location of items or limit it to certain areas of the map. So, for example, you can bias the spawn location in such a way that all the gems will tend to spawn to the right-hand side of the level, and all the gold to the left-hand side. While not immediately beneficial to our project, you can imagine how it might be useful in other situations. You may want all your enemies to spawn at a certain part of the level, or a certain item to spawn in a given area of the map. Gaining more control over your game levels will be very beneficial.

Creating unique and random game objects

With our items now spread around the levels, we turned our attention to making them more random and unique. Instead of hardcoding item variables we generated them during runtime, making the objects more varied. We used this technique to create multiple object types from a single class, such as all potions coming from the same class.

To extend this further in the project, why not try adding some random armor and/or weapons? They can be dropped by the enemies and have random sprites and statistics. You can take the same approach that we took with potions and create an ambiguous class that can generate a vast range of possibilities.

Procedurally generating art

In this chapter, we had a look at how to create art procedurally. We started with a simple approach by using SFML's built-in sprite modification functions and moved on to a more complex approach in which we rendered multiple sprite components together to create new, unique ones, giving the enemies random armor.

If you want to learn more, you should have a look at how to create art completely from scratch. There are algorithms, such as Perlin and Simplex noise, that generate 2D noise. These algorithms can be used as a base for a procedural texture. Start looking at such algorithms and take it from there.

Procedurally modifying audio

Procedurally generating audio is a complex task. Therefore, the work that we did in this chapter was somewhat brief and really limited to modifying the existing sound procedurally as opposed to their outright creation. As with art, SFML provides a range of functions to edit sounds, such as pitch and volume, which were used to give simple sounds some variance. We then created spatialized 3D sound using SFML's built-in audio functions, giving our game some depth.

Sound can be generated entirely procedurally, but it's a complex and difficult process and as such, it isn't very popular as compared to other procedural implementations. However, if you want to look into this further, you could perhaps start by creating single sounds and learn how a computer produces them. From here, it's a case of learning how to put these sounds together to create something appealing, and then generating a procedural algorithm to do so. It's not for the faint-hearted, that's for sure!

Procedural behavior and mechanics

Progressing from the simple use of random numbers and selecting values from enumerators, we implemented a much more sophisticated and meaty procedural system, giving the enemies a basic AI in the form of pathfinding. We implemented A* pathfinding, enabling the enemies to chase the player around the maze. We also created a system to generate random level goals, so now our player is periodically presented with a unique goal in return for a unique reward.

The game mechanics that we generated are rather simple, so why not have a go at generating some more complex ones yourself? You can give players an actual task that has to be completed in order to continue playing the game. Otherwise, if it was the AI work that captured your interest, you could build upon it, making the enemies smarter and more of a challenge. Maybe if they lose line of sight of the player they will stop chasing, or they try predict player movement to block you off instead of simply following.

Procedural dungeon generation

For our pièce de résistance, we implemented procedural dungeon generation. Until this point levels were loaded from a text file, but we implemented a recursive backtracker algorithm to generate a maze and then added rooms to that maze to create more open areas. Thus, levels are now procedurally generated, and we can generate a new one with a single function call.

There are lots of ways to approach procedural dungeon generation, and a number of different algorithms that can be utilized for this. If this area interests you there's plenty of room to explore. Take a look at some alternate algorithms and experiment with the implementation. Try to generate some rooms with different characteristics, or add some environmental and aesthetic features to give a level more character.

A great resource for further reading is http://weblog.jamisbuck. org/. The blog is a goldmine for everything related to maze generation and covers a number of algorithms. You should definitely check it out.

Component-based architecture

Procedural content generation revolves around flexibility and as such, I felt that touching upon component-based design would be a good way to end our work. Through component-based design, we can create a flexible code base whose inherent flexibility will make it easier to implement procedural systems.

We ran through the fundamentals of component-based design in this chapter and looked at a couple of isolated examples. A good exercise is to run through the project, moving it over to an entirely component-based approach. This will really get you familiar with the concept, and you'll be ready to use it in your next project.

The pros and cons of procedural generation

For the last time, let's have a look at the major pros and cons of using procedural generation in our games.

Pros

- It creates dynamic content
- It can save on memory usage
- It saves development time and money
- It creates a large variety of options
- It increases replayability

Cons

- You relinquish control*
- It can be taxing on hardware
- It can feel repetitive
- It's hard to script set game events
- It may generate unusable content

 * The amount of control that you will relinquish depends upon the quality of your algorithm. At the end of the day, you're the one that writes the algorithm. Therefore, you can make it do what you want.

Summary

I hope that you found the content in this book useful. The goal was to introduce you to the vast topic that procedural generation is, and I felt that working with a real game was the best way to do that. We covered the key areas of development and identified ways to use procedural generation in each aspects. Hopefully, you now have enough knowledge to use it in your own games, and can undertake further reading to learn more about the areas that interest you the most.

Remember, procedural generation isn't just one thing or one approach. It's the dynamic generation of content. There's no one right way to implement it, so experiment. Find new ways to create content dynamically and play with it. There's no wrong answer.

Happy programming!

Index

Symbol

3D sound
  attenuation 154, 155
  audio listener 152
  defining 152
  minimum distance 153
  sound position 155

A

A*
  enemy, enabling to follow path 185, 186
  implementing, in game 185
  pathfinding behavior, calling 187
  path, viewing 188-190

A* algorithm
  closed list 166
  defining 164
  F value 167
  G value 167
  H, G, and F costs 166
  H value 167
  implementing 165
  level, representing as nodes 165
  Manhattan distance 167, 168
  open list 166
  parenting nodes 168
  pseudo-algorithm 169

algorithms
  Kruskal 235
  Prim 235

Allegro
  URL 29

A* pathfinding algorithm
  adjacent nodes, finding 176-179
  coding 170
  final path, creating 184
  G and F costs, calculating 180
  H values, precalculating 174
  main loop, defining 175, 176
  superior paths, checking 181-183
  supporting functions, creating 171
  Tile datatype 171
  variable declarations 173, 174

art
  generating procedurally 266
  procedural generation, used with 113

Artificial Intelligence (AI) 18, 161

ASCII table
  URL 56

audio
  modifying procedurally 266, 267

audio component
  adding, to player class 262
  behavior, defining 260
  creating 260
  using 262, 263

audio manipulation
  about 18
  behavior and mechanics 18
  Dungeon generation 18

B

base component
  creating 248

Boolean values
  number between 0 and 1, generating 45, 46
  setting randomly 45
  spawned item, selecting 47, 48

breakpoints
  using 251
build systems
  about 23
  reference link 24

C

class diagram 24
class keyword 244
closed list 166
Code::Blocks IDE
  about 22
  cons 23
  pros 22
collision 27
color
  generating, at random 121
complex animations
  creating 115
component-based architecture
  about 238, 268
  benefits 239, 240
  disadvantages 241
  overview 241
component-based design 18
Component functions
  about 248
  component, attaching 249, 250
  component, returning 250, 251
component system
  designing 242
C++ reference
  URL 3
cryptography 3
C++ templates
  about 243
  declarations 244
  template specialization 246
  URL 247
  using 243, 245
custom package, SFML
  reference link 37

D

deterministic machines 2
Doxygen
  URL 25
DreamSpark
  URL 22
dungeon generation
  defining 204
  maze, generating 205
  rooms and mazes, connecting 206
  rooms, generating 204
dynamic libraries 37

E

enemy class
  generating 101-103
enemy sprites
  armor textures, rendering 134
  armor tier, selecting 132, 133
  creating procedurally 127
  debugging 136, 137
  default armor textures, loading 131
  default draw behavior, overriding 135
  draw setup 128
  final textures, rendering 134
  sprite components, selecting 129-131
  sprites, breaking into components 127, 128
  testing 136, 137
environment
  populating procedurally 265, 266

F

function overloading
  defining 247
  URL 247

G

game seed
  setting 43, 44
game template
  breaking down 24
  downloading 24

game tiles
  editing 137-139
G and F costs
  calculating 180, 181
GNU Compiler Collection (GCC) 37

H

heuristic 164

I

IDE
  about 21
  selecting 21, 23
inheritance 30, 31
Integrated Development
      Environment. *See* **IDE**
items, spawning randomly
  about 70-73
  enemies, spawning randomly 79-81
  enumerators, using 74
  optional parameters 74, 75
  spawn code, updating 78, 79
  spawn functions 75-77
  spawning system, expanding 73

L

level data 25, 26
level tiles 65, 66
loops
  repeating 58, 59

M

main game loop
  reference link 41
Manhattan distance 167
maze generation
  passages, carving 213-216
  preparing for 211
Microsoft Visual Studio
  about 22
  cons 22
  pros 22

modified sprites
  image, saving to file 126
  RenderTexture class, drawing 125
  saving 124
  texture, passing into image 124, 125
modifiers
  using 114
modulo operator 6
multiple textures
  combining 114

N

navigation meshes
  URL 165
Nintendo Entertainment System (NES) 10

O

object hierarchy 25
object slicing
  about 33-36
  reference link 35
open list 166

P

pathfinding algorithm
  about 162, 163
  defining 162
  URL 185
pointers 33-36
polymorphism
  about 30
  reference link 30
potential obstacles
  about 64
  keeping, within the bound of level 64
  meaningful levels, creating 64
  overlapping objects, avoiding 64
preset color
  selecting 119, 120
procedural behavior and mechanics
  defining 267

procedural dungeon generation
  about 207
  defining 267, 268
  Game and Level class, updating 209-211
  maze, generating 211
  maze view, changing 207
  rooms, adding 217-219
  URL 268
procedural generation
  about 1
  benefits 13, 14
  cons 268, 269
  defining 2
  drawbacks 15, 16
  environments, populating 17
  implementing 17
  pros 268
  unique game objects, creating 17
  used, with art 113
  using, in games 10
  versus random generation 2
procedural generation usage
  map generation 11
  space, saving 10
procedural items
  about 103
  Random Gem and Heart classes 103, 104
  Random gold class 104-106
procedural level design
  benefits 201, 202
  considerations 202, 203
procedurally generated art
  benefits 115
  drawbacks 116
procedurally generated level goals
  active goal, checking 195, 196
  defining 190
  function declaration 190, 191
  goal, drawing on screen 197, 198
  random goal, generating 191-194
  variable declaration 190, 191
pure virtual functions 32

R

random characters
  generating 55-57
random elements
  accessing, of collection 52, 53
random generation
  defining 2
  versus procedural generation 2
random item
  spawning 53-55
random main track
  selecting 143, 144
random stats
  giving, to player 50, 51
randomness
  defining 2
  pseudorandom number generation 3
  random numbers, generating in C++ 4, 5
  random numbers,
      generating within range 6, 7
  truly random numbers, generating 4
random number distribution
  defining 48, 49
Random Number
      Generator (RNG) 18, 63, 114
random number of items
  spawning 60, 61
random numbers
  URL 4
random player character
  array, returning 97, 98
  creating 87
  player class, selecting 88
  player stats, buffing 94
  random character traits 95, 97
  sprites and textures 89
  sprite, setting 89-92
  trait sprites, setting 98-100
random potion class
  defining 106
  potion pickups, determining 109-111
  random potion, creating 106-109

random tiles, spawning
  about 82
  new game tile, adding 82
  random tile, selecting 83
recursive backtracker
  about 206, 207
  algorithm 205
roguelikes
  about 16
  history 16
roguelike template setup
  about 36
  item, adding 40
  item, drawing 41
  item, updating 41
  project, running 39, 40

S

SDL2
  URL 29
seeds
  about 7
  defining 7, 8
  random numbers, generating 10
  random seeds, generating during runtime 9
  using 8, 9
SFML
  about 21, 28
  alternatives 29
  colors, working 118, 119
  defining 28
  downloading 37
  download link 37
  learning 29
  linking 37, 38
  need for 28
  reference link 29
  URL 3, 119
SFML audio
  defining 142
  sf::Sound, versus sf::Music 142
  sf::Sound, versus sf::SoundBuffer 142

SFML Blueprints
  reference link 29
SFML Essentials
  reference link 29
SFML Game Development
  reference link 29
SFML sprite modifiers
  using 117
Sfxr
  about 13
  URL 13
smart pointers
  reference link 25
sound effects
  adding 144-147
  audio listener 148-150
  editing 147
  fluctuation, creating in pitch 150-152
  sound function, playing 148
sound position
  fixed positions 155, 156
  moving positions 156-158
spawn area
  defining 66
  level bounds, calculating 66, 67
  underlying game grid, checking 67, 68
SpawnRandomTiles function
  implementing 84
sprite component
  adding, to player class 258
  creating 255
  game code, updating 259
  reference 129
  sprite behavior, encapsulating 256-258
  updated drawing pipeline 259
sprite effects
  using 114
sprites
  creating, of random color 119
  creating, of random size 123
static libraries 37
static libraries, versus dynamic libraries
  reference link 37

suitable game tile
  checking 69
  converting, to absolute position 70
  selecting 68
  selecting randomly 69
supporting functions
  creating 171
  Enemy class 172
  Level class 171

T

texture creation
  about 12
  animation 12
  sound 13
textures
  creating, from scratch 114
tile textures
  Bitwise tile maps 220, 221
  calculating 223-225
  debug changes, undoing 234, 235
  entry and exit points, adding 229-231
  if/else approach 220
  selecting 220
  spawn location, setting 231-233
  tile values, calculating 221
  tile values, mapping to 222, 223
  unique floor themes, creating 226-228

traditional inheritance-based approach
  challenges 238, 239
  circular dependencies 239
  convoluted inheritance structures 238
transform component
  adding, to player 253
  creating 252
  game code, updating 254, 255
  transform behavior, encapsulating 252, 253
  using 254
typename keyword 244

U

unique and random game objects
  creating 266
unique art
  creating 17
Unity engine
  URL 237

V

vectors
  references 186
versatility 116
virtual functions 31, 32

Thank you for buying
Procedural Content Generation for C++ Game Development

About Packt Publishing

Packt, pronounced 'packed', published its first book, *Mastering phpMyAdmin for Effective MySQL Management*, in April 2004, and subsequently continued to specialize in publishing highly focused books on specific technologies and solutions.

Our books and publications share the experiences of your fellow IT professionals in adapting and customizing today's systems, applications, and frameworks. Our solution-based books give you the knowledge and power to customize the software and technologies you're using to get the job done. Packt books are more specific and less general than the IT books you have seen in the past. Our unique business model allows us to bring you more focused information, giving you more of what you need to know, and less of what you don't.

Packt is a modern yet unique publishing company that focuses on producing quality, cutting-edge books for communities of developers, administrators, and newbies alike. For more information, please visit our website at www.packtpub.com.

Writing for Packt

We welcome all inquiries from people who are interested in authoring. Book proposals should be sent to author@packtpub.com. If your book idea is still at an early stage and you would like to discuss it first before writing a formal book proposal, then please contact us; one of our commissioning editors will get in touch with you.

We're not just looking for published authors; if you have strong technical skills but no writing experience, our experienced editors can help you develop a writing career, or simply get some additional reward for your expertise.

Learning C++ by Creating Games with UE4

ISBN: 978-1-78439-657-2   Paperback: 342 pages

Learn C++ programming with a fun, real-world application that allows you to create your own games!

1. Be a top programmer by being able to visualize programming concepts; how data is saved in computer memory, and how a program flows.

2. Keep track of player inventory, create monsters, and keep those monsters at bay with basic spell casting by using your C++ programming skills within Unreal Engine 4.

Getting Started with C++ Audio Programming for Game Development

ISBN: 978-1-84969-909-9   Paperback: 116 pages

A hands-on guide to audio programming in game development with the FMOD audio library and toolkit

1. Add audio to your game using FMOD and wrap it in your own code.

2. Understand the core concepts of audio programming and work with audio at different levels of abstraction.

3. Work with a technology that is widely considered to be the industry standard in audio middleware.

Please check **www.PacktPub.com** for information on our titles

SFML Blueprints

ISBN: 978-1-78439-847-7   Paperback: 298 pages

Sharpen your game development skills and improve your C++ and SFML knowledge with five exciting projects

1. Master game components and their interaction by creating a hands-on multiplayer game.

2. Customize your game by adding sounds, animations, physics, and a nice user interface to create a unique game.

3. A project-based book starting with simpler projects and moving into increasingly complex projects to make you proficient in game development.

CryENGINE Game Programming with C++, C#, and Lua

ISBN: 978-1-84969-590-9   Paperback: 276 pages

Get to grips with the essential tools for developing games with the awesome and powerful CryENGINE

1. Dive into the various CryENGINE subsystems to quickly learn how to master the engine.

2. Create your very own game using C++, C#, or Lua in CryENGINE.

3. Understand the structure and design of the engine.

Please check **www.PacktPub.com** for information on our titles

www.ingramcontent.com/pod-product-compliance
Lightning Source LLC
Chambersburg PA
CBHW062111050326

40690CB00016B/3282